PRAISE FOR THE KEY

"We in corporations have enormous resources at our disposal. In this groundbreaking book Lynda shows how these resources can be used both inside to bolster resilience; and outside to address global issues. The examples she brings offer important signals to how the role of corporations could develop over the coming decades. A must read for practicing managers and leaders."

N. Chandrasekaran
Chief Executive Officer
Tata Consultancy Services

"When researching a company it is obviously important to analyze the balance sheet but much more important are the intangible assets such as the quality of the people. In this important book, Professor Gratton shows what to look for in a company that can both build resilience for the future, and also make a positive difference in the world. The wealth of corporate examples from across the world is incredibly useful in showing what is possible and the impact these first mover companies can have."

Martin Gilbert
Chief Operating Officer
Aberdeen Asset Management

"Reflecting thoughtfully on her years of studying and working with corporate leaders, Gratton makes an impassioned plea for corporations to play their proper role in making the world a better place—today and for future generations."

Jasmine Whitbread
Chief Executive Officer
Save the Children

"The word over-ambitious does not exist when you look at the challenges we have to solve. There is a fundamental readjustment going in our economic system, from a rules-based society back to a principles-based society. This requires a new form of shared leadership"

Paul Polman
Chief Executive Officer
Unilever

"Contrary to Hollywood stereotypes, big corporations can be a force for good. *The Key* helps to explain why that is so and how business leaders can be part of the vanguard."

Gavin E. Patterson
Chief Executive Officer
BT Group

"Lynda has again demonstrated her unique skill at sensing the next global challenge—in her book *The Key* she challenges in a provocative but thoughtful way all current and future leaders to step up to create a better future and build their legacy. Her insights around human potential and the increasing need for us all to find our moral compass is compelling.

"This book is a must read for leaders who want to understand the new role for business, it gets to the heart of what the world needs—a sense of purpose with a new level of ownership and more importantly action!"

Dennis J. Finn
Vice Chairman and Global Human Capital Leader
PwC

"The company of the future is not the company of the past. Never before have corporations, their customers and the communities they operate in been so intertwined and interdependent. The fast-moving and dynamic forces global leaders must contend with is mind-boggling. In order to achieve the outcomes necessary for ongoing growth, executive leaders must not only reinvent themselves and their businesses every 2-3 years but must also continually ask what role their corporation will play as a force for the common good. What *The Key* does is to show, in a ground-breaking way, how the bridge between the two can be built."

Robert Kovach, PhD,
Global Executive Talent
Cisco

"*The Key* will become one of the classics of workplace leadership and management. With fascinating research, engaging style and practical wisdom, this is a real manifesto for taking action, sustainably."

Yoshito Hori
President, GLOBIS University
Managing Partner, GLOBIS Capital Partners

"We at the Aspen Institute believe passionately in the positive role leaders can play in society. What is really exciting about *The Key* is that Lynda addresses head on the question of the role of leadership and also of how leaders can build their capability to both support resilient corporations and make a difference in the world. This is an inspiring read for anyone who wants to move their eyes from beyond the present to make a significant contribution to the future."

Judith Samuelson
Executive Director,
Biz+Society Program at the Aspen Institute

"Lynda Gratton's book *The Key* is an important and inspirational call to action for leaders in corporations (and beyond) to build a future that is positive for employees, investors and communities. Grounded in real examples and propelled by solid research, this book focuses on how leaders and corporations create a future where wisdom is fostered and inner resilience strengthened. *The Key* is both optimistic and realistic, igniting our imagination and commitment to a more prosperous future where corporations actualize their potential to make a positive difference"

Jane E. Dutton
Robert L. Kahn Distinguished University Professor of Business Administration
   and Psychology
Ross School of Business, University of Michigan

"Lynda has again given us a lens into a brighter future. With prescience and insight, she has offered a way to resolve some of the most serious challenges of complex world. When large, global organizations become communities endowed with resilience and committed to service, they have the capacity to do enormous good. She offers specific prescriptions for how to use organizations to rekindle the hope that shared communities can offer. Her ideas are a call to arms and a commitment to action that will benefit individuals, organizations, and communities."

Dave Ulrich
Professor, Ross School of Business, University of Michigan
Partner, the RBL Group

"Perhaps more than at any other time, corporations have it in their power to make a significant positive impact in the world. The challenge many leaders face is how best to use this power. In this inspiring book, Professor Gratton shows how corporations can build an inner core of resilience to address global challenges in supply chains and beyond. This book takes the discussion about corporate social responsibility to a new level by clearly describing what it takes for leaders and employees to collectively make the corporation a force for good in the world."

Diana C. Robertson
Professor of Legal Studies and Business Ethics
The Wharton School, University of Pennsylvania

"*The Key* offers a novel perspective on the emerging role of corporations in society. Leadership expert Lynda Gratton offers practical insights for unlocking the hidden resources in organizations and using them to bring resilience to a fragile world."

Adam Grant
Professor of Organizational Behavior
The Wharton School, University of Pennsylvania

"Major Corporations think deeply about the future, what opportunities it presents and what challenges have to be overcome. Many have demonstrated great resilience through their innovation, adaptation, and sustained relevance to the needs of people today and tomorrow. As a consequence Corporations need to be seen and behave as part of the solution. *The Key* advocates for a stronger role for corporations and provides compelling arguments based on real life examples. Something for those inside and outside the corporate world to think about!"

Hugh S. Mitchell
Chief Human Resources and Corporate Officer
Royal Dutch Shell plc

THE KEY

How Corporations Succeed by Solving the World's Toughest Problems

LYNDA GRATTON

New York   Chicago   San Francisco   Athens   London   Madrid
Mexico City   Milan   New Delhi   Singapore   Sydney   Toronto

1 2 3 4 5 6 7 8 9 0   QFR/QFR   1 0 9 8 7 6 5 4

ISBN   978-0-07-183896-2
MHID   0-07-183896-1

e-ISBN 978-0-07-183897-9
e-MHID   0-07-183897-X

Library of Congress Cataloging-in-Publication Data

Gratton, Lynda
    The key : how corporations succeed by solving the world's toughest problems / Lynda Gratton. — 1 Edition.
        pages cn
      ISBN 978-0-07-183896-2 (hardback : alk. paper) — ISBN 0-07-183896-1
    1. Organizational change.   2. Business planning.   I. Title.
    HD58.8.G7194 2014
    658.4'01—dc23   2014001990

McGraw-Hill Education books are available at special quantity discounts to use as premiums and sales promotions or for use in corporate training programs. To contact a representative, please visit the Contact Us pages at www.mhprofessional.com.

To Charles Handy,
a beacon on this journey.

CONTENTS

PREFACE

A Love Letter to Corporations

We face profound and escalating challenges in the world—youth unemployment touches many families; income inequality and poverty are a source of shame for many of us in developed countries; and it is only the least observant who could fail to recognize the early signs of a profound change in the climate. Those of us who are baby boomers are concerned about our legacy; many youngsters are worried about the world they have inherited. Moreover, these are no longer challenges that are particular to one country or to one area and therefore can be ignored by most. Instead, these global challenges are such that if we don't do something about them, they could significantly blight the lives of our children and the generations that follow.

The question is how we address these escalating challenges. For decades, the most obvious candidates for action have been governments and global institutions such as the World Bank. These institutions can indeed play a role, but it seems to me that over the last few years there has been one kind of institution that is growing in strength and capability and is therefore becoming uniquely placed to become part of the way these challenges are addressed. That institution is the world's global corporations.

I am saying this in the full knowledge that there has probably never been a time when global corporations and those who lead them have been held in such low esteem. The bonanza years for corporations has been marked, particularly over the last five years, by the fall from grace of capitalism and corporations. I can see this in the Occupy Wall Street movement; I can hear it in my MBA class when students talk about executives "green washing" their corporations as a public relations stunt and putting the needs of their financial share-holders above all others; I can observe this in employee surveys that show that some companies are destroying human potential by creat-ing work that is dehumanizing and stressful; I can read about how some companies are exploiting resources, polluting their environ-ment, and creating a carbon footprint that puts our climate at peril.

It is completely understandable why some commentators believe that those who lead corporations have lost their moral compass.[1]

There is no doubt that the banking crisis, oil spills, excessive exec-utive pay, and corporate raiders have all fueled our natural suspicion that corporations are not good. We can view them as rapacious, evil, greedy, and self-serving. A glance at the corporate genre in books and films—*Wall Street, Wall Street: Money Never Sleeps, Syriana, Up in the Air*, and even going back to *The Godfather* and *Citizen Kane*—reinforces this. It seems that our default setting for corpora-tions is that they are not good—and that they are out to do us over.

As workers, consumers, and investors, we have become ever more vocal about how we feel about corporations and what we expect of them. As a result, perhaps more than any other time in the history of business, corporations are answerable to our opinion and our scru-tiny. Whether they like it or not, those who lead corporations have had consciousness and responsibility to stakeholders thrust upon them.

The idea that corporations are innately corrosive does, of course, misunderstand their very nature. The corporations we work for, buy from, and invest in are fundamentally collections, teams, and communities of people. Like any community, they are capable of mistakes. Through their personal growth and increasing organiza-tional capability, though, these people are also capable of developing extraordinary purpose, and from this, they are capable of profound action and volition.

Looking back, we can see our world transformed by the forces of technology and globalization that seemed unimaginable in earlier times. Looking forward, our world will transform again, undoubt-edly at a faster pace. These faster-evolving trajectories are confronting us with a whole new set of challenges to be faced and innovations to create.

The puzzle we face now is that the innovative tools from which we have benefited in the past are increasingly incapable of solving the challenges of the future. Let me explain. The last really profound shift in corporations and the technology of work took place during the industrial revolution that culminated around 1850. The technological innovations and ways of working that followed this revolution led to profound problems as workers moved into cities and much skilled craftwork was destroyed. Yet, over time, the collective endeavor and creativity of people were able to solve many of the problems the industrial revolution raised.

But this time it is different. The challenges created by this current industrial revolution are on a scale altogether greater and more global, they are emerging at a much faster trajectory, and their negative consequences will be much more difficult to reverse. Thus we need a whole new set of tools and ways of innovating that match this global scale and rapid trajectory. As we shall see, there are innovative tools of connectivity and conviviality that are developing at a fast pace, but to make real use of them, corporations will need to align them with human potential and purpose. If they can do this, they will be capable of amplifying intelligence and wisdom, enhancing emotional vitality, and harnessing social connectivity. Those who are guardians of leadership development also will be called on to look again at what it means to be a leader and the developmental journeys that take talented people to positions of leadership.

Faced with the challenges of an increasingly fragile world, it is now crucial that those who work in and lead corporations begin to aspire to and take a more central role in the affairs of the world. Indeed, my argument is that far from being one of the causes of trouble—in the right hands and in the right direction—corporations could and should play a significant and central role in finding the innovations that will allow us to face these new challenges. Indeed, corporations have the potential to become the key that unlocks these challenges.

To make this case, this book is divided into three main sections. Part I explores the transforming context in which we work and the impact these forces are having on corporations. In Parts II through IV, I describe in more detail the three spheres of action as corporations build inner resilience, anchor themselves in their communities, and address global challenges. The book finishes in Part V with a call to reimagine leadership and the role we all can play.

The forces of technology and globalization over the past 40 years have profoundly transformed the whole corporate landscape. You can see this for yourself by opening any business book published before the year 2000 (including my own). You will find stories about companies in developed countries—companies such as GE, Intel, Coca-Cola in the United States; BP, Unilever, and Nokia in Europe; and Toyota and Fujitsu in Japan. When I had first joined London Business School in 1990, I recall that fewer than 20 companies from the emerging markets where listed on the Global Fortune 500. Ten years later, that number stood at over 90.

In many ways, the history of the Indian steel company Mittal is illustrative of this shift in global power. In 1990, this Indian company was an unknown producer of steel. In the autumn of 1993, my colleague, Sumantra Ghoshal, and I had asked Lakshmi Mittal to come to speak to one of our MBA classes at London Business School. Mittal arrived with his wife, Usha, and daughter, Vanisha, to talk about his business philosophy and goals. The class listened with polite attention, but clearly our students were not overwhelmed by the presence of what they saw as a local Indian steel producer. I guess they would have much preferred to hear Jack Welsh from GE or Jeffrey Skilling from Enron. Yet fast-forward seven years, and ArcelorMittal had become the largest steel company in the world, and Lakshmi Mittal could be assured of a full and enthusiastic MBA class.

The technologies that had begun to connect corporations across the world were also connecting them to huge markets and billions of people. As a consequence, some corporations had become vast. Using value added as a measure (defined as the sum of salaries, pretax profits, depreciation, and amortization), 29 of the world's largest economies are not countries—they are corporations.[2] By 2000, ExxonMobil, at that time the world's largest corporation, was bigger than 180 of the world's 220 national economies and certainly much larger in economic size than most of the countries in which it operated. At that same time, the world's largest private corporate employer was Walmart, with 1.3 million workers. By 2012, that figure was nearer to 2 million, and if we add in the company's supply chains, the number would be tens of millions of people. Moreover, we can expect these corporate giants to continue to grow if they stay on their growth trajectory. It is therefore no surprise that between 1983 and 2001, the value of capital assets owned by the world's 50 largest corporations increased by almost 700 percent.

These colossal corporations are touching all our lives. We might work directly within corporations or in their supply chain, we may consume their goods and services, and we almost certainly invest in them either directly through our own shares or indirectly through our pensions and savings. For better or for worse, corporations are getting deeper into our lives in a way that we cannot avoid. Thus the question now arises about what it is that these colossal corporations are doing with their newfound global power and influence.

There is no doubt that these ever more powerful corporations have done some good in their communities. They have created jobs; they have brought access to credit and markets; and they have introduced new technologies, reduced the prices of goods and services, and (sometimes) increased the wealth of their host economies through the payment of taxes and wage income.[3]

Being a force for good is not new for corporations. Take, for example, the UK chocolate makers Terry's and Rowntree's of York and Cadbury of Birmingham—which were all faith-based or Quaker companies. These companies had been set up by family founders on the basis of their Quaker ideals.[4] Workers who fell ill could spend as much time as they needed to recuperate. Those who wanted literary stimulation could stroll to the library that stood on the grounds of the factories. Workers had access to schools, libraries, and hospitals. Core to Quaker beliefs was that workers should be discouraged from drinking—the scourge of life after the upheavals of the industrial revolution. Indeed, this is in part why these Quakers built chocolate factories. Their hope was that the delicious drinking chocolate they made could wean the working classes off gin, the favored tipple at that time.

I am not advocating a return to the paternalism and the values of the Quaker founders of Cadbury and Rowntree's, if indeed such a return were possible.

What I am advocating is that corporations have accrued enormous power and capabilities that they now have an opportunity to use positively in the services of their employees and communities. Corporations have become the manifestation of collaborative endeavors at the most complex level, they represent some of the most convivial ways that we can relate to each other, and their supply chains touch the lives of many.

To create a good future, it is crucial that those who lead corporations become increasingly transparent about their actions and intentions and see themselves as part of the wider world they inhabit. In other words, they must revisit the subtle questions of what the role of a corporation could and should be.

To do this, there are indeed tough questions to be faced. What can be done to build the resilience and engagement of employees in a world of increasing stress and strain? How can a deep involvement and interest in the community be more than a public relations exercise? What are the incentives and choices an executive team is faced with as it thinks about its corporate strategy? What is legitimate for workers to expect from themselves and what can and should be the expectation of those in the supply chain and corporate partners?

I started my organizational life as a seasonal employee packing chocolates at Terry's of York, and even 40 years later that initial excitement and interest in corporations has not waned. In a sense, therefore, this book is a love letter to corporations. But it's not the sort of soppy love letter I would have written to my student boyfriend back in the 1970s. It's a letter about expectations—a letter about what we as workers, consumers, and investors can expect from corporations and how we can work together to fulfill those expectations. It is a book about how to balance our social values with a well-functioning market economy.

Those of us who work in corporations want to be seen in a good light. We want to do work that is engaging and exciting. We want to be proud of what we do when we talk to others in our communities. We want to address at least some of the challenges that we and our families face. We want to be proud to tell our children where we work. And we want to be able to look them straight in the eye and say, "We have done our best."

As you will see in this book, there are corporations around the world where leaders and workers are doing marvelous things. At the same time, though, there are corporations around the world who are not doing what they could—and should.

This book is addressed to those who work in and lead corporations. It both celebrates the extraordinary feats corporations have achieved and shows the ways that the very essence of corporations can become a force of good and a key to unlock the challenges we face.

It seems to me that there is much we can ask of ourselves and our corporations. We can ask that in the place of exploitation, there is renewal. In a world of hyperconnectivity, of global sharing of abundant knowledge, and of the globalization of innovations, we can see the possibility of renewal and a profound understanding that resources are finite rather than infinite and therefore have to be husbanded through stewardship. For workers, this means the renewing of the human spirit through time to rejuvenate and working conditions that excite, stimulate, and develop a corporate purpose that brings meaning.

We can ask of corporations that their executives see themselves as part of an interdependent world, where the impact of their actions in one place and at one time is felt across the system. In this world, collaboration and alliances are more successful strategies than resource competition.

The call to companies is indeed great. In this endeavor, we each have our own role to play. For me as an academic, my only power is through the power of argument and, I hope, inspiration. For those of you who work in corporations, your role could be one of action. For those of you who consume the goods corporations create, your role could be one of making clear, through your choices and voices, that you believe, like me, that corporations can and indeed must be a force for good.

Lynda Gratton
London, 2014

PART I

❖

BUILDING RESILIENCE IN A FRAGILE WORLD

Over the coming decades, our world will be transformed by the host of emerging technologies that are shaping our interactions with work and connecting us with each other in ever more sophisticated ways and across ever more parts of the globe. These technological developments will play a continuous role in linking the regions of the world together as the force of globalization brings goods, services, and indeed jobs to ever more areas of the world. But it is not just technology and globalization forces that are transforming our world.

Each one of us is also being transformed by the demography of our situation and by our values and beliefs. The forces that are increasing the productive life spans of many billions of people around the world are also shaping the demographic profiles of the regions of the world—be that the policy in much of China for one or two children or indeed the large proportion of young adults in parts of the world such as the Middle East and Nigeria.

The past 10 years have been a decade of transitions and profound volatility, and as we shall see in Chapter 1, it is clear that there can be no return to the status quo. The transitions that are occurring in energy, economics, and geopolitics are unstable and require both constant adjustments and an eye to the long term.

To build a deeper understanding of the future, in 2008 I launched the Future of Work Consortium (FoW) in a partnership with executives from companies around the world. I was interested in finding out how they were creating ways of operating that increased their chances of flourishing in the future and indeed of bringing resilience to a fragile world. I discovered that while there are examples of short-termism, there are also companies where executives are taking a worldview and people are actively and positively building resiliency for the future.

These ways of being and indeed of making choices, sometimes seen in individuals, sometimes in leaders, or in whole corporations, are not accidental. They are not what happens when you walk blindly into the future. Instead, as we shall see in Chapter 2, they are the result of a profound determination to build resilient corporations and make a future that is positive for employees, investors, and those in the communities those corporations touch.

CHAPTER 1

TRENDS SHAPING CORPORATIONS AND WORK

O ur world is already being shaped in profound ways, and over the next decades, we can expect those forces to have ever greater velocity and complexity. Yet, as executive teams prepare themselves for the future, it is not necessary to walk blindfolded, for while the future is indeed unclear, there are sufficient signals and signs to illuminate the path ahead. Here are the seven trends that will most profoundly shape corporations and work over the coming decades. For each trend, I have raised a couple of questions that will require executives to have a point of view.

1. Rebalancing of the global markets for goods and labor
2. Growing hyperconnectivity of people and jobs
3. Emergence of talent clusters
4. "Hollowing out" of work
5. Increasing skills gaps
6. Poverty and inequality
7. Extreme weather patterns

REBALANCING OF GLOBAL MARKETS FOR GOODS AND LABOR

The resilience of every business is constantly tested by the profound rebalancing of the world. Take Lenovo as an example. In 1990, this Chinese technology company had just started to develop its own products, yet by 2005 it had bought IBM's PC business for US$1.75

billion and had become the fourth largest PC maker in the world. In 1990, South African Breweries (SAB) was a local brewer, yet by 2010 it was one of the largest beer companies in the world.

This global rebalancing will also be shaped by shifts in the location of the working populations of the world. The working population of the more developed countries will actually fall between 2010 and 2030 from 835 million to 795 million, whereas the working population of the less developed regions is expected to increase by around 1 billion people to 4.6 billion.[1]

Accompanying this population redistribution will be shifts in where innovation and new ideas arise. Historical powerhouses of innovation such as Silicon Valley spawned companies such as Google and Apple, whereas German companies such as BMW and Siemens created desirable high-end manufactured goods. Yet, from the mid-1990s onward, companies in both China and India had begun to evolve their own domestic innovation hubs, transforming from back-office and low-value manufacturing. As a result, innovation has become a global phenomenon. By 2011, 98 of the U.S. Fortune 500 companies had research and development facilities in China, with 63 having facilities in India.

- What will it take for leaders to understand this global rebalancing and the changing worldview that it inevitably brings?
- As corporations become more global and located across the world, how will knowledge and innovation be harnessed and shared across functional, business, and country boundaries?

GROWING HYPERCONNECTIVITY OF PEOPLE AND JOBS

The trajectory of low-cost connectivity is awe inspiring. By 2010, 5 billion people had access to mobile phones, and by 2020, that figure is predicted to exceed 6 billion, with 5 billion on the World Wide Web using around 50 billion devices and with low-cost access to information and services.[2]

It's not hard to imagine the beneficial impact this hyperconnectivity could have on people and their companies.[3] It means that talented people around the world can potentially access the rapidly developing global talent markets and innovations can be developed and distributed with ease. Right now, platforms such as oDesk, eLance, and Guru are able to connect buyers of specialist skills to sellers of these skills, providing access to work for web designers, software programmers, salespeople, translators, and administrators from across the world. At the same time, platforms such as InnoCentive are providing opportunities for those with tough challenges to attract individuals and clusters of knowledgeable problem solvers.

- How will corporations ensure that they benefit from hyperconnectivity by using these newly emerging platforms to join up people within and outside the corporations?
- What impact will these increasingly virtual working environments have on social connectivity, and how can trust and cooperation be supported in these low-touch working environments?

EMERGENCE OF TALENT CLUSTERS

The combination of global rebalancing and hyperconnectivity is creating opportunities for new talent pools to emerge. Migration also plays a role; the success of Silicon Valley shows the positive impact of migration, where from 1980 to 1999 almost 25 percent of startups were founded by Indian or Chinese entrepreneurs. In fact, by 2005 it was estimated these waves of immigrants had made US$52 billion and created around 450,000 new jobs. These people and others like them are creating what social geographer Richard Florida calls a "spiky world" that consists of concentrated clusters or peaks of talented and energized people generating disproportionately higher levels of innovation.[4]

These creative clusters are already located where the specialized creative classes are flocking. In the United States, for example, as long as people continue to migrate to New York City for its financial sector, Boston for its biotechnology sector, and Washington for its media focus and strategic intelligence, these American creative clusters will continue to thrive. In Europe, London will continue to be one of the world's finance and creative centers, Milan and

Rome will continue to be core clusters for fashion and industrial design, and Stuttgart, Frankfurt, and Mannheim will continue to be core clusters for high-end manufacturing. In the emerging markets, Bangalore has already witnessed the development of three strong technology clusters, Shanghai is becoming the financial capital of Asia, and Johannesburg and Nairobi could become African leaders in commerce and telecommunications.

For executives, the phenomenon of clustering presents an emerging paradox. On the one hand, technological developments will make virtual work increasingly viable and authentic, so the ideal of working on a desert island or high on an isolated mountain could become a reality. On the other hand, though, more people are moving to cities where there is a high concentration of people with similar talents, aspirations, and interests.

- What are the best ways to benefit from these newly emerging talent clusters, and how can corporations globalize their recruitment processes to attract the world's most talented people?
- These rapidly growing cities are often fragile and become the nexus of strain in resources. What role can corporations play in bringing more resilience to these cities?

"HOLLOWING OUT" OF WORK

Technological innovation has connected billions of people, but in doing so it has also undermined the demand for many middle-skill, routine jobs, through either automation or offshoring.

Right now, the sorts of jobs that are being "hollowed out" include white-collar jobs in sales, office, and administrative functions, as well as blue-collar jobs in production, craft, and operative roles. In the past, these jobs were often the launching pad for young people as they built their careers.[5] Outside the hollow middle, two types of jobs continue to flourish at either end of the skill spectrum. At the high-skilled end are the jobs of lawyers, engineers, and information technology (IT) specialists that depend on complex knowledge, expertise, intuition, persuasion, and collaboration. These are jobs where advancing technology complements and increases productivity rather than substitutes for people. At the low-skilled end of the hollow are the nonroutine manual tasks such as waiters, bank tellers, and shop assistants. These are jobs that are also inherently difficult to automate because they require the presence of someone in that location. What have been lost are the launching-pad middle-skill jobs.

- How can high-skill jobs be created, and what will it take to develop the expertise and intuition that typically come from mentoring and cross-generational coaching?
- What can be done to help those trapped in the rapidly evaporating pool of medium-skill jobs?

INCREASING SKILLS GAPS

There is no doubt that young people have always struggled to find work at certain times in the economic cycle of every country. Yet, by 2012, youth unemployment was almost 50 percent in Spain and over 20 percent in many developed countries. This is not simply the result of cyclic economic patterns; it is also the impact of profound structural changes in job markets and the nature of work that have resulted in the hollowing out of work. However, the paradox is that in many regions, although youth unemployment is high, there are also growing job vacancies. In 2010, for example, while there were 3 million job vacancies in the United States, at the same time, unemployment continued to climb. With an uncoordinated marketplace for education, with little signaling of the sorts of jobs needed for the future, and limited skill development, the skills gaps simply increase. It is interesting to note that in countries such as Singapore with highly planned economies and strong alliances between educational institutions and corporations, these skills gaps are virtually nonexistent, and youth unemployment is low.

What is making this skills gap even tougher is that there are clear signals that social mobility is declining across the developed world. A lack of social mobility will make it even more problematic for young people to transition from low- and middle-skilled roles to high-skilled ones. We can predict that these bipolar labor markets will become ever more prevalent in economies that fail to invest in wide-scale education and skills development. Moreover, a lack of investment in science, technology, engineering, and mathematics will increase the skills gap, exacerbate long-term unemployment, and entrench low levels of social mobility.[6]

- What role can corporations play in reaching out to the communities in which they work to build stronger job-ready skills?
- How can the crucial alliances among corporations, governments, and educational institutions be forged to address the complex dynamics that result in youth unemployment?

POVERTY AND INEQUALITY

Whereas in prosperous emerging markets such as China, India, and Brazil, trade and capital outflows and inflows have increased considerably over the last 30 years, this is not the case in many of the least-developed countries. To quote Joseph Stiglitz, one-time chief economist of the World Bank, "Despite repeated promises of poverty reduction made over the last decade of the twentieth century, the . . . number of people in poverty has actually increased by an average of 2.5 percent annually."[7] In 2010, the World Bank reported that some 2 billion people live in countries that are becoming less rather than more globalized—among them, Pakistan, Indonesia, and much of Africa and Latin America. In those regions, trade has diminished in relation to national income, economic growth has stagnated, and poverty has risen. Most Africans were better off 40 years ago. Income disparities are also growing within these regions. For example, the average per-capita income of Muslims, from Morocco to Bangladesh and beyond to Indonesia and the Philippines, is one-half the world average.

Despite the roughly US$1 trillion that has been spent on grants and loans to fight poverty around the globe since the end of World War II, the World Bank reports that nearly half the global population still lives on less than US$2 a day and one-sixth on less than US$1 a day.[8] It seems that the positive effects of globalization have been far from global. "The central challenge we face today," according to former U.N. Secretary General Kofi Annan, "is to ensure that globalization becomes a positive force for all the world's people, instead of leaving billions of them behind in squalor."[9]

This is also a story about inequality. Take the United States as an example. In 1976, the top 1 percent of households accounted for 9 percent of income; by 2007, that figure had grown to 24 percent.[10] And this is not just a Western phenomenon. Emerging markets are already showing signs of growing inequality: India's growing economic regions in Bangalore, Hyderabad, Mumbai, and New Delhi are quickly pulling away from the rest of the country, as are many of China's megacities. Both India and China are failing to develop as integrated wholes and have so far stopped short of using their regional competencies to construct an amalgamated platform for development. The national average per-capita gross domestic product (GDP) in India was US$978 in 2010, but in rural areas such as Bihar, the figure was as low as US$200.

What is important to realize about this growing disparity in income, is the impact it can have on the psychology and resilience of neighborhoods and societies. To illustrate this, economists Richard Wilkinson and Kate Pickett have charted the happiness of people across many societies. They have discovered that those regions with the greatest income disparity often have the lowest levels of happiness and the greatest social woes.[11] In the view of economist Raghuram Rajan, left unchecked, inequality can become entrenched, leading to uneven access to education and health care and creating the conditions for further division.[12] As a consequence, the growing fissures in the world economy will begin to surface more frequently, reinforcing social divides and factionalism.

- What role can corporations play in bringing prosperity to the families in their neighborhoods and extended supply chains?
- How can corporations enter alliances with nongovernment organizations (NGOs) to tackle poverty?

EXTREME WEATHER PATTERNS

There is a growing belief that the extreme weather patterns we are already experiencing—blistering heat in the Mediterranean, damp summers in the United Kingdom, ever more ferocious hurricanes in the United States, prolonged drought in the Indian subcontinent, the melting of the ice in the polar regions—could be a harbinger of what is to come. It seems that we are beginning to enter a new phase—"anthropocene," the period when humankind will fundamentally change the nature of the world. Just what the trajectory of this change will be is up for discussion. But there is a growing consensus in the scientific community that if the planet remains on the default path of consumption, and if nothing radical is done to overcome the global dependence on oil, coal, and gas, then the 1.1°F (0.6°C) shift in temperature that occurred over the last century as a result of rising levels of carbon dioxide is likely to be dwarfed by the shift during the next century. The most conservative estimate from the Intergovernmental Panel on Climate Change (IPCC) predicts a mean global warming of around 3.2°F (1.8°C), whereas more pessimistic models show the potential for a 7.2 to 9.0°F (4.0 to 5.0°C) increase.[13]

Given the current consequences of a 1.1°F (0.6°C) temperature increase, the impact of a shift that is nearly eight times in scale would be severe. It is predicted, for example, that a temperature increase of this scale could mean that large areas of the Amazon forest could be lost to drought and fire, agricultural yields could decrease for all major cereal crops, water shortages could affect more than two-thirds of the global population, and rising sea levels could force millions, if not billions, of people to migrate. Such an environmental transition hasn't occurred in the past 30 million years and would cause severe readjustment and long-term global conflict.[14] The "Stern Review" argues that if action is not taken, between 5 and 20 percent of world GDP eventually will be lost to climate damage, whereas the 2007 IPCC report predicts dramatic increases in carbon dioxide levels leading to arctic ice melting and spreading drought conditions.[15]

- What are the organizational practices and processes that have to be in place to ensure a significant reduction in the carbon footprint of a company and its supply chain?
- What will it take for alliances of corporations to create a surge in innovation capable of addressing some of these complex challenges of resource constraints and climate change?

CONCLUSION

These trends represent both opportunities and risks for companies—opportunities to amplify wisdom and ideas and to connect people in ever more positive and beneficial ways and the risk to the entire supply chain, the risk to manufacturing networks and local communities, the risk to company reputations, and the regulatory and financial risks that companies face.

CHAPTER 2

SPHERES OF CORPORATE RESILIENCE

Human endeavor and sheer creativity have together built everything we need to create corporations capable of thriving in the future and bringing greater resilience to a fragile world. Many billions of people around the world will increasingly have access to centuries of accumulated knowledge. In small groups or vast virtual crowds, they can exchange ideas and take the opportunity to work productively. The greatest minds will be harnessed in innovations that touch every part of the experience of people around the world. This is why some have seen the coming decades as a time of abundance.[1]

Yet the signs of an increasingly fragile world are also visible. Very often these vast crowds find it impossible to shepherd the fragile resources of the world. There seems like an irresistible urge on the part of some of those in positions of power to exploit their opportunities to the detriment of others. And the magnifying of human frailties such as greed and consumption can lead to ever more unwieldy consumption and ever greater fragility.

Having spoken to many of those who lead corporations around the world, it seems to me that most want to enter the future in an optimistic and prepared way. Yet they also acknowledge that preparing for the opportunities and challenges of the future is not straightforward. The forces that are shaping the world are working with each other to create a complex system where the real data about situations is often opaque and contested, where stakeholders are numerous, and where actions can have devastating unintended consequences. What's more, the speed of many of these forces that have technology at their heart is following Moore's law—a doubling of capacity every two years.

Many corporate leaders believe that the next 10 years will be crucial. In thinking about the breadth of opportunities available to those who lead corporations, I have framed their sphere of influence in the three concentric spaces shown in Figure 2-1—from the inner-most sphere (building inner resilience within the corporation), to the next sphere (anchoring in the community), and so on to the outer-most sphere of influence and resources (addressing global challenges)—and this is what forms the structure of this book.

SPHERE 1: BUILDING INNER RESILIENCE WITHIN THE CORPORATION

Without a core of inner resilience, those working within a corporation have neither the energy, capability, nor innovation to meet its business performance targets or indeed reach into its communities and across to global challenges. This core of inner resilience is built through the unique combination of the assets and capabilities a corporation has. A crucial part of this is the human assets of the corporation—which bring high performance through amplification of ideas and knowledge, the enhancement of emotional vitality, and the harnessing of social connections.

- *Intelligence and wisdom.* Intangible corporate wealth is created when people have the opportunity to be insightful and analytical—as individuals, in teams, and in wise crowds.
- *Emotional vitality.* When people are energized and feel vital, they are more likely to bring creativity and innovation to their work.
- *Social connection.* The social wealth of a corporation is held in the extent and richness of networks that crisscross the company and stretch outside the boundaries of the corporation into the supply chain and the wider ecosystem.

These sources of human intelligence, vitality, and connectedness are enhanced and brought into action through the way employees behave on a day-to-day basis, which, in part, is shaped by the context of the corporation—its practices, processes, structure, and by the way leaders create a purpose and a narrative. It is this combination of employees, the organization structure and form, and the leadership purpose and narrative that together creates the capabilities that are at the heart of inner resilience. In Part II of this book we look specifically at how this inner resilience is built.

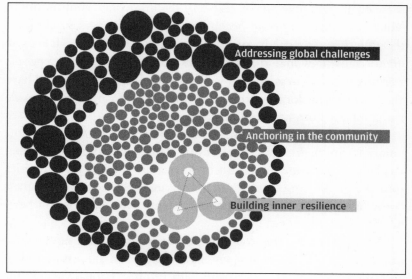

Figure 2-1   Corporate Spheres of Influence

SPHERE 2: ANCHORING IN THE COMMUNITY

Building a core of inner resilience is indeed crucial to the long-term survival of a corporation. Yet, increasingly, companies are also being called on to acknowledge that they are not independent actors but rather are deeply embedded in the communities in which they operate. In Part III of this book we take a closer look at how companies are achieving this—both in their neighborhoods and in their extended supply chains.

SPHERE 3: ADDRESSING GLOBAL CHALLENGES

The widest sphere of influence is the whole world. It seems to me that corporations have no choice but to acknowledge this outer sphere—even those parts of the world where they do not have a physical presence. They have no choice because this outer sphere contains many opportunities for the firm—potential talent pools, future customers, and sources of innovation. Yet this outer sphere also contains profound challenges—a rapidly degrading environment, rising inequality, youth unemployment, and increasing poverty. Although these challenges may not be visible in the immediate community in which a company operates, each has the potential to severely limit the growth and prosperity of the company and its workers. It is these grand challenges that are so complex that they need many people working together to solve, and so crucial that their solution will have an impact on the longer-term well-being of those within and outside the company both now and in the future.

In Part IV of this book we take a closer look at how some corporations are making a greater effort to focus on addressing global challenges. Some are doing this by leveraging their core capabilities into the global community. Often, though, the positive impact a corporation strives for in this outer sphere is created through partnerships and alliances.

Acknowledging the volatility of the world, building a fabric of resilience, and decreasing the barrier between the inside of the corporations and the outer world have profound consequences for leadership. In Part V of this book we address what this reimagined leadership is becoming.

CONCLUSION

I began with a "love letter" to corporations—a hope that the vast human and financial resources at their command could be used in a rigorous and focused way to address the challenges of our fragile world. What I have laid out here is an argument for how this could be done and the role corporations can play, but what is clear is that this external focus can only be achieved if those within the corporation—individuals, teams, and communities—are themselves resilient, and it is to this inner resilience that I now turn.

PART II

❖

BUILDING INNER RESILIENCE

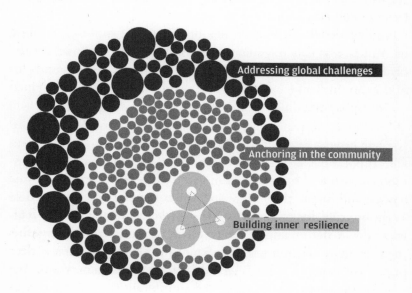

Addressing global challenges

Anchoring in the community

Building inner resilience

There are profound opportunities for today's corporations to become real reservoirs of resilience with regard to their human assets and innovative potential. These assets take three forms, which we can think of as a triangle of assets.

The first part of the triangle is intelligence and wisdom. I recall that in the 1970s in my first job as a psychologist with British Airways, the focus was primarily on measuring intelligence. The idea was that those with higher cognitive capacity would be more suited to solving the ambiguous and complex problems that fast-globalizing corporations had begun to encounter. This is why, in the search for corporate resilience, the identification and then amplification of intelligence and wisdom are so crucial—and as we shall see in Chapter 3—and why it is still seen to be so central to organizational success and resilience.

It turns out, however, that human resilience is not just about intelligence. By the 1980s, a series of researchers asked why some executives "derail" and fail to meet their potential. Their results showed that this derailment was rarely because these executives lacked intelligence.[1] Instead, as we will explore in Chapter 4, they failed in part because of their emotional vitality and insight. Faced with an increasingly fragmented and stressful working life, they simply found it impossible to reach their full potential. The second part of the triangle had emerged.

It took another 10 years before academics working in the field of human assets really began to understand the third part of this triangle of human potential. This insight came as studies of teams and corporations showed that the potential and resilience of a corporation were not simply held in individuals (however intelligent and emotionally stable they happened to be) but rather were also held in the connections between people. It seems that much of the value that people are capable of creating is brought to fruition through the strength and depth of relationships they have with others.[2] Two principal strands of research brought a deeper understanding of this.

One strand was the very detailed analysis that had begun to take place of the relationships and network structures within communities and businesses. These showed that the knowledge flows within communities rarely follow the organizational hierarchies from top to bottom. Instead, they have their own pathways, facilitated by boundary spanners—people who have networks that connect dis-similar groups.[3] These initial studies began to point to the profound impact that social capital could have on the resilience and innovative capability of a corporation.[4] A second strand of research looked at the type of people who enabled these knowledge flows and high-lighted the importance of cooperative attitudes and skills and the role the corporate context could play in enabling this core compe-tence to emerge.[5] As we shall see in Chapter 5, there was a deeper appreciation that intellectual ideas and emotional resilience could only really be brought to fruition when ideas and knowledge flowed easily between and across teams and communities.

Over time, it has become clear that the three points of the human asset triangle—intellectual, emotional, and social—are not indepen-dent of each other. Rather each is important to the other through a process of constant reinforcement. It also became clear that the context of the organization could play a profound role in amplify-ing intelligence, enhancing emotional vitality, and harnessing social connections.

The challenge is that the development of these human assets that are so crucial to resilience is being severely tested. Work is becoming more fragmented and ever more virtual, working relationships are becoming disconnected, and the accelerating pace of work is putting extreme strain on well-being. Yet, as we shall see, some companies have practices and processes that are providing extraordinary oppor-tunities for people to be connected, for work to become ever more exciting and fulfilling, and for innovation and creativity to flourish.

CHAPTER 3

❖

AMPLIFYING INTELLIGENCE
AND WISDOM

It is one of the promises of large corporations that they have the potential to find and then connect some of the most talented and creative people in the world. Some, like Google, have talent-searching practices that are developed to a very high degree. Many others routinely bring talented people in from around the world to continuously bolster their intellectual resources. This talent search is crucial because the preservation and resilience of a corporation depends in part on its capacity to solve complex and ambiguous challenges and to create networks of intelligent and wise people who can innovate. Yet, to achieve this, the knowledge, ideas, and insights of many thousands of people, indeed often hundreds of thousands of people, have to be first amplified and then connected. On the face of it, this sounds like a broad-sweeping intent. Yet, as we shall discover, in reality, it is often specific and every-day organizational practices and habits that form the bedrock of this amplification and connection.

The reality of many of the complex and ambiguous problems that corporations face is that they can only be solved by highly specialized people capable of employing rigorous insight analysis and problem solving. Companies are frequently good at solving complex problems, but often they struggle with ambiguous problems. Let me give you an example of the difference between the two. Playing chess is a complex problem. Both players understand the rules—the game starts with 60 pieces, each piece can move in an agreed way, and players take turns to move. Thus, although a game of chess between masters will indeed be complex, it is not ambiguous because the rules are known and agreed on in advance. Now imagine that you are a newlywed and it's the first time your in-laws have come for dinner. For sure this problem is not particularly complex; after all, it is only a couple of people, a dinner table, and some food. Yet the problem is rendered ambiguous because the rules of the game are not clear or indeed agreed on by everyone. Over time, of course, the "rules of the game" will emerge—what you talk about, what they like to eat, how the meal progresses. Right at the beginning, though, you don't really know how to behave, and in many circumstances, neither do your new in-laws.[1] This is what makes it ambiguous.

As we shall see, corporations across the world are building their capacity to solve complex and ambiguous problems by making use of emerging practices such as open innovation and experimentation and use of the tools of conviviality.

ABUNDANT KNOWLEDGE AND THE TOOLS OF CONVIVIALITY

Hyperconnectivity is one of the trends that will profoundly shape the way that intelligence and wisdom are developed within corporations.[2] It's not simply that these tools are creating a conduit between two people in a mobile-phone conversation. They are also creating the opportunity for what the social philosopher Ivan Illich called "conviviality."[3] This is the opportunity for people to connect not simply with one other person but potentially with thousands of others and indeed with the abundant information held on the World Wide Web.

These tools of conviviality are able to potentially increase knowledge by bringing abundant knowledge to every laptop in the world. But will this actually have an impact on intellect? Will people actually do anything with this abundant knowledge? The answer depends in part on how humankind decides to spend its time. In the 1800s, when people dreamed about the future, they predicted a life of leisure, where machines would perform the drudgework and humans could be left to experience the more erudite, cultured, and intellectual aspects of life. One part of this prediction was right: we certainly have more leisure time, at least compared with the manual workers of the 1800s. Many people also have more unstructured time, greater economic prosperity, higher educational attainment, and a longer average lifespan. However, what was more difficult for the Victorians to predict was what we would actually spend our growing leisure time doing.

We have more leisure time—and for many of us this is spent watching television. As a consequence, someone born in 1960 will have watched around 50,000 hours of TV to date. Watching most television programs is not a great way of learning. The trillions of hours spent watching TV around the world every year are both non-productive (you sit and watch) and isolating (you are on your own). However, there are signals that this may be changing in a way that can profoundly amplify and connect intelligence, ideas, and creativity. It is what some have called "cognitive surplus."[4] Freed from the passivity of television, people will start to connect to each other and, through this connectivity, generate a huge cognitive surplus of perhaps 9 billion hours a day. And the fascinating thing about this cognitive surplus is that unlike watching TV, it enables aggregation. A million people spending one hour watching TV has no cumulative impact beyond ratings. A million people interacting on the Internet becomes an additive exercise. It is the combination of connectivity, content, and interaction that makes abundant knowledge so exciting for the future.

It also seems that as we connect with each other more profoundly, we understand each other more deeply and become more empathic.[5] In the past, people tended to empathize with those most like themselves—people their own age, from their community, or of the same nationality. When billions of people are connected, they begin to empathize with like-minded others, whatever their race or gender. It is this connectivity that is creating "swarms of citizens" who are linking with each other across the globe around an issue of passion—whether it's holding corporations accountable for toxic effluent, swapping ideas about three-dimensional printing, or creating communities of employees excited about using innovation to solve a problem.

HOW CORPORATIONS AMPLIFY INTELLIGENCE AND WISDOM

These connectivity tools that people are using outside of work are increasingly having an impact inside the workplace. As a consequence, this amplification of intelligence and wisdom is becoming ever more central to how corporations are addressing the challenges they face and to building resilience. Taking a closer look at how corporations are achieving this amplification, there are four key parts of the solution, each of which I'll discuss in detail.

1. They surface ideas
2. They amplify through open innovation
3. They build insights through experimenting
4. They celebrate risk taking

Surfacing Ideas: Wise Crowds at Infosys

For most of the history of corporate life, collaboration happened when small groups of people worked together face-to-face. Yet, increasingly, the tools for amplifying intelligence are creating the possibility of sharing ideas and knowledge not just within small groups meeting face to face but also across thousands of people meeting in high-touch virtual environments.

Imagine what happens when problem solving between small groups becomes problem solving across 140,000 people—the sheer intellectual caliber of a joined-up crowd of this size and their numerous insights and thoughts. This is precisely what Indian information technology (IT) company Infosys has been attempting. The company is creating a global network that enables thousands of employees across 33 countries to have their voices heard, to exchange solutions to problems, and to have their other innovative ideas addressed. Imagine the power of this global network—watching trends, being inquisitive about what they see, bringing in the views of the outliers, and then discussing it all with thousands of others.

The executive group at Infosys that pioneered this "wise crowd" went on a journey of experimentation and piloting to really discover how best to do this. Their mission was clear—to take the corporate strategic planning and problem-solving process from behind closed doors with senior executives to something much more embracing and inclusive. In doing so, the executives had to jettison some old practices and invent and refine some new ways of working and communicating. Traditional management thinking would have the senior team locked away in a series of management retreats in a process designed to get them closer to the perfect strategic solution. In this new way of problem solving, the executives wanted to amplify the ideas and insights of thousands of people.

Listening to the Voice of Youth

The executives at Infosys wanted to upend the hierarchy of the corporation and reach out to young employees who had only been with the company for a couple of years. By legitimizing the voices of thousands of young employees, their hope was to move the expectations of employees from simply being involved in day-to-day work to taking a more active part in the long-term success of the business. These early initiatives got more traction when in 2009 a group of young people had the opportunity to present their ideas to the senior executives at the Infosys annual strategy meeting. This conversation went well. Although many of the senior executives had Gen Y children, they had limited opportunity to hear their collective views in a corporate setting.

The senior executives were then determined to create a deeper process to connect the intellectual insights from the younger generation at Infosys to the long-term decision making of the corporation. They were helped in their aspirations by rapid technological developments in virtual platforms. Combining this nascent technology with their insights from the Gen Y conversations, the executives launched a virtual corporate platform. This widened the aperture of intellectual engagement by creating a platform that enabled conversations across the corporation to proceed with ease. Within a relatively short period of time, more than 12,000 employees had engaged on the virtual platform to share ideas and to understand more deeply the strategic challenges of the corporation.

Building on the Tools of Conviviality

The executives at Infosys began to build on this early success by championing a series of events around the world that included more than 65 "town hall" face-to-face meetings, broadcasts on the company channel, virtual graffiti walls to capture ideas, "knowledge cafés" to debate key topics, chat sessions with internal experts, and an organization-wide quiz. As a result, by the end of 2010, more than 46,000 people had been involved, generating almost 20,000 inputs that were used to shape the future strategy of Infosys. For Nandita Gurjar, global head of human resources (HR) at Infosys, the momentum was extraordinary.

> For the young at Infosys, communication was a big issue. They felt it's a very top-down approach. As a result, they came up with the technology to make communication two-sided and more fluid. This comprised "Infi tv" and "Infi radio" to be broadcasted on the intranet. They also came up with something like Facebook which we call "Infi bubble" and that gets 100,000 hits every day.[6]

These conversations had really captured the wisdom of the crowds, including insights about the emerging digital consumers, thoughts about sustainability, and ideas about simplification.

Crafting a Cocreation Platform

The next stage was to give people the tools they needed to more actively cocreate and solve problems. In 2011, the company was able to launch a virtual "Innovation Co-Creation Platform" that provided the perfect medium for people to identify others with whom they could collaborate, to gain access to deeper data, and to consult with experts and submit a business case for an idea.

These processes had created a fast and continuous flow of information from around the world and encouraged rapid feedback loops. It had also allowed the most knowledgeable and excited people in the organization to become visible to senior management. By building this momentum, the executives were able to create a network of strategy champions who had real passion and deep interest in strategy. Over time, these strategy champions began to play an increasingly central role in ensuring that the ideas that emerged from the various parts of the world and across the business of the corporation could be built on, with some strategy champions devoting more than 25 percent of their time to these global conversations.

Making Real Data Available

One of the issues the executives faced as they invested more in these global strategic conversations was the way in which important confidential information could be shared. In traditional strategy thinking and problem solving, it is the executives who have sight of confidential information about the company, and this information is rarely shared with others. Yet, in the absence of real information, it is difficult for employees to have real strategic conversations. The executives realized that an open-minded attitude and good decision making relied on access to real, in-the-moment knowledge, some of which is confidential. Without the traction of such real data, these conversations simply would become hollow rhetoric. In reality, this meant sharing confidential information about issues such as industry share, profitability, and comparative competition. Have no doubt— it takes real trust in employees to be able to do this.

Harnessing the wisdom of the crowd has become ever more sophisticated as the technology has developed and as our knowledge of how to build wise crowds has become more sophisticated. The idea of harnessing the crowd also has moved from within a corporation for commercial outcomes to outside the corporation for social outcomes. As we shall see, research teams from corporations such as General Mills, Cargill, and DSM are collaborating together using similar virtual platforms to solve some of the world's most pressing challenges of hunger and nutrition.

Amplifying through Open Innovation

The reality is that some of the best ideas and innovative insights about the development of a strategy, a service, or a product do not come from inside a company but rather from outside. No company has a monopoly on ideas. Indeed, it may be that despite the best efforts of companies to attract the most creative and innovative people to work with them, these people choose not to join. There are billions of people out there, and maybe one of them has the intellect or insight that could solve the intractable problem with which a corporation has been wrestling.

Therefore, to solve some of their unusual challenges, corporations are looking outside as well as inside. This external sourcing of ideas is not new. For decades, the research and development (R&D) departments of knowledge-rich corporations have turned to contract research providers in universities, departments, or specialist research groups to address specific topics and augment their internal capabilities. Typically, these problems are specified at a high level, possibly jointly with the contracted organization, and the contractor then puts a team together by dividing the task and allocating each task on the basis of team members' skill profiles.

Although this is an efficient way of managing the process of ideation, its very nature limits scope and diversity: the teams are already within the network of alliances, and those alliances represent the current skill profile of the team members.

Imagine that the search for ideas and insights was unlimited. The power of this could be enormous. We know from research on innovation that often the most inspirational and innovative ideas often come from large, diverse networks of people, many of whom are strangers to each other.[7] Ten years ago, this unlimited search would have been unwieldy, if not impossible. Now, by using open innovation, companies are able to declare their challenge to the world and see who in the world is interested and knowledgeable enough to answer the challenge.

InnoCentive: Joining Problems and Solvers

This declaration is at the heart of the InnoCentive platform, which makes use of open innovation to connect problems to those with knowledge. Thus, instead of turning to known teams with a narrow understanding or view of a problem, the original problem is revised and expanded so as to appeal to the largest possible audience. Those interested in solving problems register with InnoCentive by declaring themselves "solvers." This pool of solvers can be extensive and can include industry experts and people from adjacent knowledge domains. In some cases, these people have solutions almost readily at hand but have yet to discover a problem their solution could address.

Why would a solver be prepared to register on InnoCentive and share his or her ideas? What the tools for conviviality have shown is that when a task is fascinating and meaningful, purposeful and complex, some people are prepared to give some of their time to address it—the crowds of knowledgeable, unpaid contributors to Wikipedia are a case in point. The purpose of Wikipedia is sufficiently inspiring that thousands of people around the world work as editors and contributors. The same is true of Linux, which is an open-source platform built by thousands of volunteer code writers working in an intricate hierarchy of decision makers.

It is perhaps no surprise, therefore, that on InnoCentive, the motivation of solvers is a combination of the thrill of solving a problem that is fascinating and the possibility of financial gain that could be considerable. The process of problem solving works like this: initially, solvers are drawn to the high-level problem, and then they begin to see how it could be made up of subtasks. Solvers then can go to a "Team Project Room" to meet others who are interested in working on this subtask. These virtual rooms are secure online workspaces designed to enable multiple solvers to collaborate as a virtual team. Once the team has worked up a possible solution, it is submitted to InnoCentive as a single proposal. Such proposals then become part of the way that the company with a problem goes about solving it.

Procter & Gamble (P&G): Connect and Develop

Some companies believe that the open innovation process is so crucial to their innovative endeavors that they have built their own capability.[8] This is the route that innovation experts at P&G have taken. Theirs is a wide portfolio of products embracing food products from Pringles to hygiene products such as Pampers, and it's a product range that needs constant invigoration and innovation. For decades, innovation for P&G came from within—from building global research facilities and hiring and holding onto the best talent in the world. This talent, comprising 7,500 researchers and support staff, still exists, but the span of their ideas has been augmented by opening up much of their innovation challenges to the world.[9]

Launched in 2001, P&G's mechanism for open innovation is the "connect and develop strategy." This works by tapping into P&G's vast global external networks to look for ideas in government and private labs and academic and research institutions and to collaborate with suppliers, retailers, competitors, trade partners, and individual entrepreneurs. Much of the operation and momentum of connect and develop depends on a network of 70 technology entrepreneurs working out of six hubs around the world. These senior P&G people first work with internal executives to identify the challenges the company confronts, defining the company's needs more tightly and then preparing a technology brief. They then engage in an initial search of the possible networks that could contain knowledge that would address the specific challenge. They do this through mining the scientific literature in related fields, looking closely at related patent databases, studying other data sources, and tapping into the wide network of research capabilities of suppliers that are collaborating with P&G.

Once the initial network has been identified, the corporation's virtual portal is used to share the technology briefs. This is both internal facing (rather like the Infosys platform) and external facing. The external portal also connects with other open-source platforms, including InnoCentive, NineSigma, and YourEncore.

Carefully defining the initial problem brief, managing the initial network of potential problem solvers, and then encouraging them to give time to solve these challenges are crucial first steps. However, where these fast-developing open innovation processes can fail is the point at which the newly generated ideas are considered by the P&G team. Often these problem solvers create an overwhelming number of uncoordinated ideas that fail to really touch the problem. Thus, at P&G, the process of screening is seen to be a crucial stage, and it occurs through an array of internal screening methods that are pushed through the entire organization. If an idea captures the attention of those on the P&G project team, it is quickly assessed on the basis of its alignment with the goals of the business and then subjected to a battery of practical questions. Does P&G have the technical infrastructure needed to develop the product? What is its real market and business potential? If, after being submitted to these questions, the idea continues to look promising, it may be tested in consumer panels, and if the response is positive, it is moved into a product-development portfolio. Once licensing or other deal structures are taken care of, the idea that was discovered on the outside enters a development pipeline similar in many ways to that for any product developed in-house. Making the shift from a dedicated internal R&D model to one of open innovation has worked well for P&G, and by 2015, the goal is for the connect-and-develop process to deliver US$3 billion toward the company's annual sales growth.

Communicating at scale and sharing knowledge can indeed make a real dent in understanding complex and ambiguous problems. But what happens when these problems are not so amenable to under-standing, even by a crowd?

Building Insight through Experiments

The power of amplifying the intellect of the wise crowd is that it creates opportunities to discover ideas, insights, and knowledge on a grand scale. However, the challenge of ambiguous problems is that there are times when no one in the crowd really knows the solution to a problem or indeed that the crowd can come to a common understanding that is wrong. When the systems within which problems are embedded are complex and the relationships between the parts of the problems are ambiguous, then understanding how problems can be solved may not be known—even by wise people.

Under these circumstances of complexity and ambiguity, joining up the crowd may make a difference, but the real insights come when new information and ideas are added. As we shall see, often this new information and these new ideas are the result of experiments that reveal the underlying structure of a problem in a more profound way.

By way of illustrating the role of experiments, let me invite you to consider two complex and ambiguous questions: What is the best way to allocate pay across a group of people? and How can the bureaucracy of expenses be eliminated? Corporations are full of problems and questions like these. Bringing together a wise crowd could begin to increase understanding of the variables within the problem and indeed even begin to build a picture of how these variables work together. When a true understanding of the problem, the variables, and the picture does not lie within the knowledge of the crowd, though, experiments can provide much-needed intelligence.

Experiments in Team Structure and Pay at Xerox

High-performing teams are becoming an ever more important part of the formula for organizational success. When teams work well, they make a real difference, and yet they often stumble. One of the complexities of teams is the way they are structured. Some teams are engaged in tasks that are highly interdependent and therefore require the input of many people to complete, for example, a design team including writers, graphic artists, and project managers. In other teams, work is structured to be highly independent and performed by individuals, for example, a sales team where each individual member is responsible for his or her own specific territory. There is also a hybrid model that combines elements of interdependent and independent work, for example, a group of researchers in a development laboratory, where each pursues independent research projects and in addition collaborates in some larger shared project. One of the reasons why teams can stumble is that the way people are rewarded can demotivate them. For example, teams that are required to collaborate are rewarded individually. Thus the question is this: What is the reward structure most likely to motivate these different types of teams?

The experiment designed to answer this complex question was the brainchild of Professor Ruth Wageman of Harvard University. As she fast discovered, who gets paid what is an area of organizational life that is replete with half-truths, close-at-hand anecdotes, and overconfident judgments—just the sort of question, in other words, where a real experimental approach could be useful. Of course, everyone has a view of how teams should be paid—but are they correct? Getting it wrong costs the corporation millions in ineffective rewards and can have a significant negative impact on how people work and perform.

In order to build a picture of the impact of rewards on performance, Wageman began an initial conversation with the management team at Xerox. Together they decided to conduct a longitudinal quasi-experimental field study with 800 service technicians working in 152 existing teams.[10] These teams varied with regard to the tasks they performed: some were engaged in highly interdependent tasks, some had to work closely with others to complete their task, in some the work was structured in a highly independent way, and other teams were hybrid, combining elements of both interdependence and independence. The interest of Wageman and her colleagues was in the types of rewards that would be best suited to these various designs of tasks.

Wageman and the Xerox management team began the experiment by measuring the initial performance and motivation of the study teams. This included group and individual performance and behaviors such as cooperation, helping, and learning. They then introduced the experimental manipulation by altering the reward system: a third of the study teams received rewards contingent on the performance of the whole team, a third received rewards contingent on the performance of team members as individuals, and a third had their rewards linked to both the team and individual team member performance. After four months and again at eight months, the performance and motivation of the teams were reassessed.

What Wageman and her colleagues at Xerox discovered was that their initial framing of the picture was wrong. They had thought that the key variable determining the performance of these teams would be their type of reward. It turned out that the crucial variable predicting team performance was not reward but rather the design of the task. In teams where work was designed to include tasks that had to be performed collectively, the productive cooperation, helping, and learning within the group increased—regardless of the type of reward system. However, Wageman and her colleagues discovered that the type of rewards did make a difference, although not in the way they might have expected. They found that where the impact of rewards was felt most strongly was in the motivation of team members rather than in the behavior of the group. Specifically, they discovered that collective rewards helped to motivate highly interdependent teams to perform well. However, for teams working on independent tasks, collective rewards did not make a difference. In these independent groups, it was individual rewards that energized members.

Wageman and her colleagues also discovered some disquieting insights about hybrid teams and hybrid rewards. What they found was that these hybrid arrangements for tasks or rewards compromised motivation and performance. The challenge and motivation of working independently were reduced, and indeed, the excitement of working in a team was compromised. It seems that hybrid teams do not experience the benefits of working independently, nor do they experience the joys of collective working. The same is true of hybrid rewards. These also send confusing messages about how to perform.

The take-away for the executive team at Xerox was the "fudge"— to create tasks and rewards that they hoped would encourage both independent and cooperative behavior was the worst way to design teams and reward structures. It is either/or. Teams excel when they are either independent, with autonomous tasks and individual rewards, or when they are interdependent, with collective tasks and team-based rewards. The middle way simply does not work. This insight from these experiments created a clear rule for how teams at Xerox are configured and how their reward structures are designed.

Experiments in Reducing Red Tape at Roche

One of the deep criticisms of corporate life is that work is too bureaucratic and inflexible. There are too many layers of people getting involved in too many decisions with too little responsibility. Take, for example, the completion of expense reports as a measure of bureaucracy. Typically, these go through layers of approval. The question is: What would it take to remove these layers of bureaucracy?

This was the topic of conversation among a group of executives from Roche Pharmaceuticals as they gathered at London Business School.[11] The group had met to talk about innovation, which is crucial to the success of a company such as Roche. As group members talked about the way they worked, it became clearer that many of them believed that red tape was absorbing too much of their energy. They are not alone in this. I hear the same plea from many executives who attend my programs at London Business School.

The intuition of the executive group was that there are alternatives to bureaucracy and indeed better and simpler ways to align with Roche's organizational values of innovation. The view of the group was that cutting bureaucracy was not only feasible but also desirable. To test this conviction, the group designed an experiment.

First, the executive group chose a bureaucratic process—the signing-off process for travel and expenses. For group members, this epitomized, in a fairly extreme form, the misalignment of values that psychologically as well as physically drains professional effort and commitment. One manager summed up the mood of the whole group when he said, "I'm responsible for US$40 million in sales but need approval to buy a US$2 cup of coffee." At that time, Roche Pharma's annual travel budget added up to US$508 million—so the stakes were potentially higher than many people had expected.

Next, the executive group set up to design a workable experiment. The group identified two pairs of matched study groups, one pair from the Basel headquarters and the other from a sales affiliate at Grenzach in Germany. In each pair, there were 50 people per group, so there was a sample of 200 people in all. For each location, one of the two groups was treated as a control group, and over the period of the experiment, that group's travel authorizations continued to operate as before. The other group in each location formed the experimental group. That group was told that as part of the pilot project, travel expenses were to be self-authorized. Subject to normal company policy (e.g., who was entitled to travel business class), group members would make the decision themselves about when to travel on business and, via the travel department, to book their flights and hotels with no further approvals. The only proviso (and this is important) was that each group member's expenses would be transparent by being posted on the intranet for others to see.

The experiment addressed three questions: Would the people who could now self-authorize be more motivated, or would they object to this level of transparency and observation? Would self-authorization be quicker, or would it become overly cumbersome as people made their own arrangements? Would group members who self-authorized their own travel spend more than those who had to go up the line for approval?

The executive group found that indeed there were real differences in the outcomes of the two study groups. With regard to motivation, in 45 percent of the members of the study groups that could authorize their own expenses, motivation increased. Perhaps more important, 83 percent believed that the approach was better attuned with Roche values. In the majority of group members, the self-authorization was more efficient and less time-consuming than the old approach. As for the costs, compared with an equivalent period during the previous year, the expenses of the experimental groups went down. Over the same period of time, the expenses of the two control groups were similar to those of the previous year.

For each of these cases, experimentation was the route to a deeper understanding of the problem and therefore of the possible solutions. This is a crucial way to amplify the intelligence of a group. So why are experiments not used more widely in corporations? In part, it is because too often there is a focus on short-term solutions. But there is more. Management by intuition is often rooted in a desire to make decisions quickly and a culture that frowns on failure. So what does it take to celebrate risk taking?

Celebrating Risk Taking at Tata

Even with the insights that experiments bring, it's not possible to be right all the time. As corporations such as Infosys found, crowd sourcing and open innovation can increase the breadth of the intellectual rigor of the place and amplify wisdom and insights. But these insights have little impact unless people feel empowered to act on them. The challenge is that in many cases these actions may not lead to the desired outcomes. So what can a corporation do to encourage the risk taking that enables people to learn more and for their intellect and wisdom to be amplified?

This question of risk taking was important to Ratan Tata as he led the Tata Group over a period of decades. By 2011, the conglomerate had businesses operating in more than 80 countries, a US$100 billion turnover, and an employee base of 450,000 people. In his final years as chairman, Ratan Tata became ever more focused on building a resilient corporation and on amplifying and connecting the vast brain power and insights of all the employees. One of his beliefs was that the best way to encourage innovation is to make heroes out of people who have dared to do things differently. With this philosophy in mind, he created the Tata Group Innovation Forum—a 12-member panel of senior Tata Group executives and CEOs from independently run companies.

From all over the world, teams submit entries to be reviewed by their peers in 10 regional rounds. In 2006, the award attracted 101 entries from 35 Tata companies; by 2012, this had grown to 2,852 entries from 71 Tata companies. The awards ceremony is held on April 26 every year—in memory of the great Indian mathematician S. Ramanujan, who died on that day in 1920. What is interesting is that there are three categories of awards. The first two are found in most companies—for the teams that have recently implemented a promising innovation and for teams that have created leading-edge pilot projects. The third category is more unusual. Called "Dare to Try," it recognizes sincere and audacious attempts to create a major innovation that failed to get the desired results. For Ratan

Tata, the reasoning is clear: "Failure is a gold mine for a great company."

Perhaps it is no surprise that the initial response to the "Dare to Try" award was lukewarm because executives, especially those in India, were hesitant to share their failures. It took time for the business around the world to participate in this category in larger numbers, with the entries growing from 12 in 2006 to 87 in 2012. Recent nominees for the award have included a plastic door for the Tata Nano car. Although this door successfully passed all the safety tests, it could not go into production because of consumer perception issues. Other nominees have included an attempt to create self-cooling tiles for buildings and the search for a low-cost drug used to cure visceral leishmaniasis—one of the developing world's more prevalent diseases. The award lives on. In 2012, winners received their awards from Cyrus Mistry, then deputy and later chairman of Tata Sons.

CONCLUSION

The amplification of intelligence and wisdom—either from inside or outside of a corporation—plays a crucial role in helping people and organizations to become more resilient. As we have seen, in a number of corporations this is assisted by the deployment of a portfolio of rapidly emerging tools that enable good ideas to be amplified and then connected.

CHAPTER 4

❖

ENHANCING EMOTIONAL VITALITY

In my book, *The Shift: The Future of Work Is Already Here*, I narrated a day in 2020 in the life of a fictitious character I called Jill. Readers saw her as she rushed through her working day, continuously hurrying to answer her incoming messages, connecting to colleagues across the world, dealing with her daughter's school performance issues, and keeping up with the barrage of information with which she was inundated. The story of Jill and her frantic day resonated with many who read the book, and my team and I went on to make a short film of Jill's life that we called *Fragmentation*. What this showed is that the tools of conviviality will indeed create extraordinary opportunities for people to connect with each other around the world. As Jill found, they will also provide increasing occasions for people to work from home and to create their own work schedules. Yet the downside is that the combination of globalization and technological developments can leave workers like Jill exhausted and drained. Rather than an aid to work, these new technologies behave more like a bad-tempered two-year old, demanding constant attention and leaving little time for reflection or innovative thought.

Jill's story may have been one I wrote about the future, but right now, across the world, cracks are already appearing in the way we work. Surveys show that people are exhausted, their well-being is deteriorating, and their emotional vitality is being drained. The result of this is that the very energy and enthusiasm that are the keys to individual vitality and corporate resilience are ebbing away.[1]

WHY WORK IS GETTING TOUGHER AND MORE STRESSFUL

It may seem that encouraging ourselves and others to work flat out, to answer that message and keep our phone by our bedside, is a sure-fire way to increase productivity. But this is a fallacy. In reality, when we lose the natural rhythm of our lives and work flat out, what disappears is our emotional resilience and those times of reflection, contemplation, and playfulness that can be the wellspring of insight and innovation.[2] Work is getting tougher and more stressful for a number of reasons.

1. The emotional spillover between work and family life can become caustic.
2. Generational friction has increased.
3. Stressful work has intensified.
4. Time has become impoverished.

It's not just being constantly hooked up to technology that is draining vitality and compromising insight and innovation. It's also the way many corporations have chosen to configure work.

Before the industrial revolution, much work took place in the home or the community at times that matched the natural rhythm of the day and the seasons. During and after the industrial revolution, an increasing proportion of work became mechanized. Many people moved their work from the home to factories, and the natural rhythm of work was replaced by the bureaucracy of time. And it is not just factory work that has followed these mechanistic principles. Office work, professional work, and managerial work also followed the rituals established in the factories of the nineteenth century— work for a fixed time in a fixed location.

Emotional Spillover Between Work and Family Can Become Caustic

When I was growing up in the 1960s, it seemed to me that this working style was probably tolerable, at least for a large part of the population. I recall my father leaving home every morning to go to the Dorman Smith factory on the west coast of Cumbria, where he was a general manager. These were indeed long working days for him, but he knew that when he returned home in the evening, my mother would have us children bathed and ready to say good night, and he could look forward to a cozy evening and a delicious supper. Without a mobile phone or home computer, his weekends were uncluttered by work and were blissfully his own. He spent them and indeed many evenings in the summer months walking in the Lakeland fells he loved and sailing on Buttermere Lake.

To imagine what was happening to my father during those years, you can think about a continual cycle of physical and emotional energy that was his working day. The energy that makes up that cycle can be both positive and negative. We experience positive energy when we are excited, feel energized, and are confident and upbeat. We experience negative energy when we are feeling downhearted, frustrated, angry, or ill at ease. Over the course of a day, our energy levels will fluctuate and potentially could move from positive to negative. How we feel at any one moment will be determined by a number of factors. One such factor is our natural state of being. For my father (and indeed for me), his natural state of being was to be positive and upbeat—and so we could expect that this would affect his energy cycle. However, the context in which we find ourselves during each day also will have an impact on our cycle of energy. There will be some situations where the context encourages us to be positive and enthusiastic, whereas other situations will leave us frustrated and negative.

What is interesting about this daily cycle is that those who have studied it have found that the context of home and work can play a profound impact. They also have found that energy created in the home and at work is not isolated—but rather can spill over from one context to the other.[3]

I did not study my father's energy during his working life in Cumbria, but I recall that mainly he had a positive cycle of energy between his work and his home. Work was a place of interesting engagement and deep friendships. When he returned home, he brought with him those positive emotions and vitality. For him, the cycle worked the other way as well. Home was a place of robust energy but also a place where his long walks gave him time for reflection and regeneration. He was able to take these positive emotions back to work.

We know from current studies of spillover that my father's experience of a positive spillover between home and work is not currently shared by most people. In part, this is so because the forces of globalization and connectivity have put pressure on anyone working now. When you are competing with the world, you have to run fast to keep up—probably a lot faster than my father and his colleagues were running.

It is not just global pressure that has changed, though. When my father returned home from work, he could be assured of four relatively well-behaved children and a decent meal on the table. My mother had attended university and was, and indeed still is, a bright, creative, and hard-working woman. Like many women brought up in the 1930s and 1940s, though, her aspirations were always to be a good wife and a good mother. As with almost all her friends at school, the idea of having a paid career after having children did not enter her head. Much has changed within her lifetime. As her daughter, I was a member of the first generation that saw the majority of women deciding to work and to strive for a career. And in their turn our daughters seem to be making the same decision.

As a consequence, right now a very small majority of men have the home life of my father. In the United States in 2011, for example, fewer than 17 percent of families had this traditional structure.[4] This is so because women are entering the workforce in ever-greater numbers, whereas a larger proportion of married couples are divorcing. Thus, rather than coming home to bathed children and a delicious supper, most parents are now scrambling to keep a semblance of order in their lives. Well, that was my experience bringing up my own two children when both my husband and I worked full time.

So here is the bottom line: the way that work gets done—in an office, following a standard number of hours—was created as a consequence of the mechanization of work during the industrial revolution. It sort of worked right up to the 1960s. The full force of the stress of global competition had not yet been felt, and moreover, women stayed at home to absorb the pressure of family life and leave the men to get on to fulfill their working obligations. This is part of the reason why my observation of my father's life during the 1960s was of a positive cycle of emotional energy between work and home.

From the 1960s onward, that support structure began to crack. More women worked, and globalization increased the stress and the working hours. And yet, despite these cracks and the pressures they created, many traditional working practices remain resolutely intact. In fact, in many corporations, how work gets done continues to look remarkably similar to the way it looked two decades ago—even though the world has fundamentally changed around it.

The negative consequences of this incapacity for organizational change have been profound. Working men are under ever more pressure to juggle hard work and family responsibilities, and although women are joining the workforce, they are rarely reaching the top of corporations.[5] The loss of this incredible source of capability and diversity is taking its toll on corporate life as companies struggle to retain their most able women.[6] At the same time, the very emotional vitality that is so crucial to organizational resilience is being compromised.

Generational Friction Has Increased

It seems that the traditional deal at work is becoming increasingly untenable and is generating a growing negative emotional cycle between work and life, and the cohort for whom this has a really negative impact is younger workers.

I caught a glimpse of this recently when my research team and I invited more than 4,000 young professional Gen Yers from across the world to talk about their experience of work. My team had built a virtual technology platform to enable them to post their ideas and to converse with others. Over a three-day period, we worked with over 30 facilitators from across the world to shape and understand their conversations. As we anticipated, this community of young people spoke of many aspects of their work—their frustration with how technology was being underutilized, the important role their colleagues played in creating a positive working place, and the joy of working with managers prepared to mentor and support them. All this we had anticipated, but what we had not anticipated was the extent to which they discussed their own health. They talked about how important it was to give time to go to the gym and to have weekends free to devote to running and the emphasis they placed on healthy eating. Many of these young people did not yet have children—so in a sense this focus was understandable. But it seems to me that it is more than this.

When the research team spoke to Gen Yers in more detail, what became clear was that like Gen Xers, they saw their working life going forward as a marathon, not a sprint. My generation, the baby boomers, viewed work as a sprint. It could be tough and at times caustic—but it was short, with retirement still pegged to the early sixties. We began our working lives in very hierarchical and traditional corporate structures, and although we ditched some of those hierarchical structures (we reduced the number of job levels, for example), there was much we did not change. We did not really attempt the much thornier and cultural challenges of where work took place or indeed when work took place. We left that to the generation that came after us.

The result was that when Gen X (born between 1965 and 1979) and Gen Y joined the workplace, they found much to frustrate them. Many had been fully submerged since an early age in a hyperconnected world. Their life experiences were deeply entwined with technology, which had profoundly influenced their social habits and behaviors. They were at ease with virtual communities and enjoyed working in peer-based environments. Thus the frustration they felt with the legacy frameworks in which they found themselves working was understandable.

It turns out, however, that differences in the use of technology and working style are not the only sources of tension between the generations. Many baby boomers, and I would count myself in this group, have been incredibly fortunate. Born into a booming postwar society, those of us growing up in the developed world were healthier and wealthier than our parents. In the developed countries of the world, we grew up in the growing affluence of society that granted us a good education (often state-funded), a positive outlook on the future (with relatively low youth unemployment), and a working life without the pressures of a "hollowing out" of middle-skilled jobs. We viewed the world as a place of positive growth unfolding in front of us and took full advantage of its fruits. We experienced continuous employment and accumulated wealth through housing booms, we did not carry an educational debt, and we expected to get a pension that the state would top up. Indeed, many baby boomers entered the workforce imagining that they could retire in their midfifties. As a consequence, we viewed life as a sprint. We thought it was fine to work hard from the ages of 20 to 50 because sometime soon after that age we could retire to enjoy the fruits of our labor—and, in many cases, a heavily subsidized government pension scheme.

The life experiences of Gen X and Gen Y are profoundly different. Gen X grew up in the shadow of the cold war, at a time of economic uncertainty and political turmoil. They witnessed growing rates of divorce among their parents (between 1950 and 1980, rates of American divorce rose from 26 to 48 percent) and earned around 10 percent less than their fathers did at the same age. They had to be more self-reliant and resilient than the baby boomers before them and more able to create a working life at a time when the certainties of lifetime employment were disintegrating in front of their eyes. For some Gen Yers, the deal has become really raw. They are saddled with educational debt, are unlikely to participate in a housing boom, and know that they will have to work into their seventies or even eighties without the safety net of a defined pension at the end of it. The globalization of work means they are under immense pressure and have to fight for their place in a world they view as a competitive arena.[7]

Stressful Work Has Intensified

Thus Gen Yers are looking forward to a marathon of 60 years of working life. This is why they are so keen to keep healthy now. For many Gen Yers and the parents of Gen Yers, the cycle between home and work has changed from the relatively positive cycle my father experienced to something much more caustic. I saw this clearly in a study I conducted with Dr. Hans-Joachim Wolfram back in 2005 of the experiences of work and home of many hundreds of people.[8] Many of those we interviewed described how they came home from work exhausted after working long hours and then found home equally challenging with the demands of family life—young children, aging parents, and dual careers. What created negative spillover from work to home were stressors such as high work demands and long working hours and the conflicts at work about what they had to do. We found that this negative cycle of spillover between work and home had a really damaging impact on people's physical and emotional energy. Those who experienced this negative cycle were less committed and passionate about work and felt that they were less likely to be innovative and creative.

For many people, work has become more stressful. This was shown clearly in a World Health Organization report that found that the percentage of workers in the United Kingdom who said that they were working "very hard" or "under a great deal of tension" has risen steadily since the 1980s.[9] The results of this stress can be devastating. Stress at work is associated with a 20 percent increased risk of heart disease and a range of other mental and physical health risks.[10] And this is not just a UK phenomenon. In a 2009 global survey of 1,000 corporations across 75 countries, more than 60 percent of workers reported that they had experienced increased workplace stress. The survey found that China (86 percent) had the highest rise in workplace stress, whereas workers in larger companies (over 1,000 workers) were nearly twice as likely to suffer from stress.[11]

Time Has Become Impoverished

Our emotional resilience is also being depleted by the way we choose to allocate our time. The mechanics of work stress can be seen in the research of Nobel Prize–winner Gary Becker, who studied time allocation.[12] His work shows that, certainly in the developed world, people are increasingly concentrating the allocation of their time on activities that can be monetized. Simply put, we spend more time doing stuff that we get paid for and less time doing stuff that we don't get paid for.

For Becker, this is of real concern. He believes that industrialization has put intolerable stress on many workers, who work too much, eat too fast, socialize too little, sit in traffic too long, don't get enough sleep, and feel harried too much of the time. It is what Boston College researcher Juliet Schor calls "temporal impoverishment."[13] This impoverishment is particularly visible in the United States and the United Kingdom, where annual working hours have increased steadily. In 1973, on average, people worked around 1,670 hours a year; by 2006, this figure had risen to 1,870 hours.

For many people, our working days have become brutal. Here is what A. G. Lafley, former CEO of Procter & Gamble, says about a working life that would be familiar to many[14]:

> I'd be up in the morning between 5 and 5:30. I'd work out and be at my desk by 6:30 or 7, drive hard until about 7 p.m., then go home, take a break with my wife, Margaret, and be back at it later that evening. I was just grinding through the day. During my first year in this job, I worked every Saturday and every Sunday morning.

The research my team and I conducted with young professionals came to the same conclusion. Like Lafley, most reported that they worked in the evening, and a very significant majority—particularly those in leadership roles—also reported that they worked over the weekend.

The simple truth about the future of work is this: there are no checks and balances on the horizon that will reduce these working pressures. We may hope for some "cognitive assistant" that will come along to somehow control our inflow of information or help us to manage the load, but we are probably hoping in vain. In fact, all the factors that are shaping these working styles—ever-increasing globalization, more sophisticated connectivity, and greater cross-border working—will simply serve to increase the pressure. Future working practices and styles could become ever more denuding of vitality. Being joined up and technologically tethered causes fatigue through constant working, long hours spent commuting to ever more crowded cities create hours of stressful travel, and the artificial global 24/7 production rhythms can increasingly sap energy.

The answer lies not in more technology but rather in the way that employees and executives think about work and about how work is done. It's fundamentally about working practices and the design and management of culture and norms. As sociologist Sherry Turkle has warned, there is the ever-present addiction to multitasking and e-mail.[15] We need to meticulously manage ourselves in the face of enormous sets of demands and bring time for reflection into the structure of the working day.

Without a way of managing and controlling the way that work gets done, the chances of building emotional vitality are slim. Instead, the sheer avalanche of data, perpetual pressure, and continual connectivity will leave employees in a state of constant anxiety and stress.

HOW CORPORATIONS ENHANCE EMOTIONAL VITALITY

This is not a good omen for the future. If their working lives leave employees exhausted, if the fragmentation of communication removes any possibility of coherence and consistency in their working days, and if the constant pressure denudes their core resilience and vitality, then the courage, creativity, innovation, and energy needed to prepare for the future will be severely compromised.

The question those within corporations face as they look into the future is how they can ensure that the corporate practices, processes, jobs, and tasks are configured in such a way that people have resilience and vitality. Human energy is a "fuel" that helps organizations run successfully. When this important but limited resource can be replenished, it fosters high performance in employees and organizations. When it is denuded, the capacity to prepare for the future is compromised.[16]

If corporations are to be places where emotional resilience is strengthened and creativity and innovation are encouraged, then they have to find a way to finish the job that my generation began—of dismantling the last vestiges of bureaucratic, inflexible work and of creating practices and processes that bring choices to employees. For corporations to build emotional vitality rather than extinguish it, there are three actions they can take:

1. Reimagine when work gets done.
2. Create weekly playfulness.
3. Build a natural rhythm.

Reimagining When Work Gets Done at BT

Weaning executives off the idea of constant work is not easy. It's a great deal easier to manage a team when they are all present, and it's easier to monitor productivity when everyone works the same hours. This is why many attempts to create more flexibility about when work does and does not get done tend to flounder. Some managers have a natural tendency toward "presenteeism"—the belief that people are only really working hard if they are in the office and can be seen.[17]

It takes determination to reimagine when and where work gets done. One company that has shown this determination to reimagine work is British telecom company BT. It employs more than 90,000 people in the United Kingdom and in over 170 countries around the globe. The reimagining was championed by Caroline Waters, who in her push for flexibility was determined to show that there was an alternative way of working. Rather than go for a major cross-company rollout of flexible working, she decided on a low-key experiment in Cardiff.

Learning Through Experiments

For those unfamiliar with Cardiff, it is the capital of Wales, and in the early days of this century, it would have taken any curious BT executive almost a day to reach this far-flung part of the United Kingdom—the perfect place, in other words, for an experiment.

The experimental group was encouraged to work as flexibly as possible. Group members could change their patterns of hours—coming in earlier, leaving later, and working on the weekends. They also could change their location of work—working from home as well as working in the office. After three months of running this flexibility trial, the results were disastrous. Those working from home became increasingly frustrated by the regular system crashes and data losses, and they also struggled to maintain their relationships with the rest of the team and felt increasingly isolated. And they were not the only ones who felt frustrated. Team managers had become incensed by the team's growing propensity to disappear on Friday and come into work late on Monday. As a consequence, managers found it almost impossible to deliver high-level 24/7 service to their customers. When the three-month report of the results of the trial went to BT's headquarters, the senior group was keen to stop the trial before it could do any more damage.

Agreeing on the Rules of Engagement

However, Waters and the development team persevered and began the long process of creating the new "rules of engagement." They agreed that there needed to be a framework of core working hours, that there had to be a more nuanced understanding of the tasks that could be home based and the tasks that needed face-to-face interactions, and that the technology needed to be simplified with a more robust user interface.

Once these new rules were in place, the trial was begun again, and within six months, the early problems had been ironed out, and team members were beginning to enjoy the flexibility afforded them. In fact, their performance was now up to the same level as that of the control group. Within a year, the experimental group, with its more flexible way of working, had begun to outperform the control group—group members delivered higher customer service, felt more engaged, and stayed longer on the job.

Twenty years after the Cardiff trial, the lessons learned enabled BT to be at the forefront of reimagining work. By 2009, there were more than 14,000 home workers, and within three years, more than 70,000 people at BT worked flexibly. Starting an experiment in a far-flung place like Cardiff turned out to be a good idea, as Waters describes:[18]

> Always experiment on the periphery of the organization rather than try to make something like flexible working a big corporate roll-out. Next, focus on developing an early learning relationship between the managers and the team members to really identify points of friction. By doing this we discovered new ways of conducting and measuring work. For us at BT, the greatest shift came when we started to measure output rather than input. Before the trial, we measured the performance of the team by a proxy of how many hours they spent in the office. After the trail, we shifted the measurement to the tasks they performed.

Waters concedes that this can be tough—when people are working flexibly, it is difficult to escape the "attendance" mind-set. However, once the metric of value had been explicitly inverted from input to output, team members found that they had the flexibility to work whenever they wanted as long as their output did not diminish. Their primary function was no longer to show up—but to produce.

Although the daily pace of work can play a crucial role in either harnessing or draining vitality, often it is the longer-term rhythm that makes the real difference. For Gen Y employees facing the possibility of 60 years of working life, work is more like a marathon and less like the 30-year sprints of the generations before them. In a marathon, the capacity to manage vitality and emotional resilience becomes a weekly, monthly, and yearly activity as well as a daily focus.

Weekly Playfulness at W. L. Gore

My colleague Babis Mainemelis was for many years a professor at London Business School before returning to his native Greece. He has spent his working life thinking about and studying the rhythm of work and the impact this has on creativity. In the case of work flexibility, the assumption is that when people can control their work, they can manage the energy and vitality cycle between work and home while also building in more natural times for recuperation and regeneration. It turns out, though, that it is not simply "not working" that can be a source of emotional vitality—the work itself also can be a source of vitality. Specifically, when the working day has within it times of unstructured and free-flowing and playful activities, then important opportunities arise for vitality to be strengthened and for creativity to flow.

This playfulness is apparent in the development of the DuPont fiber Kevlar, which is one of the most successful and profitable innovations of the chemical company DuPont. The product was created when a team explored the idea in "free time" for six months. During this period, no one else outside the team knew anything about the project. When asked why she kept the project secret, the chief chemist replied, "It was my job to spend some of my time exploring new ideas on my own. I did not need anyone's permission."[19] The same is true of the engineers at Google, who are encouraged to spend 20 percent of their time on noncore projects without a direct line to profitability or marketability. In fact, CEO Eric Schmidt believes that most of the company's new products came as a result of these side projects.[20]

It is the textiles company W. L. Gore that is perhaps best known for the way that unstructured, playful work affects the vitality of workers and the resilience of the company. Take, for example, how in one of Gore's medical products plants an engineer took advantage of free time to improve the gears of his mountain bike, inventing along the way Gore's Ride-On line of bike cables. He then went on to use that idea to develop cables using guitar strings to control the movement of oversized puppets in such places as Disney World. When he noticed that the guitar strings broke easily, he then asked how he could develop less-brittle guitar strings. To answer this question, he teamed-up with a colleague who was an amateur musician and another colleague who helped to develop Gore's non-breakable Glide dental floss. Over a period of five years, they played together in Gore's free time and in their own free time, without "asking for anyone's permission or being subjected to any kind of oversight."[21] By the end of this play time, they reinvented acoustic guitar strings, and this new product was able to capture a 35 percent share of a market where Gore had traditionally had no presence.

What is happening at these playful times at DuPont, Google, and W. L. Gore is that for a time at least, the pressures of normal working life are suspended. During these free times, people are operating outside the functional pressures of their work, they feel that they have fewer obligations to others, and they experience less pressure for conformity and consistency. It is in this space that they can explore and experiment with new ideas, behaviors, or identities. Although their "discoveries" may not be immediately useful in generating products or solutions, they create a variety of ideas that can lead to a more diverse set of options.[22,23] It's these diverse ways of working that can play such a crucial role in creating emotional vitality and building inner resilience.

Building a Natural Rhythm at Deloitte

Playfulness across a week or a month can be a real bonus to emotional vitality, but what happens in the long term? There are times when we want to come "off ramp" and change the speed and trajectory of our career for a period of time. Historically, this sort of career flexibility has been seen as a "women/mother issue" because in many families it is the mother who takes most of the responsibility for child care.[24] Yet, increasingly, the need for flexibility across a career is an issue that goes beyond the needs of young women.

Consulting firm Deloitte has been focusing on career flexibility for several years now. In 2005, Cathy Benko, a principal of the firm and leader of Deloitte's "Women's Initiative," began to examine why retention for women at Deloitte was so tough. In general, consultancy is a male-dominated industry, with long hours and heavy travel (which can be as high as 80 percent out of town). As people moved into partner-track roles, they found it more and more difficult to create a positive cycle between career and life—and this was true for men and women. Benko also tracked the evolving family structure. She found that within the firm, the traditional family of a male partner with a stay-at-home wife had changed dramatically because husbands and wives were often both working and negotiating dual careers. In examining the root cause of the issue, the firm also tracked where women went after they left Deloitte and discovered that the vast majority didn't leave the workforce altogether; most of them were still working, just at other companies. This meant that Deloitte was losing out.

Imagining a Career Path as a Lattice

As she tracked the actual career paths of employees, Benko also realized that rather than operating as a continual upward trajectory, in reality, career progression more often resembled a sine curve, even for senior partners. She called what she observed a shift from a "corporate ladder" to a "corporate lattice." As Benko remarked to me: [25]:

> The idea of a corporate ladder is deeply entrenched in our thinking and ways of operating, and it has a profound effect on our view of the world and how things are supposed to happen. Until this mental model is changed, we realized that we could not make material change at scale. So we decided to move from the idea of customization from a theoretical idea to making it very tangible.

Rather than developing a set of practices and policies to be used across the whole population, Benko and her team instead encouraged individual workers to build their own ways through their careers. Her belief was that this would enable them to evaluate their careers over both the short and long term more effectively, resulting in a career-life fit that worked for them.

To introduce this possibility of customization, the choices people can make are described along four dimensions. The first is *pace*—at any point in time, does the employee want to accelerate (through promotion) or decelerate (through staying at the same job level) his career trajectory? The second is *workload*—does the person want to work a full workload, or is he looking to reduce working hours for a period of time? The third is the *location of work*—would it be preferable to work sometimes from home for a period of time? The fourth is the *role of work*—for the next period of time, would the employee prefer to work in a project role or rather in a support role? Working across these four dimensions, it is then possible for each person to begin to design a work pattern that suits his or her unique circumstances during that period of time.[26]

By creating a more flexible way of thinking about careers, the team at Deloitte is encouraging people to create a rhythm for their working careers that is sensitive to their personal circumstances and desires. It would seem that for companies such as Deloitte, perhaps the up-or-out model, in which people either have to be promoted quickly or move out of the promotion ladder, might be growing outmoded. Their way of thinking about a working life reflects less the mechanization of work and more the natural rhythms of life. This is ever more important because more Gen Yers are demanding better work-life balance; young parents want time to share child-care duties, whereas baby boomers look to ease gradually toward retirement.

CONCLUSION

I began this chapter with the story of Jill—living a fragmented life and constantly at the mercy of a barrage of information pumped through to her by the sophisticated tools of conviviality. In the life of Jill, the caustic cycle between work and home is draining away her energy and resilience. There is evidence that the current stress at work will only increase unless those who lead corporations can learn to creatively reimagine when work gets done, think about untethering work from the office, and create a more natural rhythm of work. All this is possible, and as we have seen, there are sufficient good practices in play to act as a role model for others. It simply takes determination and courage to build a place where emotional vitality is enhanced.

CHAPTER 5

HARNESSING SOCIAL CONNECTIONS

Our relationships with each other have always played a profound role in the development of civilization. It is in conversations that knowledge is exchanged, and it is in the coordination of people in complex tasks that extraordinary products and services are created. Right now, the nature and extent of these relationships are in a phase of extraordinary transformation. Even a decade ago, Infosys would not have had the technology to connect every employee to every other employee, as it does with the "Voice of Youth." In many ways, this is just the beginning, and over the coming decade, we can anticipate ever more exciting developments.

So where does that leave human interaction? For most of the history of human endeavor, the majority of human connectivity has taken place in face-to-face meetings and conversations. These face-to-face conversations, particularly between diverse people, have created immense value as contrarian perspectives and ideas were brought together.

Yet, for many corporations, whereas face-to-face conversations may be preferable, they are increasingly impossible. For many people, in the place of face-to-face conversations has come *cyber cooperation*, where people have to forge connections and share knowledge across locations and time zones.

In responding to the reality of virtual working, corporations around the world are becoming ever more adept at creating real connectivity, even in these virtual circumstances. These emerging rules of cyber cooperation are creating more understanding and deeper awareness of what it means to manage in a virtual environment.

In addition, as we shall see, the results can even magnify human connectivity in a way that would be impossible with face-to-face connectivity.

FROM FACE TO FACE TO VIRTUAL: EVOLUTION OF SOCIAL CONNECTIONS

We want to connect with others—to exchange ideas and gossip, to tell jokes, and to work together. For much of the history of social connections and innovations such as the discovery of DNA, face-to-face conversations were the powerful medium of this connectivity. Yet, as the most recent discovery of humankind—the discovery of the Higgs boson—shows, virtual connections also can be the foundation for the harnessing of ideas and insights that are so crucial for resilient corporations.

The Power of Face-to-Face Connection: Discovery of DNA

On most autumn days in 1950, Francis Crick and James Watson could be seen conversing with each other in the fading light of the Cavendish Laboratory at Cambridge University. Together they had embarked on the arduous intellectual task of immersing themselves in many fields of science, including genetics, biochemistry, chemistry, physical chemistry, and x-ray crystallography. Although they agreed on some aspects of their endeavor, they disagreed on others. This was reasonable. The two researchers were an unlikely pair with different educational backgrounds and a 12-year age gap. They also came from rather disparate scientific backgrounds and specializations. Crick was an expert in physics and x-ray crystallography, whereas Watson was an expert in viral and bacterial genetics. Thus, at their first conversation, they found little common ground or shared language. Nonetheless, they were able to come together to crack the puzzle that many other researchers had tried so hard to solve—to understand the structure of DNA. Their enthusiasm for science had led to one of the greatest discoveries in molecular biology.

The good news is that like Francis Crick and James Watson, we humans are probably soft wired to naturally cooperate with each other.[1] In fact, there is a growing body of evidence to support this view.[2] It seems that we are essentially tribal—we are inclined to share with people we know and particularly with those in our kinship circle, we are predisposed to trust people when we can see them face-to-face, and even if at first we don't trust another, our feelings about that person are likely to become more positive the more time we spend with him or her. Thus natural cooperation takes place under the conditions that Crick and Watson found themselves in—of knowing each other well, of interacting face-to-face, and of building trust over time.

Yet, at the very time that resilient corporations desperately need cooperative, positive relationships, and alliances, they are increasingly forced to create working environments that do not contain the conditions for natural cooperation to take place. Take, for example, the people at Infosys, who are participating in a worldwide conversation with thousands of other people. Their working environment could not be more different from the world of Crick and Watson. Most often they do not stroll with the colleagues with whom they are conversing, and indeed, when they do converse with others, it is often on the Infosys virtual platform, with people whom they do not know. Thus, while many of these people may indeed be soft wired to be cooperative, this wiring has prepared them to naturally cooperate with people they know and with people from the same region or with whom they interact on a daily basis.[3] However, in the Infosys global conversations, employees are "seeing" colleagues through video conference calls, and they are conversing with people who are as likely to come from the city of Hull as they are from Hyderabad.

For those who work at Infosys, and indeed for millions of other workers around the world, cooperation has transformed from being an activity that is natural to something that is much more complex and often cyber, and as a consequence, it becomes something that has to be worked on, understood, and consciously built.

We cannot turn back the clock to reinvent the cloisters of Cambridge University; the forces of globalization and technology that have transformed the world are also inextricably moving them away from natural cooperation. Thus, while we may no longer be able to have natural cooperation, little has changed in the fundamental building blocks of cooperation. Trusting others and having respect for others remain the cornerstones of deep cooperation and knowledge sharing. Without trust and respect, it seems that knowledge gets trapped in silos, and innovation withers.

Thus, while the building blocks of cooperation, trust, and respect have remained intact, what has changed is the context of cooperation. This change has occurred along three dimensions. First, the luxury of face-to-face conversations has been replaced across the world in many corporations with the technological connectivity of e-mail and video conferencing. With this technological connectivity has gone much of the pleasure of physical intimacy and immediacy. Second, those early languid conversations in studies and university cloisters that took place over many years have been replaced with ever faster cycle times and with teams of people who are brought together to work on a task at break-neck speed. Third, while Crick and Watson may have been different in their basic science backgrounds, they had much in common. They were both men and both educated in the West at elite educational establishments. As a result, these two men had a great deal more in common than many current communities and teams where connectivity is vital. Increasingly, corporate teams and communities are drawn from men and women who have many nationalities and who also have different educational experiences and specializations.[4] As a result, the relative homogeneity of the Crick and Watson conversations are very unusual in a world of diversity. Instead, as my own research on complex and diverse teams has shown, channels of cooperation are likely to fracture and create "fault lines" across national or specialist boundaries.[5]

Therefore, at the very time when we are beginning to realize the central role that connectivity and social capital play in the resilience of corporations, we are also facing an extraordinary challenge. The corporations that build connections are facing the task of doing so even when people are not working face-to-face, when the cycle time is fast, and when those to be connected are profoundly different from each other. They are also facing the extraordinary challenge of creating cooperation and fostering ideas that address what can be incredibly complex tasks.

The task of building collaboration at speed, in a virtual context, and in a diverse group to address a complex task may seem too big to accomplish. Indeed, we might expect the benefits of connectivity to be rapidly diminishing. This is far from the truth, though. In reality, there are places around the world where the challenges of connectivity and collaboration are being met and where the power of collaboration is being felt.

The Power of Virtual Connection: Discovery of the Higgs Boson

The wonder of complex collaboration became clear on March 14, 2012, when scientists reported that they had discovered something as extraordinary as the DNA molecule. The members of the European Organization for Nuclear Research, commonly known as CERN, announced that they had finally discovered the elusive Higgs boson. This particle had been the subject of a 45-year hunt to explain how matter attains its mass.

What is really astonishing about this discovery is that it was not the result of face-to-face conversations among a small group of people. Neither indeed did these conversations take place in the cloisters and halls of rarefied academic institutions such as Cambridge University. Rather, this was a feat of cyber cooperation on an extraordinary scale, involving incredible amounts of data and a large number of people collaborating across the world. In understanding how this feat was achieved, we can come closer to building a clearer way of thinking about the nature of cooperation in global and diverse corporations.

To understand how this complex collaboration was achieved, it is important to realize that the teams associated with CERN were working on a common task.[6] Their task was to analyze and understand the data created by the CERN experiments. The creator of these data is the Large Hadron Collider, which is a particle accelerator with a circumference of 27 kilometers, built on the scale of London's Circle line and lying beneath the countryside of Switzerland and France. The experimental conditions that generate these data are extraordinary. The equipment is constructed with tolerances to a billionth of a meter, it operates at temperatures of about −456°F (−271°C), and it accelerates subatomic protons to energies of 7 trillion electronvolts. The data created through these experiments are gigantic. Roughly 15 petabytes (15 million gigabytes) of data are produced annually, and that's enough to fill more than 1.7 million dual-layer DVDs. This mass of data cannot be held in one site, so it is distributed to hundreds of sites and thousands of scientists around the world.

Rather than face-to-face conversations in the Cambridge cloisters, scientists from over 170 institutions across 34 countries work together. To do this, the data are initially distributed to 11 large computer centers—in Canada, France, Germany, Italy, the Netherlands, the Nordic countries, Spain, Taipei, the United Kingdom, and two sites in the United States. These so-called tier 1 centers then make the data available to over 160 tier 2 centers. Teams of scientists then access these facilities through tier 3 computing resources, which can be local clusters in a university department or even individual personal computers.[7] The communities working on these findings are incredibly diverse, with more than 20 disciplines involved, including bioinformatics, medical imaging, education, climate change, energy, and agriculture.[8]

The discovery of the Higgs boson is the result of complex cooperation on the grandest of scales. It is why contemporary research articles from the CERN community often carry more than 100 author names—such is the extent of this cooperative endeavor. In understanding how this feat was achieved, we can come closer to building a clearer way of thinking about the nature of cooperation in global and diverse corporations.

HOW CORPORATIONS HARNESS SOCIAL CONNECTIONS

Complex collaboration can be successful and indeed can succeed at a scale and speed that dwarfs natural cooperation. In fact, it seems that the very technologies that are pulling us apart can also join us together. Yet, to do this, we must be prepared to look with a fresh eye at what it means to cooperate and, like the CERN physicists, be prepared to use every collaborative tool that technology has provided. This is by no means an easy feat, nor is it straightforward. What is clear is that the individual skills and organizational capabilities that build and support these cyber collaborations and virtual networks are a great deal more sophisticated than the managerial skills and organizational practices needed to build cooperation in familiar, similar, and long-lasting communities. It is possible for collaboration to be built, even in this emerging world of cyber collaboration, and as we shall see, the executive teams most adept at this are able to make use of four broad actions:

1. Create transparent performance commitments.
2. Balance cyber trust and friendships.
3. Communicate constantly.
4. Understand the role of generosity.

Creating Transparent Performance Commitments at Morning Star

Trust and commitment are at the heart of complex collaboration. We are more likely to trust people when we believe them to be competent and when we see them delivering on their commitments. The challenge is that it is difficult for others to see the commitments an individual has made to others and the extent to which those commitments have been met. However, there are emerging examples of how these commitments can become transparent. Take, for example, the way in which the senior team at the Californian food-processing company Morning Star has brought transparency to commitments. Although the company is small by the standards of multinational corporations, the process it has developed is an interesting way of looking at how commitment-based trust can be developed.

Founded in 1970 as a tomato trucking operation by MBA student Chris Rufer, Morning Star has become the world's largest processor of tomatoes. The company is managed on the basis of the commitments employees make to each other. This process of commitment making acknowledges the countless interdependencies that exist between people as they go about their daily tasks.

The commitments are expressed in a practice called the "Colleague Letter of Understanding" that becomes the thread that connects every employee with all those with whom they are engaged in joint tasks. The process begins when an employee crafts the commitments he or she has made with his or her colleagues. Once made, these commitments are shared with team members and across into the other teams of the company. Each commitment is built from a series of detailed "stepping stones" that describe the tasks people have committed to and describe the way that the performance of those tasks can be measured and tracked by others. In order to bring greater transparency to this, twice a month the detailed financial accounts of each business unit are published and made available to everyone. It's this combination of commitments and transparent financial accounts that has proved so important in building trust among people. Simply put, an employee is much more likely to trust someone who he or she doesn't really know if that employee can see that the person has a history of meeting his or her commitments.

Initially, the webs of commitments were written on a paper document that every employee completed. Then, on an annual basis, these written statements were reviewed with those involved to ensure agreement. This worked fine when the business was small, but as it grew, the whole process became unwieldy. By working with a technology company, the executive team was able to create a commitment-based software program that visually built a network of the commitment ties between people for all to see.

This technological innovation was crucial because it transformed a process that was static into one that became dynamic. As a consequence, at any point in time, the commitment network can capture the real changes in individual responsibilities. It also brought increased transparency to the commitments because people were able to view with ease their own and others' commitments. It turns out that this is crucial for complex collaboration. When people engage in a shared task and know what they and others are responsible for, then the whole task runs more smoothly and builds a stronger degree of trust among the communities.[9]

Balancing Cyber Trust and Friendships at TCS

The challenges of complex collaboration became crystal clear to me through the Future of Work Consortium. During an early stage of the research, my team and I asked over 3,000 executives from 50 companies to rate a number of their corporate practices and processes. We were interested in how important they believed these corporate practices to be for the future and their own perceptions of the current development of these practices. We then ranked all the corporate practices on the basis of risk. Those at the top of the risk ladder were corporate practices that were both important for the future and rated by the executives as currently underdeveloped. Taking a look at the results of this ranking of risk, what was fascinating was the extent to which anything to do with complex collaboration was at the top of the risk ladder. It seems that across the world, executives report that they struggle to create corporate practices to encourage people to work cooperatively across boundaries, be they functional boundaries or different generations. They also ranked as a major area of risk to the capacity to build high-performing virtual teams.

This perception of risk is understandable. As corporations have grown and globalized, fewer and fewer of their cooperative endeavors are natural, and more and more are complex and virtual. Take, for example, a member of the Tata group, Tata Consultancy Services (TCS). By 2012, this technology company was employing more than 238,000 people with more than 110 nationalities across the world. Of these, more than 70 percent were technically savvy Gen Yers, and 85 percent of the work of the firm was conducted virtually. It has proven to be a resilient business model that requires a global delivery network of employees working from anywhere, anytime to serve customers around the clock. It seems to be working. The average growth rate of the firm is 21 percent, and in the 2011–2012 fiscal year, TCS achieved annual revenues of over US$10 billion (£6.6 billion).

An outcome of the global business strategy is that for almost all employees, being able to collaborate across time zones and with people who are very different has become a standard working practice. Yet, as the executive team will acknowledge, supporting this complex collaboration is tough, particularly when these networks cover more than 55 countries.

So how do the executives at TCS go about building trust and cooperation in a virtual context? It seems that there are three ways corporations such as TCS are reinventing collaboration.

Focusing on Performance

The network of commitments and trust in performance is just as important to people across TCS as it is to those at Morning Star. For TCS, the heart of these commitments is the strategic goals of the corporation, which are communicated through a technology platform that enables every employee to track and monitor his or her own performance against these goals and shows how others across the company are progressing. As Nupur Singh, head of the HR function in Europe, comments:

> We encourage collaboration by encouraging a leadership style that is not about micro managing. We want people to trust each other. So we encourage leaders to define the end results, the accountability, and their responsibility. A leader defines the vision, sets the boundary but does not control until the outcome phase, and creates freedom within the boundary. Facilitators take the lead when required. It's not a power game, and commitments between peers are crucial.[10]

It seems that like the executives in the home-working experiments at BT's office in Cardiff and the lattice career path at Deloitte, the TCS executives have seen the beauty of measuring performance outcomes rather than time inputs.

Building Cyber Trust

Like the executives at Morning Star, the team at TCS has seen how commitments and accountability can smooth the path to successful complex collaboration and problem solving. However, although these commitments are important, they cannot stand on their own. What is also crucial to complex collaboration is communication—in fact, masses of communication.

Frequent communication is a powerful determinant of natural cooperation, as the discovery of DNA by Crick and Watson illustrates. Their continuous conversations over a long period of time became the foundation for innovation and insight. It turns out that such frequent communication is as important for complex collaboration. Just how important is shown in a piece of internal research conducted by a team at TCS that monitored the communication patterns and performance of virtual teams. This team discovered that one of the key indicators of team performance is the extent and depth of communication. The teams that communicated most also trusted each other more, and this lubricated their cooperation and ultimately was an important determinant of their performance.

What exactly is happening in this frequent communication that makes it capable of supporting trust and ultimately building performance? Clearly, some of this virtual communication will be about the progress of the task. But this is not all—the crucial role that constant communication plays in these high-performing virtual teams is that it provides an opportunity to showcase a person and his or her capabilities. It is this showcase that encourages others to trust. As Nupur Singh reflects:

> We have discovered that trust is the real factor that makes a difference in the highest performing teams. Our culture is "trust someone until they are unworthy of trust." People have to live up to the trust. To support this, much effort is focused on ensuring that people have the competency to "live up to trust."

There are various ways that Nupur Singh believes her colleagues at TCS increase the likelihood of people living up to trust.

Living up to Trust

First, when commitments and performance are visible and shared in the moment, it's much easier to give instant feedback rather than wait for the annual ritual of performance appraisal. The executive team at Morning Star had come to the same conclusion when it designed the network of commitments. At TCS, these commitments are enhanced by the assignment of a facilitator to each team. The facilitator's role is to work with the team to observe closely their progress and to coach them in building performance.

Next, being able to "live up to trust" is boosted by encouraging every team member to continuously update and enhance his or her skills. In the spirit of virtual working, a global training platform provides access to over 10,000 web-based courses on technology and a wide range of domain knowledge and soft skills such as coaching and mentoring. Team leaders are also specifically trained in how to manage virtual teams.

The TCS executives have discovered that visible commitments, team facilitators, and online training support are necessary. However, this is not enough. It seems that even cyber cooperation needs the warmth and affection that only face-to-face relationships can bring.

The challenge for a global company such as TCS is that face-to-face meetings are very costly. Typically, face-to-face meetings involve flying people across the world to be together—just the sort of activity, in other words, that increases the carbon footprint of the company and drags employees away from their families. Thus, if teams are indeed going to meet face to face, it's crucial that every encounter delivers as much impact and value as possible. As Nupur Singh comments, "Face-to-face meetings have a high premium as it is in these circumstances that trust can be fostered."

Balancing cyber cooperation with the intimacy of face-to-face meetings is crucial. Therefore, for example, most projects begin with a kickoff meeting that brings the whole community together in one location for a few days. There is also the practice of *Maitree* (which means "friendship" in Hindi), whereby employees and their families spend time together in activities from theater to yoga, origami, and flower arranging to get to know each other better. Trust is also encouraged by building wide networks of working relationships and friendships. For example, every employee has the opportunity to work every two to three years on a project or assignment in another country.

These executive decisions—visible performance metrics, constant training to build competence, initial face-to-face meetings, *Maitree*, and overseas projects—are all designed to create the trust that builds cooperation. Yet, fundamentally, trust and cooperation are about the culture and norms of the place. In building a culture of cooperation, I and others who research cooperation have found that the early period of socialization is crucial. So what is TCS doing to support a culture of cooperation in the first 90 days?

It seems that when a newcomer joins, he or she is immediately immersed in a series of socialization steps that introduce them to the value of positive collaboration. The newcomer has a phased induction and integration program that starts on day one of joining, followed by networking events such as breakfast clubs, reaching-out sessions where they meet the leadership team, business-units meetings, and conversations.

Once the newcomer is on a team, there is much focus on the design of work. Like the executives at Xerox, the TCS executives have discovered that when tasks are designed to encourage interdependence, they are more likely to build cooperation. Therefore they are thoughtful in the design of work and of the workflows that encourage reciprocity. What of pay? Again, recall the Xerox experiment that showed that people on teams are very sensitive and attuned to the way they are paid. At TCS, the decision has been made to encourage teamwork by ensuring that pay differentials are not too great. The executive team realized that when pay differentials are large, people are less likely to trust each other and less likely to collaborate with each other. Therefore, keeping pay differentials as narrow as possible creates a stronger bedrock for collaboration.

Constant Communication at Cisco

I saw how this need for constant communication that the TCS team found to be crucial was also key to how employees at U.S. software company Cisco have learned to cooperate with each other. The same forces that are shaping the working day at TCS in Bangalore, India, are also shaping the working days at Cisco in San Jose, California. As one of the main architects of the cloud, it is no surprise that like those at TCS, the executives at Cisco have been in the vanguard of new ways of collaborating. As a core member of the Future of Work Consortium, I have seen how the collaborative practices at Cisco work on a day-to-day basis. One of the particular challenges for the teams working on the cloud architecture is time compression. Natural cooperation tends to evolve slowly over time as people spend more time together and build a mutual view of reputation. However, faced with projects with compressed time, the challenge for the Cisco teams is to do cooperation at speed and with dispersed membership.

As befits a technology company, what is interesting about the way that Cisco executives have approached virtual collaboration is their use of collaborative tools. The task is large, and in order to connect the thousands of project teams, the company built an intranet that enables more than 110,000 employees and contractors to connect, communicate, and collaborate with each other. This is crucial because most Cisco employees spend as much as half their time working from home, whereas more than 40 percent are located in a different city from their managers. Executive Robert

Kovach, who works on the organizational development and learning aspects of Cisco, describes the sheer breadth of this communication endeavor:

> There have been over 600,000 Webex meetings, 110 million conferencing minutes per month, 2.4 million intranet web pages exist with an additional 42,000 wiki pages, and 2,000 new videos are uploaded each month.[11]

In Kovach's view, it's the sheer scale of connectivity that really makes a difference to collaboration.

Like the TCS executives, though, the Cisco executives discovered that the way these teams are managed is also crucial. They have evolved a dynamic way of working whereby each leader is intimately involved with sharing the goals of the business rather than simply setting tasks and monitoring. They also have thought hard about where collaborative work takes place. As a result, across the world, Cisco offices have been redesigned. By 2011, there were nearly 1,000 conferencing facilities allowing multiple-participant meetings in high definition, some on life-sized screens, with more than 240 cities in 59 countries around the world linked with telepresence capabilities.

Encouraging virtual collaboration has had many advantages, as Robert Kovach reflects; it has made a significant impact on the travel and therefore the all-important carbon footprint of the company. In 2011, for example, 211 million air miles were avoided and 90 percent cost savings achieved. This virtual way of working also has had a positive impact on the way people work collaboratively with each other. In Kovach's view, building high-performing virtual teams has been a real advantage to the resilience of the corporation. There have been a number of occasions when the executive teams have been able to deal speedily with a crisis because they have had the collaborative practices and culture that enabled emergency executive meetings to be arranged at very short notice with participants around the world.

Understanding the Role of Generosity

I was intrigued by TCS's Nupur Singh's comment "Trust someone until they are unworthy of trust." Now that's interesting. For me, it hits at the very heart of a philosophy of human nature. Let me ask you to reflect on this. Do you trust someone until they are unworthy of your trust? Do you believe that most people are prepared to cooperate? Or do you believe that most people are operating in their self-interest and therefore can only be induced to cooperate? These are important questions because our attitude toward the answer becomes the basis of how cultures are created within corporations and ultimately the practices and processes that are designed within a corporation.

This question of trustworthiness is one that my colleagues, Sumantra Ghoshal and Peter Moran, reflected on in an article entitled, "Bad for Practice," published in 1996.[12] Their observation was that for decades the view of human behavior has been gloomy. Powered by the way economists interpret the motives and behavior of people, the prevailing assumption was of *Homo economicus*. Essentially, the economic argument goes, people operate on the basis of being rational self-interested maximizers. In other words, when faced with the choice of cooperating with others, people are most likely to make a choice about how to behave based on what will maximize their personal outcome.

It seems that this question of who and when to trust is not simply a theoretical mind game. If the executives of a company believe that people are essentially self-interested maximizers, then the structures and practices they build will be designed on the basis of this assumption. By doing so, they are creating a self-fulfilling prophesy in the sense that those treated as if they operate on the basis of self-interest will, over time, begin to behave in that way.[13] Of course, the reverse is also true. If an executive believes that people are able to act with generosity and cooperation, then that executive is likely to create a context that assumes this and, by doing so, encourages people to be cooperative and trusting of others. What is interesting about the experiences of the TCS executives is that their assumption of trustworthiness, through this process of self-fulfillment, increases the likelihood of others behaving in a trustworthy manner.

The intricate dynamics of trust and cooperation have become clearer with recent developments in game theory and mathematical modeling. One of the researchers engaged with the question of trust and cooperation is Harvard University's Martin Nowak, who approached the question of cooperation not from a philosophical vantage point but rather as a mathematician who uses game theory and simulations to deepen insight.[14]

Generous Tit for Tat

Nowak studied the tension that exists between being cooperative and self-interested in a game called *prisoner's dilemma* which has been used by psychologists to study cooperation. The game proceeds through a series of rounds in which a pair of players has to decide whether to cooperate with each other. By studying the outcomes of the choices they make and the probability of subsequent choices, what he and other game theorists have been able to recreate is the evolution of cooperation across a relatively short period of time.

The prisoner's dilemma game works like this. In every round of the game, each player has an opportunity to act. The player can choose either to cooperate with the other player or to stop cooperating. As a consequence of these choices, there are three possible outcomes to each round of the game: both players can decide to cooperate—a positive outcome; both players can decide not to cooperate—a negative outcome; or one player can decide to cooperate while the other player decides not to cooperate—this outcome is called a defect. In this defect outcome, when one player cooperates and the other player defects, this leaves the cooperator in a position of being exploited.

The game is repeated over time, and after each round of the game, the players make their next move. As the game progresses, there are various long-term strategies players can adopt. They can use a tit-for-tat strategy—in other words to reciprocate cooperation only when the other player first cooperates. In a sense, this tit-for-tat strategy seems like it would make sense in a working situation. Surely, it is best to cooperate after someone has cooperated with you. But it turns out that this strategy is not quite so simple. Most important, a tit-for-tat strategy assumes proximity; you have to see and know the actions of the other in order to predict future action. It also requires constant repetition so that reciprocity is built over time. Thus this tit-for-tat strategy is best within a long-lived community whose members are working closely with each other, not—in other words—in virtual teams.

Moreover, as the research team found, this tit-for-tat strategy rapidly breaks down when the other partner fails to reciprocate. It is no surprise, therefore, that the most resistant cooperative strategy the researchers found was what they termed "generous tit for tat." This goes beyond tit for tat in the sense that even if the other player does not reciprocate when the first player has cooperated, there is still an opportunity for cooperation to continue. Straight tit for tat can be too harsh and unforgiving. Add a sprinkling of forgiveness and trust, and then watch how the other behaves in the next round.

This short digression into the world of game theory brings with it greater insight into Nupur Singh's words: "Trust someone until they are unworthy of trust." It is this corporate attitude that provides enough room for cooperation to flourish. The implicit contract is "Failing once does not make you unworthy of trust—but fail more often and others will begin to lose trust in you."

Collaborative Tipping Points

This modeling of cooperation that game theorists have been engaged in looks primarily at the cooperative actions and choices between two people. In reality, though, the sprawling, intricate communities and teams of most businesses are made up of multiple relationships among many people. Here the work of the game theorists has provided a glimpse into how wider networks behave. To do this, they have modeled cooperative strategies via mathematical simulations. For example, Nowak ran hundreds of simulated prisoner's dilemma games in order to observe the emerging cooperative dynamics. What he discovered was fascinating. The simulations showed that over time, populations of players are able to develop stable cycles of cooperative patterns. However, these stable cooperative patterns can be broken at the point where new players, who are programmed to use the rules of self-interest rather than the rules of cooperation, began to enter the game. When this occurs, the pattern of cooperation rapidly erodes, and in its place, a cycle of self-interest and chaos continues until more players are prepared to begin to cooperate with each other.

One of the interesting propositions Nowak tested with these mathematical simulations was the point at which the number of self-interested players entering the game would break the cycle of cooperation. He discovered that cooperation continues as long as the percentage of those entering with self-interested rules is less than 32 percent of the total population. At this tipping point, the community rapidly disintegrates into individual self-interest, and cooperation is destroyed.

Of course, one can argue that these are mathematical models rather than real life experiences. However, field experiments conducted on cooperation have come to the same conclusion. For a culture of cooperation to emerge, at least 65 percent of the people have to have strong personal values of cooperation and sharing and must be prepared to use those rules of cooperation when they are working with others. This is why, for example, companies such as TCS put such a large store on recruiting naturally cooperative people and then enhancing their skills through training and development.

CONCLUSION

At a time when technology, globalization, and generational differences are putting pressure on the natural capacity of people to cooperate, business strategies are calling for more cooperation. As we have seen, companies are making significant investments to ensure that trust and collaboration are being built—even when people are working virtually and collaboration has to take place across boundaries. Creating a network of positive, engaged people also provides a crucial foundation for scaling and mobilization.

Yet there is a growing view that while this is important, it is not sufficient. Increasingly, those who lead corporations are also being held to account for what they do in their neighborhoods and supply chains—and it is to this that we now turn.

PART III

❖

ANCHORING IN THE COMMUNITY

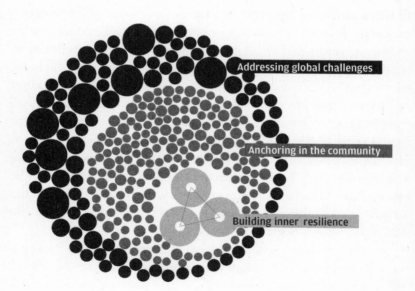

Addressing global challenges

Anchoring in the community

Building inner resilience

For decades, the leadership role of building an inner core of resilience was sufficient. Although corporations did indeed operate in a wider external context, this was seen to be in some way a context that could be controlled or even ignored. Executives schooled in the art of business strategy were encouraged to view the world outside the corporation primarily as a field of competitors to be battled with or of consumers to be lured. If the "outside" of neighborhoods, supply chains, or regions was to be considered, it was kept in the periphery of a corporate social responsibility function rather than seen to be central to the strategy of the business.

However, this passive view of the role of the external context of the corporation has to change, and in some companies, it is changing fast. In its place is emerging an acknowledgment of an ever-growing permeability between the "inside" and the "outside." Increasingly, the world outside the boundaries of a corporation does matter, and rather than a context to be controlled, executives are realizing that the world outside can dramatically impinge on the inside and therefore on the latitude of choices available to them. The challenges of climate change, poverty, inequality, and youth unemployment each have their own trajectory of corporate impact. Unpredictable weather patterns and rising sea levels will create uncertainties in supply chains and transportation; poverty and inequality will bring growing societal fissures and become the breeding ground of unrest and terrorist groups that will have global corporations in their sights; and the specter of youth unemployment will both create skill gaps that jeopardize talent pools and also bring the instability and lack of social mobility associated with bipolar labor markets. As a result, it seems clear that the world outside a corporation can no longer be viewed simply as a battlefield of competition, disconnected from the activities within the corporation. The world outside the corporation matters—and it is beginning to matter a great deal.

Yet it is not just escalating global challenges that are breaking down the boundaries between the corporation and outside worlds. The dissolution of these boundaries is also hastened by changes in the expectations of consumers and employees. It seems that consumers and employees are increasingly viewing corporations as potentially positive players in the world rather than simply as players in the competitive landscape. As we shall see in Chapter 6, these groups have emergent expectations about how corporations work as neighbors and, as we shall see in Chapter 7, expectations about how corporations can work as global institutions in tackling the world's accelerating challenges.

It seems that now is the time to break down the boundary between the inside and the outside and to see the corporation in its totality. If corporations are to be sufficiently robust and successful over the coming decades, their resilience has to be seen not only in the context of inner resilience but also as a factor of outer resilience—in the neighborhoods in which they reside and in the extended supply chains that serve them.

CHAPTER 6

BEING A GOOD NEIGHBOR

A t a time of decreasing state support in many countries around the world, coupled with significant demographic and societal shifts, neighborhoods are becoming increasingly fragile. For some corporations, such as those in the information technology (IT) sector in India, the lack of neighborhood schooling puts their growth strategy at risk, and being a good neighbor is about building job-ready skills. Yet, even in the most developed and wealthiest nations, such as the United States and Japan, there are always neighbors in need of help—be they the elderly or the poor. As we shall see, though, it takes focus, determination, compassion, and resources for a corporation to be a good neighbor. When corporations reach out into their neighborhoods to become good neighbors, they typically do so in three ways:

1. They build vibrant and resilient neighborhoods.
2. They bring compassion into the neighborhood.
3. They build job-ready skills in the community.

BUILDING A VIBRANT AND RESILIENT NEIGHBORHOOD AT ZAPPOS

Tony Hsieh is CEO of the U.S. online retailer Zappos.com and has been able to build a corporation that is both profitable and makes a positive contribution to its neighborhood. To do this, he took Zappos from an online shoe retailer with US$1.6 million in sales in 2000 to one that had over US$1.64 billion in sales in 2010—and he has sold the company to Amazon along the way. Yet, despite these changes, the people employed at Zappos continue to see their business as one of the best places to work in the United States. Inside the corporation, Hsieh's real passion is corporate resilience in the form of the healthy and happy lives of his employees. This is how he describes this[1]:

> We want the person to be the same person at home or in the office because what we've found is that's when the great ideas come out, that's when their creativity shines, and that's when true friendships are formed—not just coworker relationships. When people are in that environment, that's when the passion comes out and that's really what's driven a lot of our growth over the years.

Yet this inner resilience is not all. What has been fascinating is how Hsieh has worked to ensure that the emotional, high-touch way of working inside the business is mirrored outside in its immediate neighborhood.

A particular focus has been the location and design of Zappos' offices. This is important because how the executives of a company plan their offices to physically sit in their neighborhood—the bricks and mortar of the places—signals much about their attitude toward their neighborhood. It's a clear and physical manifestation of the relationship between corporation and place—the inside and the outside. Let me explain what I mean.

Removing Physical Barriers

There are some corporate offices that distinctly signal that the corporation and its people are different from and removed from the community in which they are situated. This is my overriding impression, for example, of the Infosys campus in the Indian city of Bangalore. To the casual observer, the campus looks like a fortress. Within the soaring walls of the circular campus lies a pristine area where employees can work, eat, relax, and even sleep. It feels like it is located a million miles away from the chaos of India that assaults the senses within minutes of leaving the gates of the campus. Many other Indian IT companies have similarly removed themselves from the chaos of Indian cities with the same impenetrable high walls. This is not just an Indian phenomenon. Looking at the latest designs for Apple's headquarters in California, it seems that designers and executives are thinking along similar lines to the Indian IT companies, building an office around an inner cloistered open space that is available only to those inside. For Infosys, the strategy is to remove the campus and its employees from the squalor of the streets of Bangalore. For Apple, the strategy is to increase the focus and creativity of its teams by building a total environment removed from the distractions of everyday life. Yet, whereas this makes total sense, it does create a strong physical and psychological barrier between the inside and the outside.

So what is so interesting about the design choice that Tony Hsieh and his team at Zappos have made is that it has reversed the prevailing Silicon Valley approach. Instead, they consciously decided to bring the outside in. To make this vision a reality required a significant coalition of multiple stakeholders, including real estate agents, economic development boards, and corporate executives. The process began in 2011 when Hsieh realized that Zappos would soon outgrow its offices in Henderson, Nevada. The chosen place to relocate was the City Hall building in Las Vegas, which overlooks the downtown neighborhood. The strategy behind the move was to enable over 1,200 employees to be housed under one roof and really integrate into the community. The move provided an opportunity for Hsieh's values about organizational culture to become reality. This is how he describes his logic[2]:

> Happiness is really just about four things: perceived control, perceived progress, connectedness (number and depth of your relationships), and vision/meaning (being part of something bigger than yourself).

Hsieh's vision began with the launch of the "Downtown Project," which aimed to turn this derelict core of Las Vegas, with its liquor stores and weekly hotels, into a major city bustling with economic and social prosperity. This is important, for whereas most tourists see the bright lights of Las Vegas, few visit downtown Las Vegas with its blocks of run-down casinos and cavernous gift stores. Less than two miles to the north there is the so-called homeless corridor, a patchwork of soup kitchens and air-conditioned shelters that protect the area's thousands of homeless people from the life-threatening 115°F (46.1°C) afternoons during the summer.

Engaging with the Community

The Zappos plan was to take over this area of the city and build a new campus that would make a positive contribution to the resilience of this fragile neighborhood. The inside of the campus was built on the guiding principle of serendipity, encouraging people to wander around and create their own sense of community. A clear signal of this sense of community was that all employees entered through a single door.

The culture and way of working inside the campus were then reflected in the design of its immediate neighborhood as a new live-work-play destination for Las Vegas' emerging creative class. In his thinking, Hsieh was deeply influenced by the book, *Triumph of the City*, in which Harvard Kennedy School of Government's Edward Glaeser argues for the value of cities. Glaeser believes cities can revitalize and become a key incubator for new skills and the site for creative clusters to emerge and that this unleashing of productivity comes from the spontaneous "collisions" between different types of people, which spark ideas and create deeper relationships that lead to more ideas.[3]

With seed money of US$350 million, Hsieh began to buy empty lots, to seed new businesses, and to subsidize local schools. The corporate team also was actively involved in providing initial funding for dozens of high-tech startups and creating real estate projects. Importantly for community roots, Hsieh then went on to make a US$1.5 million deal with Teach for America to bring 1,000 core members and alumni to live and teach in the area. In short, he is doing everything he can to make the area an attractive place for professionals and entrepreneurs to live. If Glaeser's argument is correct, then it would be expected that this creative cluster would attract a plethora of supporting businesses, including cafés and restaurants, real estate businesses, dentists and doctors, employment services, couriers and messengers, private hospitals, and retail stores. In fact, the city's economic development team has estimated that the Zappos move will have an economic impact on downtown valued at more than US$336 million.

What Hsieh and his team at Zappos have understood is that resilient and vibrant corporations can reach out beyond their inside to use their physical design to support and strengthen the fragile communities of which they are members.

BRINGING COMPASSION INTO THE NEIGHBORHOOD

The capacity and interest of a corporation to connect to its neighborhood can be signaled through the way it physically sits within its community. It also can be signaled through the way employees support their local neighborhoods.

The Yakult Ladies

There are occasions when the outer world of a business impinges on the inner world in a dramatic manner. This drama unfolded on March 24, 2012, in the Saitama Prefecture in Japan when a 75-year-old woman was found dead, her body lying next to her emaciated 45-year-old mentally disabled son. She was discovered by the visit of a Yakult drinks delivery lady who visited the home and saw that the newspapers had not been collected for several days; the woman also recalled that the old lady had not looked well the last time she had visited the previous week. It was her call to the police that saved the life of the son.

In many developed countries of the world, the chances are slim of a person regularly knocking on the door of a neighbor. In fact, in many cities, old people and the disabled feel isolated and cut off from their community—even when this community is full of businesses and corporations. Yet this is not so in many cities in Japan, where for more than 40 years teams of women employed by the Yakult Corporation have been calling on elderly people in their neighborhoods. For the Yakult Corporation, the way of reaching out into the neighborhood has not been through buildings but rather through the purposeful actions of many thousands of salespeople. The creation of the Yakult Ladies with a positive remit to keep an eye on the elderly in the community has become a crucial part of the way the corporation anchors itself in the community.

The case of elderly communities in Japan is important to the wider world because the demographic profile of Japan will be replicated in other advanced nations over the coming decades. It is no surprise that in Japan the burden of elder care on the state and on individual caregivers is increasingly seen to need a society-wide solution. Indeed, across the country there is a growing expectation that corporations will be called on to play a greater role in supporting the communities of older and ever more isolated citizens.

The way that the Yakult Corporation has been able to work with its communities is in part a reflection of the business model and ethos of the firm. Founder Minoru Shirota created the Yakult probiotic drink with a vision that true health comes from physical fitness combined with good mental, social, and cultural well-being—a view he summed up in the phrase, "Working on a Healthy Society." This philosophy became the foundation for the Yakult Corporation and the idea behind the door-to-door delivery service of the Yakult Ladies. By 2012, there were over 80,000 Yakult Ladies working in 15 countries, of which 43,000 are in Japan. Each of these employees is given training and then allocated to a specific area, delivering around 200 bottles a day and earning a commission on each bottle sold, thus becoming financially independent. Typically, a Yakult Lady is around 42 years of age and has family responsibilities. In Japan, her children are looked after in over 1,373 day-care facilities while she travels by bicycle, cart, or on foot into her community, where she meets her customers and checks on the safety and well-being of the elderly in her community.

In many ways, the Yakult Ladies are a reflection of the history of the company and the role that these people play both in urban and rural Japan. Across the United Kingdom, other communities of workers are also making a difference in their neighborhoods—encouraged in part by the decisions made by a local grocer in 1914.

The John Lewis Partnership

This man was John Spedan Lewis, and the company he founded became the John Lewis Partnership, which by 2013 had become one of the United Kingdom's largest department store groups with a network of shops and Waitrose supermarkets stretching from Aberdeen in the northeast of Scotland to Cornwall in the south. The John Lewis Partnership is Britain's largest and oldest example of worker co-ownership, with more than 81,000 partners owning the retailer's 38 department stores and 285 Waitrose supermarkets. The partnership also has the rare accolade of being one of the most successful retailers in the last five years, riding out the storm of recession with more resilience than many others.

When Lewis took charge of one of the Lewis family's unprofitable stores, he promised his staff that when the shop became profitable, they would share in the profits. By 1929, he had created a trust to take over the assets of the company and run it as a partnership. Etched outside the entrance to its London headquarters, in large chrome letters covering the entire wall, is the following message:

> In 1914, John Spedan Lewis laid the foundations for a different kind of business. His vision was of a great commercial enterprise whose success would be measured by the happiness of those working in it and by its good service to the general community.

For decades, the John Lewis Partnership has worked to follow John Spedan Lewis's aspiration to build resilient communities and neighborhoods.

Accountability is key, and the senior team at the John Lewis Partnership legitimizes and celebrates the actions they take in their neighborhoods by reporting them in the same way they report their performance actions and financial outcomes. In fact, every year since 2001, the company has publicly reported what it has achieved, setting out the policies and principles it is pursuing, summarizing how it is managing its environmental impact, and pointing out how it is working with suppliers and local communities. This reporting is underpinned with the aspirations of successive executives. Here is current Chairman Charlie Mayfield talking about the partnership:

> The John Lewis Partnership faces similar Corporate Social Responsibilities challenges to other major retailers but in one respect our response is very different. That's the energy and passion of our Partners, who, as co-owners of our business, drive our work to operate as an ever-more sustainable and responsible business.

Such is the importance of the local neighborhood that up to three years before a full-line John Lewis store opens, a team sets to work to understand the culture and diversity of the surrounding neighborhood and the manner in which the partnership can best support its needs. As a result, for example, in a diverse city such as Leicester, the needs of over 24 different communities were understood; in Cardiff, all recruitment material was printed in both Welsh and English; and when John Lewis Stratford opened, almost 80 percent of partners came from the local community. As a result, studies show that most people believe that the stores have a positive impact on their neighborhood.[4] Jeremy Collins, who is the property director for the partnership, puts it like this:

> At the end of the day, it's important to understand that John Lewis is a long-term investor. When we invest in a city or town, we don't just build a shop; we build relationships with the local authority, fellow retailers, the Partners we employ, and the community as a whole so that together we can create a thriving and vibrant environment from which we all benefit.

This reporting also covers the commitment the partnership makes to community initiatives. Whereas the commitment is at least 1 percent of pretax profits, in reality, it is often more, with community initiative contributions totaling US$18 million in 2011–2012—equivalent to 3.07 percent of pretax, prebonus profits.

All John Lewis Partnership partners are encouraged to offer their time to support local, regional, and national initiatives that help to build more vibrant, economically sustainable neighborhoods. In 2012, this amounted to over 28,000 hours in voluntary community activities. The people who want to make more of a contribution by working full or part time in their communities are supported through the Golden Jubilee Trust, and every year more than 50 people decide to do this, with the partnership taking on the partners' full pay to cover the placement. In late 2011–2012, a local volunteer scheme was launched with the aim of increasing partnership hours to 75,000 spent in local communities.

Located across towns and cities, John Lewis shops also play an important role in providing meeting points that are often central to their communities. Space equipped with Internet access and audiovisual facilities is available for events ranging from volunteer recruitment fairs and activity classes to regional meetings and staff training courses.

How Corporations Encourage Compassion in the Community

Corporations have an extraordinary opportunity to bring resilience to a fragile world by ensuring that the communities of which they are members are themselves resilient. This support can take many forms—from the physical buildings that Zappos has created to incubate clusters of entrepreneurs, to the vast chains of Yakult Ladies who deliver daily care to their neighbors, or the way that teams at the John Lewis Partnership are leveraging their unique skills into their communities.

It is interesting to reflect on these experiences and ask why workers, either individually or collectively, decide to do the right thing in their neighborhoods and communities. Certainly, there is growing evidence that many people are soft wired to be cooperative and altruistic. However, it seems that another aspect is the corporate context in which they work. Although some corporate contexts serve to encourage this natural altruism, others, often inadvertently, serve to discourage these acts of compassion, generosity, and kindness. If corporations are to become good neighbors, then it's crucial that they understand how to encourage acts of generosity—and then act on that understanding.

Legitimizing Acts of Generosity

There are many subtle ways that the context of a corporation can discourage generosity, for example, by creating a way of working that squeezes out any nonproductive time that people have during the day through a relentless focus on money-creating tasks. Thus, when corporations successfully support their neighborhoods, there is always an understanding that employee involvement is not seen as nonproductive time but rather as core to work. Take by way of illustration the experiences of the Yakult Ladies. I have no doubt that if a productivity expert reviewed a Yakult Lady's work schedule, her first recommendation would be to significantly decrease the amount of time spent with each client. Talking to and supporting elderly clients could be seen as a nonproductive use of their time. And yet, by signaling the importance of these acts of generosity, the executives at Yakult have legitimized these home visits by building them into the daily work patterns. The tacit agreement is, "It's okay for you to spend time talking with your aging clients, and in fact, we acknowledge and celebrate these acts of generosity."

Through Reducing Toxic Spillover

An exclusive focus on productivity is not the only way that generous and altruistic acts can be discouraged. The way that daily, weekly, and annual patterns of work are shaped can leave very little time for other activities in the evenings, on the weekends, or during sabbaticals. It is only when we have time and emotional and physical vitality that we can make a difference in our communities. One of the reasons that the community work of the John Lewis Partnership is so successful is that people have the energy after work, during their lunch breaks, and on weekends to actively leverage their work skills and competencies into the community.

Yet, in many corporations, the spillover from a depleting, tough workday is sufficiently draining to discourage active community engagement. Indeed, there is a growing body of empirical research that shows the impact of this toxic cycle. The sociologists who study work rates have discovered that when hours of work increase, social acts in the community tend to decrease.

This puts an even greater emphasis on flexible working and work that does not feel toxic and draining. It would seem that when companies such as BT and Deloitte bring flexibility to how and when work gets done, not only are they building the emotional resilience of their employees, but they are also creating space for acts of generosity.

By Going beyond a Utility Perspective

There is another, rather more subtle way that corporations and the financial markets discourage acts of neighborhood generosity and altruism. They do this through the way they signal the importance of the monetization of human time. This signals that all time should be accounted for through markets and that all time must be monetized if it is to be perceived as valuable. Following this argument, anything that cannot be monetized has little intrinsic value.

Over time, this subtle perspective serves to downgrade acts that don't have a clear monetary outcome. When this occurs, our intrinsic motivation in doing a meaningful or generous act is overtaken by our concern for extrinsic motivation and monetary reward. There are some who argue that this shift in motivation from intrinsic to extrinsic is a relentless march in many contemporary societies. This is the argument of political philosopher Michael Sandel.[5] He believes that as a consequence of this extrinsic perspective, some of the good things in life are corrupted or degraded as they are turned into commodities. He has this to say about how economic principles have attempted to create a science of human behavior based on a utility perspective that focuses primarily on extrinsic motivation:

> At the heart of this science is a simple but sweeping idea: in all domains of life, human behaviors can be explained by assuming that people decide what to do by weighing the costs and benefits of the options before them and choosing the one they believe will give them the greatest welfare or utility.

Reflecting on earlier examples, one could ask what would be the outcome if the Zappos leaders, the Yakult Ladies, or those working for the John Lewis Partnership chose to take the economic and market mind-set. What would be the result if they chose to engage in the weighing of costs and options? Under these circumstances, would they engage individually or collectively with their community? What would be the cost and benefit of doing so?

The question may seem bizarre, but Sandel's argument is that implicitly this economic and market-led way of thinking about human motivation has been a key factor in shaping the context of many companies. It is why, for example, so much corporate energy and resources are focused on the remuneration process with their finally delineated bonuses and share-option schemes. The goal is to appeal to the extrinsic motivation of employees. The fact that empirical evidence shows that bonuses play a very limited role in encouraging high performance is research that is often ignored.[6]

This economic assumption is that all human behavior is influenced by the market—and therefore that incentives are the cornerstone to why we behave. But, as Sandel argues, this perspective crowds out the notion of empathy, acts of generosity, and indeed anything else that money cannot buy. When the only standards of a corporation are those of utility and the market, then this devalues many of the behaviors and norms worth caring about.

Sandel gives the example of research by behavioral economist Dan Ariely. He tells the story of the American Association of Retired Persons (AARP), which asked a group of lawyers if they were willing to provide legal services to needy retirees at a discounted rate of US$30 an hour. The lawyers were appalled at this offer and refused. As Sandel reflects, the AARP had appealed to the lawyers through their extrinsic motivation and through the market for their time. Yet, when the AARP asked if they would provide legal advice for free, many of the lawyers agreed. Once it was clear that they were being asked to engage in a charitable activity rather than a market transaction, the lawyers responded charitably.[7]

It seems that when corporate strategy treats all human motivation as if it were market-driven and seeks to monetize all activity, then the effect is to downplay the natural human tendencies for altruism and generosity. Yet, when corporations legitimize and celebrate these community actions, they can encourage a more generous and altruistic motivation. This happens when a corporation develops the culture and practices that encourage and enable people to be what they are destined to be—altruistic and cooperative. In so doing, they recognize the potential in a single act of generosity and are able to seize on it and amplify it for the many.

BUILDING JOB-READY SKILLS IN THE COMMUNITY: THE INDIAN IT COMPANIES

Across many neighborhoods of the world, inequality is rising, and people are struggling to find work in a job market that is becoming increasingly specialized and hollowed out. This is certainly the case in India, where those with privileged access to networks and education are able to join the global elite, leaving behind tens of millions in rural poverty or living in the slums that ring Mumbai and Delhi. Youth unemployment rises as the gap increases between the technical and engineering skills needed in India's booming IT sector and the poor educational attainment of many young people. It's the skill gap on a grand scale.

The Broken Educational System in India

India may seem like a wellspring of highly educated professionals, thanks to the many doctors and engineers who have moved to the West, and the legions of bright, English-speaking call-center employees may seem to represent, to many Western consumers, the cheerful voice of modern India. Within India, though, there is widespread recognition that the government has not invested enough in education, especially at the primary and secondary levels. Barely half of fifth-grade students can read simple texts in their language of study, only about one-third of fifth graders can perform simple division problems in arithmetic, and most students drop out before they reach the tenth grade.

These statistics stand in stark contrast to China, where a government focus on education has achieved a literacy rate of 94 percent of the population, compared with 64 percent in India. In a 2012 survey of childhood literacy and mathematical ability, the children of Shanghai were ranked top (more competent even than Finnish children, who have historically taken the lead) compared with Indian children, who ranked in the bottom 10 of the country league tables. The demographics are also important here; nearly 500 million people, or 45 percent of India's total population, are 19 years of age or younger.

This lack of education and skills is bad news for the rapidly growing Indian IT industry that relies on a large home market of work-ready skilled youngsters. The challenge of youth unemployment and the skills gap, however, is not one that can be easily solved by a single company acting within its neighborhood—what is required is the coordinated action of many.

Being Prepared to Invest in the Entire System

To address poor neighborhood education, a group of India's IT companies is experimenting with ways of facing up to the skills gap. As Infosys CEO Kris Gopalakrishnan explains, "If Indian IT companies had simply accepted the workforce available in the country, they would be a fraction of their current size, as would their employment levels and market shares." Gopalakrishnan is not alone. Across the Indian IT sector, executives in companies such as Wipro and Tata Consultancy Services (TCS) have realized that they have to work together to invest in the entire system that builds workforce skills. As Nandita Gurjar, head of HR at Infosys, says:

> All that has been achieved could not have been possible without an alliance with Tata and Wipro. When all of us came together, it became very difficult for the government to ignore us. The scale that has been achieved lies in the power of this alliance. In fact, for our out-of-India efforts to achieve the same level of success, we need to apply the strategy of alliances there as well. For example, in the United States, we cannot hope to achieve scale unless American companies come forward as well.

The focus of the IT corporations has been to operate on all parts of the complex system that results in high youth unemployment and creates a skills gap. One of the first steps was to work together to influence the Indian government to open up more engineering universities.

The next step was to work together to improve the employability of young people and equip them with a range of work-ready skills by reaching out to school children in their neighborhoods, by working closely with engineering institutions and business schools, by helping teachers understand what corporations require, and by designing work-ready curricula. In so doing, these corporations have taken over some of the educational tasks that typically would be handled by the government and educational institutions. What was required was a great deal more than simply changing institutional structures or adding resources. Instead, there had to be a complete transformation of the science and engineering curricula and a redesign of how teachers teach.

Changing the Way Students Learn

Each company has played a role. At Wipro, for example, founder and Chairman Azim H. Premji used the resources of his foundation to help train new teachers and guide current teachers into overhauling the way students are taught and tested at government schools. This overhaul is crucial in India, where typically students are drilled and tested on reproducing passages from textbooks and are then required to regurgitate their learning. For example, the foundation is engaged in a five-year project working with 1,500 schools in the Indian state of Uttarakhand to improve primary education. The focus is to change the way pupils learn, from rote learning to writing their own stories and working on independent projects.

There is also a network of employees in regional hubs who work with more than 1,000 colleges to train teachers in a curriculum they have created and made available on the foundation intranet. The focus is firmly on work-ready skills. As Nandita Gurjar from Infosys told me:

> We see this as a supply chain issue—we have built a five-year model of requirements, and we work with academies and governments to make it happen. We want to drive excitement in IT in children across India—we want to charm them about IT so that more say, "I want to be an engineer when I grow up."

There is also an understanding that this type of signaling has to happen before young people make a decision about what to study. Thus a whole series of initiatives has been targeted at school children from the age of 15 years. For example, since 2008, more than 680,000 schoolchildren from around India have learned about IT through a two-week course designed by the teams at Infosys to raise their skills and aspirations. To support this course, every year more than 10,000 Infosys employees teach in local schools, and for those who decide to take a sabbatical to teach full time, the corporation pays 50 percent of their salary. As Nandita Gurjar remarks:

> The objective of this training is to make an Indian person into a fully fledged global citizen. Our aim was a curriculum that gets people ready not just technically but as a whole. For example, we even now have courses in place to teach people to eat with a knife and fork. This may all sound very basic, but in India, where the majority of people eat with their hands, it is these little things that make a huge difference.

In parallel, in 2002 TCS launched an academic interface program designed to support work-ready skills. The range of initiatives under the program includes faculty development programs, internships for students, workshops, and an outreach program where TCS trainers talk to students. By 2012, more than 670 institutions in India and over 180 outside India had been involved in the program.

Using Corporate Assets

One of the key assets these IT companies have is their training campuses. I remember being amazed at what I saw when I first visited these campuses. At Infosys, for example, the training campuses in India are set up to train 45,000 employees each year. The centerpiece is the Global Education Center in Mysore, where groups of 14,000 entry-level programmers are trained together in a 23-week training course. During this time, students live on campus, are fed in the numerous canteens catering to the vast range of Indian regional foods, and are able to make use of the e-learning and simulation facilities.

These IT campuses are also used increasingly to support the community. School teachers from across India are encouraged to come for two months to the Mysore Global Education Center to understand how IT corporations work and what is expected of a global workforce. The program works with over 400 engineering institutions, and its launch has reached more than 7,000 faculty members and 153,000 students.

Across India, alliances of this sort that bridge various stakeholders have been crucial. As Nupur Singh from TCS remarks:

> A lot has been accomplished through our alliances with other organizations, academia, IT engineering and business students, and most importantly, the government. When all these multiple alliances come together, right from developing curriculum, training teachers, offering internships, creating access to the IT industry, the impact is enormous. We have created global alliances with valuable competencies of innovation and scaling—we hope to address global challenges.

CONCLUSION

Neighborhoods are a crucial part of the life system of a corporation. When neighborhoods flourish, corporations flourish. Yet there are many reasons why leaders should think of their corporations as somehow independent, and indeed employees should feel that the barriers to outside generosity and altruism are too high. As we have seen, when corporations are able to get this balance right, they seem to do so in two ways: by identifying the real needs of the community and leveraging their resources to address those needs and by building a portfolio of activities to bind them to their communities.

CHAPTER 7

❖

CREATING RESILIENCE
IN SUPPLY CHAINS

Every couple of months, the IKEA catalogue used to thump through my letterbox—before I enjoyed the excitement of the company's online catalogue. It's the wunderkind of consumption, a reminder of the supremacy of markets, and a living testament to the power of globalization. It's also a weighty tome. It's not unusual for it to have 300 pages. Worldwide, approximately 208 million copies of the catalogue were printed in 2013, more than double the number of Bibles expected to be printed in the same period.[1] Within these pages are arrayed a marvelous world bazaar of 12,000 products that could grace homes, from plants and living-room furnishings to toys and kitchens. The 332 IKEA stores can be found in over 38 countries from the United States to Australia. One can only marvel at the complexities of the supply chain that makes, assembles, ships, and places these millions of goods into IKEA stores across the world.

Should the executive team of a corporation such as IKEA care about what happens in these supply chains? After all, the workers in these supply chains are mostly invisible—found working in the factories of some of the poorest nations in the world or on the farms and plantations in far-away countries. Even if IKEA executives did care, the vastness and expanse of the supply chains makes them unwieldy to take action within. It is not just IKEA that has a vast hinterland of suppliers. Take the U.S. service company ManpowerGroup, which has calculated that its third-tier suppliers constitute a network of over 14 million people reaching into every part of the world. It is certainly more convenient for executives to keep these invisible millions at arm's length, shrouded by outsourcing contracts and wrapped up in third-party agreements.

As consumers, should we really care about the conditions in the supply chains of the goods and services we consume? As a fan of iPhones, should I care that the assembly of my unit takes place in the Foxconn factories at Zhengzhou or Taiyuan in China that, although possibly good by local standards, are places that few of us would want our own children to work in? Should I care that the budget tee-shirts I buy are manufactured in a factory in Pakistan where the fire regulations are nonexistent?

These are tricky questions for leaders, workers, and consumers. As consumers, we can approach the question of conditions in supply chains from a variety of perspectives. From an economic perspective, our inner economist may say something like, "The role of corporations is to minimize the cost of a supply chain and maximize its profitability. My role is to consume what they produce." After all, without a tightly controlled supply chain, the extraordinary inexpensive clothes we buy would not be possible. The humanist within us may feel disquiet at some of the stories we hear about conditions in supply chains. It might whisper to us, "How do you feel when you hear that those clothes are made by young people, often children, in appalling conditions?" The pragmatist within us (and I speak for myself here) simply reaches for the latest iPhone, takes it out of that gorgeous black packaging, and gets on with using one of the design and marketing icons of the modern age. It seems that it takes a very special sort of consumer to really care enough to take action on the activities within the supply chains of the products they consume.

The same is true for executives in corporations. Even when corporations do intervene in supply-chain issues, sometimes the results are not those they expected and can lead to unintended consequences. Studies from UNICEF, for example, show that the public furor that took child workers out of the garment factories of India and Pakistan simply resulted in some moving from factory work into prostitution as a means to continue to support their families economically.[2] Often the challenges of poverty and labor constitute complex dynamic systems where the unintended consequences can simply serve to exacerbate the problems the intervention was there to reduce.

HOW CORPORATIONS ANCHOR THEMSELVES IN THEIR SUPPLY CHAINS

Yet, despite these complexities, it is possible for corporations to actively work within their supply chains to build resilience. The energy and focus to do this often arises from the values and business model created by the founders or by the determination of current senior executives. Those corporations that successfully anchor themselves into their supply chains often work on the following three areas:

1. They take responsibility for the extended supply chain.
2. They build a social business model.
3. They invest in local communities.

Taking Responsibility for the Extended Supply Chain at IKEA

What Andreas Franzen saw in the dimly lit, often filthy factories in the outer reaches of Western supply chains changed the way we as consumers think about where our stuff gets made. It was 1998, and this Swedish documentary maker had taken an undercover camera and sound crew into the factories of India and Pakistan. What he saw chilled him—filthy factory floors littered with debris, factory air often filled with the fumes of chemicals destined to destroy lungs, and antique machines with no safety guards that routinely ripped the fingers from their operators.

But this was not the worst. Huddled in these factories were children, often working long, long hours and rarely having anything in the way of education. He saw children as young as five and six working in dyeing factories with foul-smelling, toxic dyes, sitting for eight hours a day in dimly lit rooms working on huge carpet looms, and breaking stones and carrying bricks on their frail, underfed bodies. Most of these children had nothing in the way of education and prospects, and many would be dead before the time they reached adulthood. What Franzen had glimpsed was a vision of hell in the underbelly of the supply chain.

The documentary that Franzen and his team made was to take this vision of hell from the hidden corners of the world onto the television screens of millions of people. His film sparked protest campaigns throughout Europe. What was clear to the executives at IKEA was that as a marketing and sales company, it was almost impossible to introduce codes of conduct that guaranteed that child labor would not be used. However, across Europe, consumer outrage began to take its toll on sales figures, and what became clear was that the executive team would have to reconsider its attitude toward those in the company's supply chain. By September 2000, the executive team created a code of conduct, "The IKEA Way of Purchasing Home Furnishing Products (IWAY)," which described what IKEA expected of conditions in its supply chain. The executive team then asked all suppliers in the supply chain to sign this code of conduct, and those who could not sign were given three months to introduce an action plan. If after that time adequate changes were not made, the company ended its relationship with those suppliers.

In order to police the code of conduct, the procurement team was strengthened and made many unannounced visits to suppliers and subcontractors in South Asia. If child labor was found, the procurement team asked the supplier to act in the best interests of the child. The team did this by implementing a corrective and preventive action plan that included education and training. Following the action plan, the procurement team then visited the school attended by the child and made additional unannounced visits to the supplier. If after this period of time the corrective action was still not taken, then IKEA terminated all business with the supplier. Since IWAY was introduced, more than 165,000 audited improvements in working conditions have taken place in supplier factories around the world.

What the IKEA team soon began to realize was that policing and monitoring were in fact only part of the solution; if the company really wanted to make a sustainable and long-term difference in its supply chain, it would have to be more than police. So the team began to work cooperatively with international agencies such as UNICEF and Save the Children to create an agenda for change.

Building Multistakeholder Initiatives

Child labor, like many challenges, can be represented as a complex dynamic system in which any intervention can have unintended as well as intended consequences. Understanding and positively acting on the dynamics of these complex systems often takes a multistakeholder approach. It is only through the shared lens and perspectives of stakeholders such as governments, corporations, and NGOs (nongovernmental organizations) that the full system can be understood and acted on. This multistakeholder approach became a foundation for the continued work of the IKEA team in its global supply chain. For example, in August 2000, the team launched a community-development project in collaboration with UNICEF to establish learning centers for working youth in India. The aim was to combat the impact of the earliest child labor interventions that had resulted in needy children simply moving from the factory into the brothel. As Per Heggenes, CEO of the IKEA Foundation, explains:

> By working together for the past 10 years and contributing more than €100 million to UNICEF projects in India so far, we have created opportunities for more than 74 million children. By thinking long-term and teaming-up with UNICEF, we're giving hope to many millions of families.[3]

Similarly, IKEA's partnership with Save the Children has so far helped 65,000 children in the Indian cities of Gujarat and Maharashtra move out of child labor and into the classroom. The goal is that by 2015, more than 10 million children in 20,000 villages will have improved access to quality education.

The issue of bringing the outside in becomes particularly pertinent for corporations that, like IKEA, have vast supply chains. This is the case for both food manufacturer Danone, a corporation headquartered in France, and Natura, a Brazilian cosmetics company with a supply chain extending into the fragile region of the Amazon basin. The story of how they have reached out into their supply chains and neighborhoods reinforces the importance of these initiatives and the benefits that can accrue from them.

Building a Social Business Model at Danone

Danone is one of the major dairy and food producers in the world, and from the beginning, the corporation has been guided by the values and philosophy of founder Antoine Riboud. In 1972, Riboud made a speech in which he set out what he viewed as the relationship between the inside of the corporation and the outside of the supply chain[4]:

> A company's responsibility does not end at the door to the factory or the office. The jobs it provides shape whole lives. It consumes energy and raw materials, and in so doing, it alters the face of our planet. The public will remind us of our responsibilities in this industrial society.

When he said this, Riboud was referring to a French company with a footprint primarily in France. Those who have visited the verdant rolling hills of Normandy will know how French farmers live, and those in the European Union will be aware of the subsidies the farmers receive. Their life is tough, but in general, it's a good and comfortable life. Thus, "taking responsibility outside the factory door" was not such a stretch for a company such as Danone.

For Franck Riboud, Antoine's son and Danone's current CEO, this issue of what goes on beyond the doors of the factories has become a great deal more complex. Danone now has a vast global footprint with operations in 90 countries and more than 100,000 employees. It has a supply chain that touches the lives of many local suppliers and retailers, from dairy farmers in Normandy and southwestern France, to roadside fresh-food hawkers in Mexico City, and to grain and dairy farmers in the Ukraine and Egypt.

By the early 2000s, Danone's international presence was moving into countries that were significantly poorer than those in Europe. Suddenly their producers and local consumers were very different from the French dairy farmers and Parisian housewives who bought Danone's yogurt. Increasingly, executives were working in regions that business professor C. K. Prahalad had referred to as the "bottom of the pyramid."[5]

The Bottom of the Pyramid

The argument Prahalad made about the bottom of the pyramid was this: historically, Western multinationals have developed products for Western tastes and Western purses. Shampoos, soaps, drinks, yogurt, biscuits, and pain relief tablets were all made in Western factories and at a cost that put them beyond the reach of low-income consumers. A villager in rural India might want to wash her hair with Head and Shoulders, a Hindustan Unilever shampoo, but the cost of the bottle would be way beyond her means. Prahalad championed this impoverished consumer and reasoned that whereas a low-income person will not be able to buy a bottle of shampoo, she might be able to buy a single sachet. Or the whole pharmaceutical manufacturing and supply chain could be reengineered so that pain relief tablets could be sold at an affordable cost. This emerging idea of *frugal innovation* has been very influential for executives such as Franck Riboud as they thought about their roles in their neighborhoods and supply chains. More recently, this argument has been championed by Harvard Business School's Michael Porter.[6] He argued that making a positive impact in poor communities can only be sustainable if these companies follow an economic model that is sufficiently robust to make a profit.

Building a Social Business Model

Riboud had a chance to rethink how his corporation provided nutrition to low-income communities in a conversation in 2005 with Professor Muhammad Yunus, founder of the Grameen Bank. They began to share their ideas and convictions about how to bring progress to the world's most impoverished people and discovered that their areas of expertise were complementary. Yunus was a pioneer of community-led low-cost financing; Riboud was a pioneer of the development of low-cost nutritional foods and their manufacture and distribution at scale.

The outcome of this creative conversation was an agreement to launch Grameen Danone Foods. Their aspiration was to follow Prahalad's advice about frugal innovation and the bottom of the pyramid. They aimed to create community-led projects that would both produce low-cost nutritional foods and also follow a sufficiently rigorous business model to enable the projects to be economically sustainable.

Their first trial of this joint venture was the building of a yogurt plant in Bangladesh. They followed the social business model to create value that would be economically self-sustaining while creating wealth for customers, employees, and regions where the company operates. By 2007, the first plant was up and running, producing affordable yogurt. What separated this yogurt from the local yogurt was that it was fortified with micronutrients such as iodine, zinc, iron, and vitamin A. This fortification is crucial in the fight against "hidden hunger," which stunts the lives of millions of young children. Yet, whereas the impact of the fortified yogurt on the local population was important, what had a greater impact was the effect on the supply chain. The plant employs 177 full-time employees from the local communities, providing vital support to families in a region of extreme unemployment. It also employs over 800 Danone sales ladies, who like the Yakult Ladies, take yogurt to be sold individually to people in the neighboring towns, creating networks of support and neighborliness. The milk itself comes from over 370 microfarmers, who are small-scale herders scattered throughout the region. Without a dairy plant, the milk these farmers produce typically goes no further than the village and is the victim of unpredictable demand. With a local dairy plant, they can be sure that their milk can be sold every day, and the fixed price encourages them to make future investments in cattle.

This social business model has been extended to other regions across the world. In the West African state of Senegal, the La Laiterie du Berger project has built a local dairy that collects and pasteurizes the milk of over 600 local herding families, whereas in Algeria, the Sahazine project has brought Danone research expertise to produce and sell a range of snacks designed to combat the problem of iron deficiency in the local population.

From these early pilots, the executive team began to scale these initiatives by launching danone.communities. This is a mutual fund of over US$100 million set up with the goal of encouraging social business initiatives to fight malnutrition and poverty around the world. The fund is managed and marketed by the Crédit Agricole group in partnership with local stakeholders and NGOs and has about US$8.7 million available to invest. In 2009, the corporation also launched the Danone Ecosystem Fund with a US$137 million endowment designed to create value and wealth in the Danone supply chain of farmers, suppliers, subcontractors, transport and logistics operators, distributors, and local community authorities.

Leveraging Through Powerful Corporate Learning

When a corporation leverages its internal capabilities and processes into its communities, the results can be profound. One of the marks of Danone is its decentralized organizational structure that gives local autonomy by emphasizing decentralized decision making and peer-based networks. This means that when broad goals are set at the top of the corporation, much power and resources are delegated to local teams, which are freed up to develop their own initiatives and responsibilities to meet the corporate goals.

What is fascinating is the way that the Danone teams have then been able to use this same internal practice to build resilience into their supply-chain communities. The key is the DAN 2.0 process, which uses social media and the internal Danone intranet to support networks of people throughout the world to exchange their experiences and ideas. This has created a robust and dynamic community of people across the company who share and develop their deep expertise in building and sustaining local social business. The community has been further strengthened by the creation of a series of social innovation laboratories that share best practices across the community. By 2009, there were some 120 social business initiatives from 70 Danone subsidiaries across the world.

Investing in Local Communities at Natura

For a company operating in one of the world's most sensitive environments, company behavior in its neighborhoods and supply chains can be even more crucial. This is the situation for Natura Cosméticos, which was founded in Brazil in 1969 and produces eco-friendly cosmetics, fragrances, and personal hygiene products. By 2012, it had become one of the largest cosmetic companies in the world, with a market share of 23 percent in its Brazilian target market, revenues of US$2.31 billion, and an international market share that has increased from 4.4 to 9 percent in five years.[7]

The vision of the company and its attitude toward consumers and producers were laid down by founder Antonio Luiz da Cunha Seabra, who used the phrase "*bien estar bien*," which can be translated as "well-being and being well."[8] This connects the inside of corporate and individual inner resilience with the outside of the community and the supply chain.[9] *Well-being* is the relationship people have with themselves and their bodies, whereas *being well* describes the relationships with other people and with nature. Since the founding of Natura, this purpose has been the guiding principle for a host of practices that include the way products are sold, the research and development focus, and the way that people are treated in the supply chain.

Publicly Shared Goals

Since the beginning, Natura executives have recognized that the company's environmental, social, and business interests are intertwined. The current CEO of Natura, Alessandro Carlucci, has made a number of public resource commitments to his employees, shareholders, and consumers. One such commitment is that no habitats will be harmed in the making of Natura Cosméticos products. This means using sustainable extraction, running carbon-neutral processes, and making recycled and recyclable packaging and materials.

These publicly stated goals have created an internal rallying point for employees. They mean, for example, that when a product is being developed, a detailed analysis of its environmental impact is created with the proviso that any new product has less environmental impact than existing products. It's a stringent requirement, and it's absolute. If a new product can't live up to this principle, it does not become part of Natura's product line.[10] As for all corporate supply chains, meeting these principles is essentially an exercise in alliance building and stakeholder management. As CEO Carlucci reflects:

> Of course, this does not only depend on us—on Natura. We have such a strong and significant network of relationships with our stakeholders that, step by step, day by day, we reach the objectives of all those who share the same values.[11]

The supply chains are particularly sensitive because many Natura products use ingredients from the Amazon rain forest. Since 2000, the company has worked with the Amazon families that grow and harvest tropical plants and fruits such as cupuaçu, açaí, and andiroba. These supply chains extend throughout the Brazilian Amazon, with more than 1,500 families scattered across 16 communities. Like the Danone dairy herders, these supply chains reach into fragile social and physical ecosystems, and like Danone, the corporation has made a significant investment in their sustainability. The goal of the Amazônia program is to build investments of US$500 million by 2020 to be used to develop a research center in Manaus, capital of the state of Amazonas, where researchers and scientists will study the regions and preserve local biodiversity. The program also plans to expand the Benevides plant in Pará, which manufactures vegetable oils and soap. With these initiatives, Natura aims to increase the purchase of Amazonian raw materials from 10 to 30 percent and double the number of families in its Amazon supply chain.[12]

Investing in Local Communities

One of the most fascinating aspects of the Natura business model is the way that the corporation manages its extended sales force. Like the Yakult Ladies in Japan, Natura operates throughout South America with a large direct-sales network of more than 1.4 million women called *consultoras*. This is the largest direct-sales force in Brazil and the third largest in the world. This network of women can have a profound impact on their families and communities because in general they are paid more than their peers—the median monthly salary is 16 times the national minimum wage. The saleswomen also have an opportunity to take a share in the profits and ownership of the company. While many corporations are cutting back on their direct-sales forces, the Natura group continues to grow—up 16 percent in 2011. This is not just a Brazilian phenomenon; outside Brazil, the number grew by 23 percent to reach 230,000 *consultoras*.

What is also interesting about this sales force is how these women feel about themselves and their jobs. In a sector with legendary high turnover, the *consultoras* stay. Many top sellers have been with the company for more than two decades, and most *consultoras* (95 percent in fact) are really happy in their jobs. CEO Carlucci believes that many factors contribute to retention, but two are at the top.

First, customers want to buy our products. We offer good value, so they are easier to sell than other products from our competition and provide consultants with a nice profit. Second—and most important to me—our consultants feel they really belong to a community, that they are part of a company that wants to offer excellent products and generate value for society, the environment and their community. They are engaged with the philosophy of the company. We try to treat them as people, not just numbers.[13]

CONCLUSION

The forces of globalization and technology are creating ever more extensive supply chains, and the conditions within these supply chains are becoming ever more transparent as swarms of citizens have enhanced sensibilities and more sophisticated sensor mechanisms. In some of the supply chains in which large global corporations operate, there are people who go to bed hungry and children who are suffering from malnutrition.[14] These are people on the outside of these corporations, and while their plight might be observed, they can be thought of as "not our problem." There are many reasons why executives and employees should choose to look away. Yet, as the experiences of Danone, Yakult, and Natura have shown, many employees want to get involved, and when their special competencies are used, the results can be impressive.

PART IV

ADDRESSING GLOBAL CHALLENGES

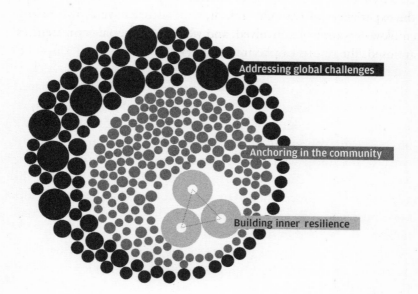

Addressing global challenges

Anchoring in the community

Building inner resilience

We stand at a fork in the path. Our world is being reshaped by globalization, hyperconnectivity, and technological conviviality. The resulting communities are transcending national boundaries and encouraging talented people to engage actively in the affairs of the world—wherever they happen to be born. With this globalization and technological conviviality have come challenges that are perplexing and hard to solve. Across the world there are a generation of young people who have no strong relationship with work or the institutions of work, and while there is unprecedented wealth for some, others have less, and inequality is rising. This growing youth unemployment and widening gap between rich and poor are creating an ever-stronger breeding ground for dissatisfaction and malcontent. At the same time, a scramble for resources is playing out across much of the world, bringing with it the specter of significant climate change.

At this fork in the path, what role can those who lead and work in large corporations play in bringing resilience to our fragile world? It seems to me that global corporate institutions are growing in strength and capability, and as a result, they are becoming uniquely placed to become part of the way that these challenges are addressed.

It is the combination of the sheer variety of corporations and their unique signature processes that makes the landscape of corporate ecology such a potent force for change and innovation.[1] This variety is embedded in how a corporation's culture and capabilities are shaped by its distinctive history, specific environmental and societal context, and the aspirations and courage of its CEO. The resulting signature processes are then honed and shaped by the extraordinary competitive pressure under which many corporations operate—which in the words of Joseph Schumpeter bring "creative destruction."[2] It is the creativity of this process of destruction that has honed the capabilities of corporations—and my argument is that it is these capabilities that now should be used in the service of the world.

There are already signs in the corporate landscape that some corporations are actively leveraging their unique capabilities. In Part IV, we will look in detail at three clusters of capabilities where corporations are particularly strong: in their research and innovation capability (Chapter 8), their capacity to scale and mobilize (Chapter 9), and their ability to build alliances across multiple stakeholders (Chapter 10).

CHAPTER 8

❖

LEVERAGING RESEARCH AND INNOVATION CAPABILITIES

I t takes an extraordinary amount of resources to create a corporation capable of high levels of innovation. Imagine the care that teams at an innovative corporation such as Google go through to find and then retain some of the cleverest people in the world. Almost all of what they do—design of the Google campus, flexible ways of working, and share-option schemes—has been honed over time to deliver one capability—clever people capable of working cooperatively together.

It's not just Google. Across the world, a number of corporations have made significant investments in developing their assets and core capabilities in innovation and research and development. Over decades, they have attracted highly specialized and creative people and then developed their human resources policies to create practices and processes that retain and motivate these specialists. They know that these highly talented people have the potential to create disproportionate amounts of value from the resources the organization makes available to them.[1] They know that their most talented software programmers or pharmaceutical researchers can create a new line of code or a new drug that has the potential to bankroll the entire corporation for a decade. They also understand that these talented people are not amenable to hierarchical managing, that they can be spiky and hard to work with, that they can prefer to keep their knowledge to themselves rather than share with others, and that they often hate overly bureaucratic structures. Thus, over decades, corporations that rely on these clever people have honed a way of tuning into and leading them and have built ways to ensure that the deep knowledge of these experts can be shared with ease across the boundaries of the corporation.

HOW CORPORATIONS LEVERAGE RESEARCH AND INNOVATION CAPABILITIES

Across the world, clever people are volunteering to address global challenges and thus are leveraging the research and innovative capabilities of corporations in significant ways. By so doing, they often take one or more of the following actions:

1. They identify, build, and link core capabilities.
2. They leverage deep insight.
3. They use specialist skills.

Identifying, Building, and Linking Core Capabilities at DSM

I can always spot the Dutch students in my classes at London Business School. They are almost always the tallest in the class. It's not just London Business School students, compared with any other race in the world, these young people, brought up in the dairy-rich lowlands of the Netherlands, have the longest legs of anyone. It was not always the case; those born in the Netherlands in the "Hunger Winter" during and immediately after World War II were not so lucky. Deprived of fresh vegetables, many suffered from "hidden hunger" that later led to health issues, including a higher susceptibility to diabetes.

In Europe, "hidden hunger" has been alleviated, but across the world, it still haunts the poor. In fact, it is estimated that as many as 2 billion people across the world live with hidden hunger that impairs the mental development in 40 to 60 percent of infants in the developing world, debilitates the health and energy of 500 million women, and leads to more than 60,000 deaths during childbirth annually. If current trends continue, the lives of more than 450 million children globally will be affected by stunting in the next 15 years as a result of malnutrition.[2] This also can have a devastating economic impact.

The World Food Program (WFP) has calculated that malnutrition can decrease a country's gross domestic product (GDP) by at least 2 to 3 percent when a 1 percent decline in developing-country growth rates traps an additional 20 million people in poverty.[3]

Perhaps it's the national understanding of hidden hunger that has led researchers at the Dutch natural science company DSM to work so hard to solve the problem. The corporation began in 1902 as a mining company and then shifted its competency base steadily from mining into fertilizers, and by the 1950s, it had the expertise to research and manufacture plastics for the growing consumer boom in Europe. Over the next two decades, the innovative capability of the firm developed further into specialized research in life and material sciences. By 2012, it had become a leader in innovating around nutritional foods and dietary supplements, personal care, and pharmaceuticals, employing 22,000 people in Europe, North America, and China. During this period, the research and innovation capabilities were being continually strengthened through the support of Ph.D. students in local universities, the attraction and development of young graduates, and the attachment of university professors to research teams.

Building Complementary Assets

Since 2007, the executive team at DSM has leveraged these research and innovation capabilities into building resilience in a fragile world. The team has done this through partnering with teams at the WFP, which is the world's largest humanitarian agency and feeds around 90 million people in over 80 countries every year. This joint project is lead by Fokko Wientjes, and the alliance between DSM and the WFP is a story of complementary assets, as Wientjes remarked to me:

> The whole story of this partnership is about complementary competencies as there is contributing from both ends and benefitting from both ends. DSM brought to the table content knowledge and innovation capabilities, whereas WFP had an outreach that DSM couldn't match. WFP is a good convening partner in a way that DSM would never be able to pull off as they have the patience and capabilities to bring people together.[4]

This partnership has grown over time and has made some important breakthroughs. For example, the partnership has developed ultralow-cost sachets of vitamins and minerals that can be added to food. To date, more than 12 million people in countries including Nepal, Kenya, Bangladesh, and Afghanistan have received these supplements.

The partnership works as a consequence of teams from both organizations being prepared to and capable of collaborating together. As in all complex teams that are working across organizational boundaries, trust between the groups is crucial. As Wientjes comments, "What is crucial is to secure integrity of the partnership—we need to make sure that integrity is not at stake, and there needs to be a readiness to work together." The readiness to work together comes because the problems the teams are trying to solve are so crucial.

In my own study of the performance of complex teams, I have used the notion of *ignition* to capture the energizing impact of a meaningful joint task or exciting questions to bond team members together.[5] I discovered that what is particularly crucial in teams where members come from different backgrounds is mutual respect and a shared goal. Here it is the combination of DSM's life-sciences expertise and WPF's on-the-ground knowledge and field observations that really boosts innovation. This potential is then ignited by important questions, such as "How do we create an ultralow-cost nutritional sachet?"

An interesting aspect of the partnership between DSM and the WFP is the differing cost bases from which they operate. Corporations such as DSM have significant overheads, their research scientists around the world are paid competitively, they work in well-furnished offices, and their pensions are generous. This is why, historically, Western companies such as DSM have struggled to produce goods that could be sold to people who are paid less than a dollar a day.

Learning Through Frugal Innovation

In working with the WFP, the executive team had to change the way it thought about the company's revenue streams and its product development. It was clear from the start that the work they did in these partnerships and the products they created would never meet the normal revenue streams the executive team would demand from most of their products. Thus, in tackling projects around hidden hunger, the executives had to take the projects offline as a revenue stream. This created extraordinary learning opportunities.

The executives discovered that when confronted with real poverty and what C. K. Prahalad has called the "bottom of the pyramid," they had to fundamentally change their mind-set on how product innovation works. What was clear was that the research and cost base of micronutrients in the developed markets was way too high for countries such as Ethiopia and Somalia, and indeed for UN institutions such as the WFP. What the research teams were forced to confront as they worked together and with others in the field was a complete reinvention of an economically sustainable product. As Fokko Wientjes reflects:

> For us, the value is in donating staff and time; this is crucial to learning. It's not about pouring in millions of euros—but rather creating mutual benefits with shared beneficiaries. This builds resilience into the program. We treat it as a program, just like any other DSM program, with a finite time scale and an understanding that once the knowledge has become embedded in WFP, then it will become part of their operating procedure.[6]

Although the partnership between DSM and the WFP began with teams of scientists, it quickly widened to include many other people across DSM. Across the world, employees organized and participated in events that raised awareness of malnutrition; they supported WFP projects with on-ground research assignments in countries such as Zambia, Guatemala, Kenya, and Bangladesh; and they worked as volunteers on various projects.

Creating a Web of Insight

What has proven really important to the success of the project has been the combination of research- and lab-based insights and on the ground knowledge. This combination is crucial because when it comes to nutrition, the storage, transportation, and end use can have a significant impact on the viability of micronutrients. It is this local insight, from WFP teams on the ground and a network of local non-governmental organizations (NGOs), that brings real insight into these issues. As Fokko Wientjes described to me:

> We once sent 50 DSM volunteers to spend time in Kenyan refugee camps watching how refugees live. They then created a protocol on how best to tackle nutrition issues in refugee camps.
>
> Volunteers are also sent to different developing countries to examine the costs of diets because, together with awareness and education, budgets are also important. So these volunteers conduct research to find incomes and the costs of products available. This is essentially a data-collecting exercise so as to make a compelling case. This information is then cascaded through web-based tools to our partners, which is a database consisting of articles. For instance, this information has been an integral part of WFP, assisting it in explaining effectively the various dimensions of this problem to various stakeholders. It is also available to all the WFP staff. DSM gives out this information to UNICEF as well because it makes stronger cases when both humanitarian organizations are relaying the same message.[7]

What is interesting about research-led companies such as DSM is that not only do they have the expertise to attract and retain clever people, but they also have built platforms for the retention and sharing of this knowledge. It is this combination of assets that has been so important to the leveraging of DSM's innovative competence into the partnership with the WFP.

Leveraging Deep Insight at Google

Where is the first place you go to when you want to find something or check a fact? It seems that for billions of people around the world, the go-to place for places, people, and events is Google. The complexities of the algorithms behind this seemingly simple act of "googling" are extreme. This is why the executive team at Google has brought in some of the smartest mathematical brains in the world to create these algorithms. Every year, more than 1.5 million people apply to join Google. If they are selected, they are pampered in the Google offices, fed free food, encouraged to "bring their dog/parrot to work," provided with concierge support, and use slides to get from the office to the canteen. The list of pampering is endless and legendary.

The point is this: innovation-led companies such as DSM and Google rely on their capacity to attract, retain, and motivate some of the cleverest people in the world. They do this in their unique style to attract unique people. At DSM, the question posed to some of these clever people was how to eliminate hidden hunger. At Google, the question was altogether different. It was a question about technology and the incitement to violence.

At the heart of Google is the capability to harness technology and the brainpower of its 34,300 employees to improve the ways people across the world connect with information. Google Ideas was launched to leverage this technological and networking power and to harness this power to tackle some of the toughest human challenges.[8] The leader of Google Ideas is Jared Cohen, and over the last couple of years, Google Ideas has encouraged people across the corporation to leverage their technology by focusing on extreme gangs and money laundering.

Empathizing with the Tragedy of Gang Violence

For Cohen and his colleagues, the reasoning is this: one of the challenges of the twenty-first century is the way extremist gangs destroy the livelihood of those who become members while also putting terror into the communities in which they operate. In an interesting paradox, the tools of connectivity and conviviality that have enabled "citizen crowds" to be convened in an instant have also been used by terrorists and violent gangs. Thus both citizen empowerment movements and violent gangs have made use of YouTube to broadcast their messages and Twitter and text messages to connect in a moment. For the engineers at Google, who are watching the emergence of networks around the world, this reality is deeply concerning. They have witnessed how extremist groups have taken advantage of new Internet technologies to spread their message. For Jared Cohen and his colleagues, the connectivity and conviviality technology that corporations such as Google have created have to become a part of the solution rather than simply the conduit for the problem.

This issue of violent extremism is pressing. The explosion of youth unemployment as a result of the combination of globalization of labor markets and the "hollowing out" of work has left some regions of the world with little by way of gainful employment for their young. It is the developing countries and those with the most fragile economies and political structures that often have the highest proportion of vulnerable young people. North Africa and the Middle East now have the highest percentage of young people in the world, 60 percent of the citizens of these regions are under 30 years of age, twice the rate of North America.[9] With an unemployment rate of 10 percent or more, North Africa and the Middle East also have some of the highest regional rates of joblessness in the world. For the young people of these regions, the rate is four times that.[10]

The youngsters growing up in fragile countries with high unemployment rates are at greatest risk. Some of them will be actively recruited by the extremist religious or ideological groups that they perceive to be closest to them in identity or proximity. By 2012, this was already apparent in war-torn or unstable regions of the world, such as Afghanistan, Somalia, and parts of Pakistan. Psychological studies show that young people, most often men, join violent gangs to create a sense of shared status. Once this status is created, it is almost impossible for those young people to leave the gang—by doing so, they lose all their kinship and status.

Leveraging Convening Power

Cohen's own understanding of the creation and legacy of extreme groups deepened when he worked at the U.S. State Department, which sent him to Iran, Iraq, Syria, and Lebanon to document militant organizations and interview their members. During that period, Cohen deepened his knowledge of the mechanics by which young people become involved with militant organizations. By retracing their socialization process through interviews, he discovered that many young people turned to violent gangs because they had no network of their own to turn to for support. As Cohen described, "They were broken souls who would rather have had a pen in their hand."[11] When he traveled to Colombia and Guatemala on behalf of the State Department, he found a similar situation.

Yet, as socialization and identity studies have shown, getting gang members out of their gangs is tough. To tackle this problem, Cohen and the team at Google Ideas launched an initiative in the summer of 2011 by arranging a meeting—which they called the "Summit against Violent Extremism" (SAVE), in Dublin, Ireland. Ireland has a long history of extremists, with thousands of Irish Republican Army (IRA) and paramilitary terrorists waging war on each other for many decades. Yet Ireland is also a place where a peace settlement had been drawn up and extreme terrorist acts had decreased significantly. The aim of the summit was to understand more deeply what draws young people to these groups and what can be done to redirect them.

The summit brought together more than 80 "formers"—from inner-city gang members and right-wing militants to violent nationalists and religious extremists—for three days of debates and workshops. The formers have rejected violence and actively work against extremism either through their own or other nonprofit organizations. Members came from Asia, the Middle East, Latin America, North America, and Europe. The summit also included survivors of violent extremism, along with more than 100 delegates from civil society organizations, academia, technology companies, government, media, and the private sector.

After the summit, a number of actions were taken. One was to set up an online network of former violent extremists, survivors of violent extremism, NGOs, academics, think tanks, and private-sector leaders called Against Violent Extremism (AVE). The AVE website is managed by the London-based think tank Institute for Strategic Dialogue, Google Ideas' partner. The website was designed to initiate a global conversation on how to prevent young people from becoming radicalized and how to deradicalize others. As Cohen remarks:

> Until now, there has never before been a one-stop shop for people who want to help fight these challenges—a place to connect with others across sectors and disciplines to get expertise and resources.[12]

A second initiative has focused on using Google's search capabilities to expose and disrupt global criminal networks by launching a campaign against the secrecy and impunity of drug cartels, organ harvesters, cyber criminals, violent radicals, and traffickers in arms and people.[13] The project is an alliance with the Igarapé Institute, a Brazilian security-development think tank, and the Peace Research Institute of Oslo, an international conflict-research institute. Cohen sees it this way: "We believe that technology has the power to expose and dismantle global criminal networks, which depend on secrecy and discretion in order to function."[14]

The campaign was launched at a two-day summit entitled, "Illicit Networks: Forces in Opposition," in Los Angeles in July 2012. Reflecting the extremist process, the summit assembled victims, law enforcement personnel, politicians, academics, and technology experts to devise strategies to combat global criminal networks that claim hundreds of thousands of lives and cost an estimated $1 trillion each year.[15] Stewart Patrick, a senior fellow at the Council on Foreign Relations who helped organize the event, said:

> It might sound like a different path for Google, but technology companies today have a lot of powerful tools for bringing transparency to these illicit networks, to fight back against corruption, and to empower those who are trying to combat transnational crime.[16]

The Google engineers may seem very far from the nutrition researchers at DSM, but what both have shown is that it is possible to leverage deep corporate research and innovative capabilities in the service of a global challenge that is threatening an ever more fragile world.

Using Specialist Skills at Boston Consultancy Group

Save the Children is now almost 100 years old and works to improve the quality of life of children in 120 countries. Historically, it has worked through a decentralized federation of 29 independent organizations. Over the years, the teams at Save the Children have become ever more adept at forging partnerships and innovative collaborations with corporations that share its vision of a better world for children. These alliances tend to be long term rather than one-offs and range from designing multistakeholder partnerships to addressing specific problems confronting children and galvanizing support for Save the Children's programs.

In 2010, the international board of Save the Children decided to bring its federation of independent organizations together by selecting, for the first time in the history of the organization, an international chief executive. They chose Jasmine Whitbread, and her first task was to decide how best to build a deeper and more nuanced capability to tap into various alliances and partnerships to tackle child poverty. This is how she describes her approach to me:

> These "Big Issues" demand "Big Coalitions" and cross sector participation. An NGO like Save the Children may have a clear purpose, but it needs to ally with large companies to create the scale and have an impact.[17]

To do this, Whitbread decided that one of her major priorities was to reinvent Save the Children as a twenty-first-century organization that could mobilize people with different views and agendas around a common cause. She realized that while the organization had been competent at creating partnerships, internally there was a growing realization that its governance and structure had begun to hamper its global capability. Its federated and decentralized structure certainly built local understanding and flexibility, but increasingly it damaged the capacity to achieve greater global scale and scope at speed. In trying to understand how best to accomplish this goal, Whitbread worked closely with members of the strategy consultancy Boston Consultancy Group (BCG). Founded in the 1960s, the firm has more than 6,000 consultants who have developed capabilities in corporate strategy, organizational architecture, and culture change. The founder of the partnership, Bruce Henderson, was fond of quoting Archimedes, "Give me a lever and a place to stand, and I will move the world." He was the first of a succession of senior partners who continue to work to leverage the firm's assets and capabilities for social good and to build a more resilient world.

The partnership between Save the Children and BCG goes back more than 20 years to the 1990s, and since that time, successive groups of BCG consultants and partners have supported Save the Children executives on a variety of organizational development issues. The work to prepare Save the Children for the twenty-first century evolved into a series of projects including multiple secondments of BCG consultants and partners.

Creating Many Channels of Involvement

By 2012, the BCG managing director responsible for the Save the Children relationship was Craig Baker who was spending about one day a week on the program, both leading the BCG team and advising the executive team. About this, he remarked to me:

> I myself devote one day a week to such global partnerships and do not differentiate between them or any other business client. The only difference between the two clients is that one gets us revenues and the other doesn't.[18]

The relationship between the two organizations goes deeper: some associates are engaged through the firm's social-impact secondment program and typically spend 12 months working with one of the social-impact partners; others have taken a social-impact leave of absence, often helped by BCG to find opportunities to work with NGOs on a leave-of-absence basis; others are part of a 12-month social-impact immersion program that deepens the experience and skills of those interested in such an experience. Some, like Craig Baker, are engaged through client projects that offer employees a chance to work at a client company on a project basis. Of the 6,000 consultants in the firm, more than 750 have chosen to participate in social-impact projects in 2011, and many others become involved through local volunteer opportunities.

These partnerships can be deeply satisfying to participants, and many also have been an opportunity for participants to broaden their skills. As Craig Baker remarks:

> Our people develop both intellectually and professionally, and this enhances our ability to attract and retain the world's best talent.[19]

For Save the Children, the work with a strategy partner such as BCG has created an opportunity for the organization to better leverage the collective strength of its independent national members to serve the needs of children around the world. In an interview with Jasmine Whitbread she described that this is how she sees it:

> Getting all 29 members of Save the Children to agree to one shared strategy that involved huge organizational change

would never have been possible in such a short time without the invaluable help of BCG. BCG's insight, process reengineering, and change management capacity, not to mention credibility and can-do approach, continue to support us through this ambitious strategy to achieve more for children.[20]

CONCLUSION

Successful, knowledge-rich corporations such as DSM, Google, and BCG are full of crowds of talented, creative people. Some of these people want to leverage their capabilities into tackling big global issues. It is this innovative capacity and willpower that, perhaps more than anything else, is particularly well developed in making this link between capabilities and problems. However, as we will see, it really takes mobilizing capabilities to convert great ideas to a scale capable of making a real difference.

CHAPTER 9

❖

LEVERAGING SCALING
AND MOBILIZING

The first time I walked into the London headquarters of Standard Chartered Bank, I was enchanted by a set of sepia photographs of tents in the deserts of Arabia. These were the first trading posts of what was then the Standard Bank of British South Africa. The photographs were taken around 1865 and show the first employees of the bank, resplendent in pith hats and linen suits sitting on tables under canvas tents. They had traveled from London to be the bankers for the traders who led their caravans of camels bearing silks and spices across the trade routes of the desert. Along the wall was another set of photographs that showed the bazaars of Calcutta and Shanghai, where the first offices of the Chartered Bank of India, Australia, and China were founded in 1853.

By the 1870s, companies such as the Standard Bank had begun their early lessons in building the capability to mobilize resources and knowledge and to scale their products and services across the world. The executives at the Standard Bank had begun by experimenting with how to set up branches in Calcutta; they had worked out how best to select managers who could be trusted not to run away with the assets in those dusty Arabian tents and how to move their assets from one place to another in a safe and secure way.

Over the next hundred years, other local companies also began to learn to hone their skills in scaling and mobilizing. Indeed, those who were successful at developing this capability became the foundation for the multinational companies of today. To these early capabilities in scaling and mobilizing could be added the capability of working across geographies. Those first London employees of the Standard Bank who had been chosen to work in the Arabian desert spoke the languages of the region and knew something of the customs of its people, and those who joined in Shanghai would be selected for their expertise in Mandarin. From their first steps in globalization, these early multinational corporations had begun to learn how to become embedded in local cultures, how to learn the language and customs of the place, and how to trade and engage in local commerce.

This expertise in scaling and mobilizing continues to be held in high esteem in contemporary corporations. Young executives are chosen for promotion on the basis of their cultural sensitivity, and senior executives are assessed on their capacity to describe a purpose that resonates across the regional networks of the corporation. Many corporate resources are then used to build an infrastructure that enables ideas and products to flow at speed and at low cost around the world. The organizational architecture—who reports to whom and the protocols of decision making—is constantly tweaked to ensure that the organization finds the sweet spot between centralization and decentralization.

The result is that over many years—indeed, for some companies, even hundreds of years—successive executive teams of large corporations have honed their scaling and mobilizing capabilities.

HOW CORPORATIONS LEVERAGE SCALING AND MOBILIZING CAPABILITIES

Some of these corporations now have discovered that it is possible to actively leverage their own scaling and mobilizing capabilities in the service of their community and indeed into the broader challenges of building resilience in a fragile world. Taking a closer look at how this has been achieved, there are three actions that seem to be crucial:

1. They build a case for action.
2. They mobilize around a cause.
3. They make use of scaling capabilities.

Building a Case for Action at Unilever

It's interesting to reflect on what we personally can do to make a difference. For those of us who are baby boomers, the question is particularly acute because wrapped up in this question is our own sense of legacy. I was reflecting on this as I talked with Paul Polman, CEO of Unilever. We are about the same age, so I guess that both of us are looking back as much as looking forward. He leads the corporation that brings you Dove soap, Knorr soup, Ben & Jerry's ice cream, and products like this to you and over 2 billion other consumers every day. We were both presenting at the Peter Drucker Conference, which is held in Vienna every year to celebrate the life and work of one of management's greatest thinkers. Reflecting on his own life, Polman had this to say:

> I have three children. When I think about my own life, it's clear that we have had an easy time of it. Thinking about my own parents, my father never went to university, but he wanted his six sons and daughters to go to university—so he worked really hard as a young adult to make sure this happened. It was second nature for him to work for the greater good. For my generation, compared with my father, we have had an easier time of it. In fact, we have created comfort and taken it for granted. We have become a "we generation": we wanted it all, and in doing this, we have stolen resources and taken away job opportunities from the next generation. We now have to fix it. We can make a difference. We can try to correct and put the world on a better path. We have to try this.[1]

Of course, the scope for Polman to make a difference is infinitely greater than mine and probably yours. But there are many CEOs right now who have a global scope like Polman's but have chosen not to use it. When Polman joined Unilever in 2009 as their CEO, one of his first decisions was to publicly commit the whole company to halve the environmental footprint of its products and practices by 2020. He also set a sustainability target that by 2020, no less than 40 percent of the corporation's total energy requirements would come from renewable sources. The long-term goal was that this would be 100 percent. At the same time, he also committed to Unilever's shareholders and employees that the business would double its revenues by 2020.[2]

His vision resonated with the long history of Unilever, which is steeped in the ideals of sustainability reaching back to the founder of Lever Brothers, Lord Leverhulme, who built a business to manufacture soap so that "cleanliness could be commonplace." This heritage continues to be important, as head of sustainability Gail Klintworth remarked:

> When Paul came to his job, this was a little easier. What he did was to take what was inherent in the company and raise it to a cross-company strategy. To do this, he went internally and externally with a bold goal. What was the really bold part was that we made a public commitment without actually knowing how to achieve it. This is something that is very unusual for CEOs.[3]

Setting and Monitoring Goals

By April 2012, Polman was presenting the first results of the "Sustainable Living Plan," which was to be the first part of a 10-year program with initial initiatives in palm oil, as well as sourcing agricultural raw materials more sustainably and reducing the amount of energy used throughout Unilever's operations. In a series of presentations across the world, he invited campaigners, NGOs, and others to question Unilever on its work. The progress report he discussed listed both the successes and where the corporation was off plan (including the sustainable sourcing of sunflower oil) as well as where it had missed its target (on improving heart health). The report showed that the company had moved from 14 percent sustainable sourcing within one year to 24 percent without any negative impact on growth.

For Polman, this sort of public commitment is crucial, as he remarked at the Drucker conference:

> Any system where too many people feel they are not participating and feel excluded will ultimately lead to rebelling against the system. We need to be a proactive actor, not just bystanders. There are forces at work, which through social media are connecting billions. I see these social networks

increasingly organizing themselves. As consumers, they are demanding transparency. On top of this, the shift to the East and the change in the economic balance has exposed our institutional system. Politicians struggle because of their short-term focus and are having a hard time understanding the power of connected people.[4]

CEO visions and goals are one thing, but it's really in the day-to-day actions of millions of people that these sustainability goals come to life. What is tricky is that these goals are not simply for the Unilever factories and regional offices; they are also for the total value chain and range from sourcing, to manufacturing, to transport and refrigeration, all the way through to the consumers' use of the products. In effect, this is the whole life cycle of over 1,600 products in 14 geographic locations. This means that employees need to take a scientific approach to the environmental footprint in each geographic location to understand the baseline data and then extrapolate going forward. In some cases, this also means making a financial case for change. For example, in the design and building of all new Unilever factories, the architects and planners are tasked with halving the current environmental footprint. This requires making investments that would not meet the normal discounted yield but could be calculated to have significant benefits in the longer term. It also involves reaching out to the billions of customers who use Unilever products every day to encourage them to use the products in a more sustainable way. Imagine the skills and organizational capabilities required to make this happen. This is research and innovation and scaling and mobilizing on a grand scale.

Creating a Program for Change

It rested with Gail Klintworth and her team to support this scaling and mobilizing. Klintworth had come from leading Unilever's South African business, so she was well versed in the DNA of the corporation and how it makes change happen. She began by using her small team to assemble a network of over 100 champions from across all the businesses and all the regions in which Unilever operates. Together they used the tried-and-tested Unilever approach to scaling and mobilizing by first creating working groups for each product category in each factory and across every function. The task of these working groups was to put in place their own plan on how to deliver to the sustainability goals. Next, the goals where embedded into the performance-management system so that meeting these sustainability goals was tied into the annual remuneration assessment and by 2013 had become a key part of the performance appraisal of all of the presidents of the businesses. This is how Klintworth described the process to me:

> It's about change management over a massive network. We followed the normal change processes: understand the vision and goals and ensure that there is buy-in, align the goals with performance targets and remuneration, and ensure that there are early wins. We also wanted to make this part of leadership development, helping people to think how they make difficult decisions. So we are preparing sustainability case studies to be used in all our leadership training. It's important that we get intellectual buy-in to the goals and targets and bust the myth that the sustainable solution costs more. But emotional engagement is also crucial. For example, we take people to see what's happening in the plantations in Malaysia so that they can experience firsthand both the positive and negative impacts we have on our communities.[5]

The sustainability goals touched every person in Unilever, for when the teams began to monitor and analyze the specifics of carbon use, they found that a significant proportion was used within the company rather than in the products and supply chain. Commuting to work every day, sitting in large air-conditioned offices, and flying around the world to meet colleagues and customers were all significant creators of carbon dioxide and are unsustainable in the long term.

Reducing this required a complete redesign of the way that people work. This also brought home the realization that sustainability is not simply about natural resources; it's also about creating working practices that are energizing for people. Over time, teams across the corporation began to experiment with what could and would work. To do this, they ran pilot programs across the company to look more closely at various ways of working: which tasks could be achieved productively from home without the high carbon cost of commuting and office work and which were more "cooperative-rich" and so needed a range of face-to-face options. Over time, the corporation began to invest in local hubs[6] built nearer to people's homes and so giving them a chance for face-to-face interaction while still significantly reducing the number of commutes and meetings. Like the executive teams at Cisco, the design team also made significant investments in collaborative technologies so that over time people developed the habit of using video conferencing rather than simply getting onto a flight to meet people. By 2010, the capacity for "telepresence" had been implemented in over 24 countries, resulting in more than 5,000 meetings producing both cost savings (travel costs have fallen by US$19.8 million) and sustainability benefits (in 2010, 43,000 tons of carbon emissions were avoided).

What the teams at Unilever had done was to begin to fundamentally change the way that work gets done. This involved creating clear expectations of performance, putting in place measures of outcomes rather than hours of work, and encouraging managers to coach rather than supervise. Dismantling the vestiges of bureaucratic work is not easy because it involves making change across the whole supply chain and requires deep and cooperative alliance building with suppliers and distributors. This path is not without its dangers, as Polman told the *Harvard Business Review*[7]:

> If we hit all our targets on this plan but no one else follows suit, we will have failed miserably. We are trying to show that you can be successful as a business and at the same time show the financial community that this should be one of the better drivers for their investments. At the heart is the development of strong alliances with NGOs, governments, and other corporations.

As Gail Klintworth reflected in a conversation with me:

> Advocacy and policy influence are crucial. We had to identify the key areas where we need to work with policy makers and governments to make the right kind of shift. The credibility and vision of the CEO are crucial to having the right conversation with the right people.[8]

What Polman is attempting at Unilever is to lead the corporation down a path that is not a scramble but rather a more purposeful path.

Mobilizing Around a Cause at Standard Chartered Bank

To take a closer look at how scaling and mobilizing can be used against global challenges, I want to return again to the offices of Standard Chartered Bank. This time my purpose is not to admire the sepia photographs but rather to learn more about how the employees across the corporation have been part of an initiative that has made a positive impact on the sight of more than 31 million people across the world.

Imagine what it takes to make a difference at this scale. In part, the scale of the endeavor reflects the global scale of the corporation. From those early days of the Arabian tents, the bank now has a network of over 1,700 offices across some of the fastest-growing and also some of the poorest places on Earth in Asia, Africa, and the Middle East. The sheer survival of the bank since the 1850s stands as a testament to its inner core of resilience. In a sector that has undergone extraordinary stress during a number of financial crises, the bank has steadily grown its assets and profits. What has been crucial to this is not only the bank's ability to build an inner core of resilience but also the values it aspires to bring to its employees, customers, and neighbors.

Like Paul Polman at Unilever, Franck Riboud at Danone, and Antonio Luiz da Cunha Seabra at Natura, CEO of Standard Chartered Bank Peter Sands does not see corporate purpose as a choice to be made between economic and social value in a zero-sum game. Rather, his leadership purpose is to both meet shareholder expectations and to be "Here for good."[9]

Identifying a Resonating Cause

The thinking behind saving sight began in 2003 when then CEO Mervyn Davies used the opportunity of the bank's 150th anniversary celebrations to invite staff from across the world to consider how best the bank should celebrate. His only proviso was that their ideas had to be about giving back to the bank's communities. Across the network of the bank, avoidable blindness was identified as a cause that people felt really passionate about and that many felt had been neglected in their own communities. They could see, often firsthand, the economic and social consequences of members of their community being visually impaired.

Studies at that time showed that more than 300 million people were seriously visually impaired, of which 45 million were blind, whereas 90 percent of avoidable blindness occurred in the developing world—where many of the branches of the bank were located. What's more, without concerted action, the number of blind people was projected to increase from 45 million to 76 million by 2020. Perhaps most worryingly, blindness is a problem that disproportionately affects women, who were twice as likely as men to become blind, due in part to unequal access to appropriate eye care. The economic and social consequences of blindness are huge and rising; estimates of the annual cost of lost productivity were expected to rise from US$200 billion to US$300 billion by 2020. Yet 80 percent of the world's blindness is avoidable—through either prevention or treatment—and for as little as US$30, someone's sight can be restored.

Agreeing on the Goals for Action

In 2003, the Seeing is Believing (SiB) program was launched with the goal to restore the sight of 28,000 people in the parts of the developing world where the bank had a presence. That number represented one person for each of the bank's employees at the time. With the exception of a small team based at the London headquarters and responsible for overall management, the program was entirely resourced by the voluntary fund-raising activities of employees across the world. In order to boost this commitment, it was decided that every dollar an employee group raised would be matched by a corporate fund—and by 2012, the bank had crossed the halfway mark of raising US$100 million by 2020.

Across the bank, people became involved by engaging in their own communities on projects with local NGO partners. CEO Peter Sands and his team signaled the importance they placed on this by encouraging every employee to spend three days of paid leave on a variety of community investment programs, including SiB. By 2012, with more than 87,000 employees, this added up to a quarter of a million potential days of employee energy and focus. As a result, by its ninth year, SiB had reached over 31 million people—funding more than 2.8 million eye surgeries, training more than 84,000 health-care workers, performing 5.9 million eye-care screenings, and distributing over 273,000 pairs of eyeglasses across Asia, Africa, and the Middle East. The SiB team also partnered with local NGOs in India to establish 78 vision centers in an innovative model of community eye care that by 2012 was being rolled out in other countries.

Making Use of Scaling Capabilities: Vodafone and Safaricom

For us in the developed world, we take for granted our ability to bank our money and draw that money out of the bank at will. For over a hundred years, an infrastructure of branch offices and, more recently, cash machines has reached even the smallest of towns. Can you imagine how it would be if you did not have access to banking?

Imagine keeping your money under the bed or hidden in the biscuit box. This is dangerous, the money earns no interest, and transfers cannot be done with ease. Moreover, because you have no financial record, you will struggle to take out credit or buy insurance for your health, your home, or your old age.

The Fragility of the "Unbanked"

For many people living in underdeveloped countries, access to banks is something they have never taken for granted. The reasons are clear. Take, for example, a vast and rural country such as Kenya. Imagine the capital investment required to build a network of thousands of bank branches in the major towns and to move money physically from one branch to another across roads that can be knee deep in mud in the rainy season. With most people in Kenya earning less than a dollar a day, it is no surprise that major banks have simply focused their operations on the large cities of the country. The result is that the retail banking infrastructure in many developing countries is poor, leaving most people with no way of saving or transferring money.

This was the case in Kenya, where fewer than 2 million bank accounts served the country's population of 32 million people. Go to Kenya right now, and you will see how that dismal situation has begun to change. At every street corner in even the smallest of towns there are individual retailers who, in effect, are bank tellers capable of receiving money and providing a banking system. They don't sit behind the bars of a bank branch—for Kenya continues to have very few bank branches. These retailers are the very same people who sell mobile phone airtime in the form of scratch cards. They are part of Kenya's fast-growing mobile phone network, which works from a relatively well-developed network of booster stations across the country and ultralow-cost handsets.

As a consequence, the average Kenyan does not have what you probably have—a bank branch network. But what they do have is something you may not have—they can use their mobile phone to transfer money. They do this by becoming M-PESA Safaricom users (the local Kenyan telecom) and then registering their identity with their local mobile phone retailer through either their national identification cards or passports. They can then exchange their cash for electronic money and put this into their e-float. It's free to register, and transaction costs are low. By 2012, more than 25,000 retailers had signed up as M-PESA agents—far outnumbering Kenya's 850 bank branches.

The impact has been profound.[10] Nearly 60 percent of Kenyan households use M-PESA for person-to-person transfers, as well as to pay for everything from school fees to mobile phone credit to electricity bills. Of these, over 80 percent use M-PESA for saving. The capacity to move money fast across the vast distances of Kenya can be lifesaving.[11] In a country with limited unemployment and health insurance, the flexibility of M-PESA encourages networks of friends and extended family to create risk-sharing practices.[12]

The M-PESA system was designed and built by an alliance led by the UK telecom company Vodafone and its African partner Safaricom. This is a formidable achievement that tested the innovative, scaling, and alliance-building capabilities of both corporations and the banking and government partners with whom they worked.

Overcoming Obstacles

Step back for a moment and imagine the financial, social, cultural, political, technological, and regulatory obstacles that had to be overcome to build and deliver M-PESA. First, it required creating a well-functioning and trustworthy working partnership between stakeholders who included a global telecommunications company, a number of local banks, a variety of microfinance institutions, and the Kenyan government. From a legal perspective, this alliance had to cope with complex and often contradictory regulatory requirements. Second, with the average Kenyan earning a dollar a day, any service to the Kenyan population would never meet the return on equity (ROE) that most corporations demand. Therefore, there had to be a way of bringing substantial resources to the project outside the normal ROE goal-setting requirements. Third, for a telecom company such as Vodafone, financial services is not the core business—M-PESA has little to do with the voice or data products that drive Vodafone's revenue streams. Moreover, the task was to develop the project outside Vodafone's core market because Kenya is a relatively small market for Vodafone. Finally, the project called on significant scaling and mobilization capabilities. The speed of the project required training of hundreds of thousands of people across Kenya. Moreover, it meant understanding the needs and aspirations of millions of customers who had no prior experience with banks, who were often semiliterate, and who faced routine challenges to their physical and financial security. Yet, despite all these hurdles, by 2102, millions of Kenyans could do something that people in developed countries take for granted—save their money, pay their bills, and send money to their parents and children when needed.

The project to build M-PESA began in 2000 with US$1.6 million seed funding from the Department for International Development (DFID) in the United Kingdom. At that time, Nick Hughes, a member of Vodafone's corporate social responsibility unit, had been thinking about how using a mobile phone to transfer money could have an impact on some of the economic factors of poverty.[13] The task was to move from a great idea into a scalable action. With Vodafone's Kenyan partner, Safaricom, and CEO Michael Joseph, the idea quickly gathered momentum.

Using Corporate Project Parameters

The project rapidly ran through its initial financial investment, and the decision was made to increase the corporate funding to ensure that it could continue. Over the period of the next five years, an alliance of institutions worked closely together to get the project off the ground. This involved the telecoms Faulu Kenya, a leading microfinance institution in Kenya, and the Commercial Bank of Africa, which provided the traditional banking infrastructure. By 2005, the project was ready to go live. Looking back on this time, Vodafone project leader Christele Delbe reflects:

> Mobile cash was completely unproven. At any one time, there are many projects within Vodafone that we are thinking about. Obviously, we prioritize those with the greatest potential for returns. What was interesting about this project is that while the financial return would always be below our ROE criteria, we could see the social return. The project required significant upfront investment. It worked because the link with the initial challenge allowed us to make this investment and then defer the costs over a couple of years. The partnerships with DFID and Safaricom allowed us to reduce our upfront risk.[14]

To mobilize at speed and scale, the project was treated like any other Vodafone product development with project leads, a clear project plan with multiple accountabilities, and project monitoring and feedback.

One of the fascinating insights from the M-PESA initiative is the extent to which the service has enabled a much deeper and richer understanding of how economies such as those of Kenya work at a micro level. Teams of researchers have studied the positive impact on poverty of enabling money to be transferred easily. Their results are one part of an emerging worldwide conversation across the telecom industry with NGOs and indeed governments. For example, the telecom industry's body—the Global System for Mobile Communications GSM—has actively brought together the various telecom companies from across the world to build deeper alliances with governments and financial institutions. What has also emerged from these discussions is the importance to projects such as M-PESA of the right type of regulation market. One of the impacts of M-PESA has been to encourage telecom regulators across the world to open a debate with corporations and NGOs about the impact they can have on financial inclusion. The alliance was further boosted when in 2012 the Bill and Melinda Gates Foundation committed US$500 million to M-PESA projects over five years.

CONCLUSION

Corporations really make a difference when they can amplify their research and innovative capability and then scale the very best ideas with speed and dexterity. However, some challenges are really tough to meet. They involve many stakeholders with potentially conflicting agendas. This is where real alliance-building capabilities come into focus.

CHAPTER 10

❖

LEVERAGING ALLIANCES

It was more than a decade ago that I first saw a diagram of the ecosystem of alliances for a global corporation. I was in the Finnish headquarters of the telecom company Nokia, and at that time, the word *ecosystem* was just beginning to be used to describe the multiple alliances a company had with its suppliers, partners, and competitors. The diagram illustrated the extent of these relationships as a network with fine lines connecting the partners both with Nokia and with each other. It was an extraordinary sight. There were alliances with code developers such as ARM Holdings, with the chip manufacturers such as Philips, with factories all over the world that manufactured the phones, and with distribution companies that ensured that the billion parts that Nokia was moving around at any point in time could be found and catalogued. At that time, the senior team at Nokia was in the process of creating one of the world's most complex ecosystems of alliances.

Over time, many more of these ecosystems and their alliances have emerged in sectors such as pharmaceuticals and aerospace. These had become industry sectors that were just too complex for any one company to supply all the answers. This was illustrated at the time in Nokia's alliance with ARM Holdings. ARM Holdings is a community of some of the most talented code writers in the world, spun out of the engineering and mathematics departments of Cambridge University. Most have Ph.D. degrees, they do incredibly complex work, and they are the main competitors to Intel. The Nokia executive team, with its emphasis on mobile phones, could never hope to build such a team from its roots in Finland. However, it did not need to build internal competencies. Instead, it simply had to become very skilled in managing the alliance with ARM Holdings. Over time, the Nokia–ARM Holdings network became just one of hundreds of similar alliances the team at Nokia was building.

It was the inspiration of the Nokia ecosystem diagram that encouraged me to go on to spend more than five years researching the collaborative relationships that underpin these alliances by spanning internal and external corporate boundaries. I wrote two books about it, *Hot Spots* and *Glow*.[1] In a sense, the books were a celebration of this precious capability that in some companies had been fashioned in the most exquisite manner.

What I had learned about these alliance capabilities was that they depend on people across organizational boundaries being prepared to appreciate each other's point of view and then to trust each other and to be skilled in managing the conflicts that emerged. I also discovered that having a strong shared view of the goal of the alliance is also crucial.

It has never been more important that alliance capabilities are used to build resilience in a fragile world. The challenges that create this fragility are becoming harder to fix as they emerge ever faster and have so many potential unintended consequences and competing demands. Moreover, their solution requires multiple stakeholders— each with their own agendas and capabilities.

In their simplest forms, these alliances are between an NGO and a corporation, each bringing its unique capabilities and assets. At their most complex, they involve building alliances across multiple stakeholders, each with their own perspectives, capabilities, and challenges.

IMPACT OF MULTIPLE STAKEHOLDERS

The difficulties of bringing stakeholders together to fix these escalating challenges became apparent to me when I chaired a session on the challenges of youth unemployment at the World Economic Forum's meeting at Davos in the Swiss Alps in early 2012. The session brought together multiple stakeholders interested in the field of youth unemployment. This included an array of economists and labor academics from the Wharton Business School, representatives from a number of governments from around the world, a clutch of

NGOs working on skill gaps, and a few social entrepreneurs devoting their financial and human resources to solving this problem. It did not take us long to agree that the need was great. We were staring in the face of what could become a lost generation.

But what also rapidly emerged was the complexity of building multiple stakeholder alliances around complex issues. We heard how in many regions the schools and colleges seemed to be developing their curricula in isolation from market needs and job-ready skills. We also heard how corporations, faced with a lack of the right talent, often simply rushed into the "tragedy of the commons," seeing it as a war for talent and pushing up the prices of those who had the skills rather than developing the skills of the many. And we heard how governments, often faced with a constant churn of political priorities and short-term voter-friendly initiatives, failed to set clear long-term strategies.

Yet we also heard how when these stakeholders are aligned, the impact can be amazing. We can see this right now in Singapore, where youth unemployment rarely goes above 6 percent. This is the result of cooperative alliances among multiple stakeholders which I saw first-hand as a member of the board of Singapore government's Human Capital Institute. Every stakeholder is encouraged to play a unique role. Singapore schools and colleges are encouraged to develop their curricula with an eye to the likely skills needs of the country, and there is much signaling to youngsters about what skills will fly in the emerging economy. The government plays its role: the Economic Development Board, led then by its highly talented chairman Leo Yip, is mandated to provide high-value jobs by attracting new high-value businesses to the country and supporting the growth of entrepreneurs; the Ministry of Manpower backs early skills development in crucial areas such as engineering and science and makes sure that high-talent immigrants are ushered into the country without too many hassles; and the Ministry of Education safeguards Singapore's world-class schools to guarantee that the most talented families who want to relocate to the country can be assured of their children's education. At the same time, the leaders of corporations are encouraged to reach out into their communities to make a real difference and to train their employees. Perhaps, then, it is no surprise that when Unilever decided to set up a second campus, it choose Singapore and when the business school INSEAD built a second campus outside France, it made the same decision. As the Singapore experience shows, ensuring that youth unemployment never goes above 6 percent takes both an understanding of the dynamics of the system of employment and a great deal of concentrated and coordinated action by a wide group of stakeholders.

Of course, you may be thinking that it is relatively easy to coordinate stakeholders in a small and highly educated country such as Singapore that has one of the world's most professional civil servants to guarantee that these alliances work with ease. And there is no doubt that there is some truth to this view. However, as we have seen, an alliance of sorts is emerging in India focused on job-ready skills where the information technology (IT) giants (such as Wipro, Infosys, and Tata Consultancy Services) are working with each other and with teachers on the development of a work-ready curriculum to tackle India's chronic low standards of education.

What I learned from my experience in looking at youth unemployment and working with the Singapore Ministry of Manpower is that there are multiple stakeholders, each of which has strengths it can bring to an alliance. Often, however, these stakeholders also bring factors that make it hard for them to address the challenge on their own. This is why alliances across multiple stakeholders can be so difficult and yet can also be so effective. These stakeholders each can potentially bring their own unique capabilities:

- Governments can bring fiscal and legal frameworks.
- Multilateral agencies can create convening power.
- NGOs can bring passion and on-the-ground experience.
- Swarms of citizens can bring scale and immediacy.
- Social entrepreneurs can bring ideas and resources.

Governments Can Bring Fiscal and Legal Frameworks

Massachusetts Institute of Technology economist Daron Acemoglu and Harvard University's James Robinson have argued that in part the capacity of businesses to flourish and citizens to live purposeful working lives is determined by the incentives created by institutions such as law, education, and fiscal policy and that politics and government determine what institutions a nation has.[2]

When governments succeed in taking action, as the Singaporean government has with youth employment, it is often through their capacity to develop key infrastructure and policy frameworks and to roll out initiatives that relate to human rights, public health, and education. Indeed, in many advanced economies, government is often the biggest "business" of all and can therefore lead by example. In their own relationships with their employees and supply chains governments can set the precedent by consuming differently and by planning effectively and efficiently. Governments can encourage prosperity by creating positive-feedback loops within the economy, by creating a fair distribution of resources that prevents the elites from undermining them and reducing the debilitating impact of inequality, and by building a positive and stable fiscal context in which challenges such as poverty and unemployment are addressed.

Yet governments themselves face substantial problems. Most have been through the deepest global economic slump in 70 years, and this has tested the resiliency of their institutions, of their markets, and indeed of capitalism itself. Moreover, a consequence of this is that much of their energy has been focused on trying to solve these economic problems—with the crisis around the euro simply serving to make matters worse. The global economy in which they operate remains weak, and they are operating within what has evolved into an increasingly interdependent system—a system in which domestic policy, even in the largest economies, is shaped by global developments. In addition, slow growth and high unemployment in much of the world have contributed to more divisive politics. And this, of course, works against more cooperative regional and global solutions.

Governments and their elected officers are also constrained by their jurisdictional boundaries and short election cycles. Democratically elected governments are constantly seeking ways to please their electorates and can shy away from providing unpalatable data or taking a tough line of action.

Multilateral Agencies Can Create Convening Power

In many alliances, international development agencies such as the United Nations play a key role. Set up, owned, funded, and controlled by the governments of the developed countries, the role of these international development agencies is specifically to focus on issues through various development-related projects, including the World Bank, the Organisation for Economic Co-operation and Development, and various UN agencies such as the International Labour Organization and the International Monetary Fund. Many were created during the final stages of World War II, and their design was heavily influenced by the United States and the United Kingdom.

Since the end of the cold war, multilateral agencies have set a variety of goals bound up with the notion of development. However, although their intentions have been laudable, there are criticisms that their actions have lagged behind. As Harvard professors Joseph Bower, Herman Leonard, and Lynn Paine report in their study of executives' perspectives on multilateral agencies,[3]

> First, went the argument, they are not managed particularly well; they are bureaucratized, bloated, and self-interested. Second (and perhaps related), many felt that the existing institutions have been systematically undercut by the lack of cooperation from important national governments—most notably the United States, Russia, and China. Finally, and perhaps more crucially, most observers note that the main international institutions on the landscape today were never designed to deal with the issues that are now arising or with the threats to the economic progress.

Yet significant multilateral agencies and corporate alliances have emerged. In the late 1990s, the World Bank launched the Business Partners for Development program designed to understand more clearly the benefits and challenges of partnerships. In 1999, then UN Secretary-General Kofi Annan announced the Global Compact, an attempt to bring together the world's largest corporations to encourage voluntary adoption of universal basic standards relating to human rights, the environment, and labor. By 2004, it had more than 1,600 members, including several hundred multinational corporations. This is not a regulatory body but rather a voluntary framework of principles, and as such, it lacks "teeth." As George Lodge, from Harvard, and Craig Wilson, from the World

Bank, remark, "The wonder is that it has taken the United Nations Development Program and multinationals so long to begin to get together and that the connections are so slight."[4] However, as we have seen, many of the most interesting initiatives that combat poverty— such as that created by DSM and the World Food Program—are brokered by the convening power and patience of multilateral agencies. Members of these agencies are able to pull stakeholders together around a single issue and by doing so tailor the competencies of these stakeholders to improving the situation.

NGOs Can Bring Passion and On-the-Ground Experience

Nongovernmental Organizations (NGOs) are playing an increasing role in creating resilience in a fragile world, particularly because most have concerns that center on human rights and the natural environment. There are many of them, and their numbers are growing fast. Those that have seen membership climb the fastest include Amnesty International (39,000 in 1987 to 108,000 in 1992), the Sierra Club (114,000 in 1970 to 555,000 in 1996), and Greenpeace (250 in 1971 to 1.7 million in 1996). Whereas some of them indeed are of the "attacking variety,"[5] most seem to prefer to work in partnership with corporations.

Many NGOs are deeply trusted in the communities in which they operate.[6] In a survey conducted in 2012, people in 16 of 23 countries said that they trusted NGOs more than they trusted business. Historically, NGOs have been trusted most in developed markets. By 2011, though, they were gaining trust in emerging markets as well. In Brazil and China, for example, where trust in NGOs is on a par with trust in business, it seems that higher economic levels have come with a greater concern for environmental responsibility, education, and public health, the very province of NGOs.

NGOs benefit from being up close with the challenge and seeing exactly what is going on day by day. This can be crucial to understanding the complex dynamic systems in which problems operate. What the NGOs also can bring is an unswerving focus on and passion for a single issue in a way that brings both clarity and measurement. Take, for example, the role of Save the Children, the purpose of which is so clearly embedded in its title. Its role is simply to make a significant positive impact on the lives of millions of children across the world. Unswerving purpose such as this makes it relatively easy for NGOs to set priorities in a way that governments and corporations juggling many needs are rarely able to do. What is more, in the tense situations in which many of these challenges are played, of all the players, often it is the NGOs that are the most likely to be seen as nonpartisan and trustworthy. This creates an opportunity for them to play a key brokering role in complex political situations.

Yet many of these local NGO initiatives suffer from a profound lack of scale and an inability to mobilize at speed. They simply don't have the personnel and resources to make a real difference beyond the locations in which they work. Moreover, although the more global NGOs are passionate and deeply knowledgeable about local conditions, they don't necessarily have that deep expertise in all areas. This is why, when Save the Children wanted to transform its organizational capability to become more responsive across the globe, it was to the strategy consultancy BCG that it turned.

Swarms of Citizens Can Bring Scale and Immediacy

Just as corporations mobilize "wise crowds" internally, so the tools for connectivity and conviviality are being used outside corporations to enable communities of interest to arise with ease and to mobilize large swarms of people in a very short period of time. Freed from a heavy diet of television watching, more and more people are using their "cognitive surplus" to engage with something more meaningful.[7]

These swarms can and will have a profound impact—joining up people across the globe and identifying people from many locations with similar values and aspirations. Right now people with similar interests are sifting through WikiLeaks to find government misdeeds, forming flash groups over issues of the moment, and connecting with each other in virtual communities that are becoming increasingly significant. Bad news spreads quickly and through multiple channels because users of YouTube, Twitter, and Facebook are able to expose the deviant actions of corporations and governments to huge audiences. If something is significant enough to go viral, it probably will. Once unleashed, the power of these "twitstorms" is enough to sweep even the most agile corporate public relations agencies off their feet. Online communities such as Avaaz bring people-powered politics to decision making worldwide. Avaaz is a shared infrastructure that is easily mobilized in support of causes selected by the members—and by spring 2012, it had 9.1 million members.

With the combination of increasing scale and the ever more sophisticated tools of monitoring and accountability, we can predict that the power and influence of swarms of citizens will only increase. What's more, rapid globalization and Internet coverage have enabled these conversations to go from local or regional conversations to truly global conversations. They have created what John Ruggie, from Harvard's Kennedy School of Government, has called a "transnational space" that goes beyond the boundaries of governments. He sees this as signaling the emergence of a "global public domain: an arena of discourse, contestation, and action organized around global rule-making—a transnational space that is not exclusively inhabited by states and which permits the direct expression and pursuit of human interests, not merely those mandated by the state."[8]

It is not at all surprising that young people are using their "digital native" status and environmental concerns to play a particularly active role in this transnational space. Take, for example, the community Net Impact, whose mission is to mobilize a new generation to use their careers to drive transformational change in the workplace and the world. This is a community of young people who value courage and putting their values to work for good, who want to inspire and support one another to build a sustainable future, and who want to have a positive impact by using their careers to transform their lives, their organizations, and the world. Based in the United States, the community has over 300 chapters, strong global connectivity, and an annual conference that attracts more than 3,000 people. The community began more than 20 years ago with a small network of MBA students who wanted to make a difference. By 2012, it had become a global community of over 30,000 student and professional leaders working within and beyond business to tackle the world's toughest problems.

Social Entrepreneurs Can Bring Ideas and Resources

Back in 2010, I met Blake Mycoskie of TOMS Shoes, at a conference in Norway. His idea is one of simplicity: encourage people to buy simple shoes made in a renewable way—and for every shoe sold, the company gifts one to a person in a developing country.

Social entrepreneurship such as that practiced by Blake Mycoskie is not new. In many ways it is the legacy of the philanthropic Quakers who used their industrial fortunes to build housing and libraries. What is new is that more often these are people who are using their technical savvy to make a difference. Some, such as Mycoskie, have used simple technology, whereas others have been really smart in their use of rapidly emerging "frugal" technology. Take, for example, a water-purification system capable of providing decent drinking water to villagers. Social entrepreneur Dean Kamen, borrowing a metaphor from the story of David and Goliath, calls his initiative Slingshot, and in developing this idea, he has brought together the tools of low-cost frugal technology, deep connectivity, and abundant knowledge.[9]

Often these social entrepreneurs work in tandem with corporations to achieve scaling of capitalization and scaling of energy. For example, Dean Kamen entered into an alliance with Coca-Cola to build, distribute, and most important, use Coke's enormous supply chain (the largest in Africa) to help maintain Slingshot.

People across the world have their eyes set on following in the path of Blake Mycoskie and Dean Kamen. My colleagues at London Business School tell me that the electives on social entrepreneurs attract a huge following, and the same is true in business schools around the world. Foundations such as the Aspen Institute are supporting this move by creating case studies of social entrepreneurs that are being used in business schools across the world while also supporting the community of scholars and professors who are teaching the subject.[10] I see this firsthand when I teach the young global leaders at the World Economic Forum headquarters in Geneva. Brought from all over the world, this is a group of over 30 young people who are just beginning their journey of social good.

What is clear is that social entrepreneurs such as Blake Mycoskie and Dean Kamen bring passion, often deep understanding in a particular issue, and sometimes large sums of money to dent the problem. However, like the NGOs, they also can lack scale, and this is why so many of them partner with corporations when it comes to really making an impact.

HOW CORPORATIONS LEVERAGE ALLIANCES

All these stakeholders—governments, multilateral agencies, NGOs, swarms of citizens, and social entrepreneurs—undoubtedly try to do their best. Yet each one is limited for reasons of history, competency, scope and reach, financial constraints, and multiple political agendas. However, in combination with the assets that corporations can provide, the power of these various stakeholders can be strengthened. When corporations are able to play a significant and active role in alliance building, often they build on the following three factors:

1. Understanding contributors
2. Building verification processes
3. Creating boundary spanning across the alliance

Understanding Contributors at Partners in Food Solutions

It's hard to know how best to make a difference, and sometimes it's a moment's revelation that shows the way. Back in 2009, Peter Erickson, who headed up the research and development (R&D) department at General Mills, was working as a volunteer, packing meals for needy children in Africa. Food companies such as General Mills have long donated money and surplus food to fight hunger in Africa. Headquartered in Minneapolis, Minnesota, General Mills is one of the world's leading food companies, and food contributions are a big part of its outreach program.

What struck Erickson as he packed meals for children in Africa was that he—with a Ph.D. in nutrition and 30 years of experience—could surely better leverage and use his resources. With this thought in mind, he began to talk with the wider community of General Mills' 1,300 scientists, engineers, and nutritionists. The question he asked was this: Would they be willing to volunteer their technical and business expertise to make a more significant difference in terms of hunger in Africa? Three hundred immediately said they would, and this sense of support and excitement from these early conversations gave Erickson the momentum to move forward.

The view of the community was that the real win in addressing hunger in Africa was not to continuously ship food from the United States to Africa but rather to work on the ground enhancing the resilience of local suppliers, producers, and farmers. This can be tough; many of these farmers have little education about how to increase their yields, food processing is often archaic and wasteful, and storage standards compromise quality and safety. As a consequence, much of their food deteriorates on its long journey to market.

Take the case of the East African country of Malawi, where a corn-soy blend is an important part of the diet, particularly for the many people living in refugee camps on Malawi's borders. For years, the World Food Program had distributed this fortified corn-soy blend because it is a key source of micronutrients, protein, and digestible energy and feeds over a million children a day. As we saw in the example of DSM, the nutritional fortification of this corn-soy blend has been crucial to tackling "hidden hunger." However, this is not an ideal solution for two main reasons: first, the corn-soy blend has to be shipped from the United States, and second, it is often nutritionally compromised as a result of the way it is cooked in the refugee camps.

Erickson and the team he gathered around him asked this question: What knowledge do we have within General Mills that would enable us to extend the shelf life of the corn-soy blend to 12 months and to ensure that it is cooked properly? The most obvious solution would be to adopt the traditional model and send out skilled volunteers to work face-to-face with the farmers in Africa. The challenge was that General Mills as a corporation, unlike Danone or Standard Chartered Bank, has a very limited number of people working on the ground in sub-Saharan Africa, so scaling and mobilizing were always going to be a hurdle for them. This is in part why the team decided instead to turn to alliance building.

Establishing Virtual Knowledge Communities

One of the core capabilities of a corporation such as General Mills, DSM, and Google, is the sheer breadth of the R&D knowledge it holds across the corporation that has been codified through a knowledge-management system. The decision was taken to tap into this knowledge network and to operate remotely from the U.S. headquarters. The thinking was that this would more rapidly achieve the scale in a corporation with limited on-the-ground presence.

The initial project was to build a knowledge-rich collaborative platform that would enable the General Mills volunteers to describe the specific knowledge and experience they could bring. From this initial identification, these individual volunteers where then able to group themselves into specialist communities and to identify where synergies between the clusters could emerge. Projects from the field then could be brought to those working on the virtual platform, and once launched, General Mills' project-management system would kick in, enabling teams to monitor activities, commitments, and goals.

What this means, for example, to an NGO group working on the ground in Zambia is that it can initially scope the project and then go into the General Mills' platform to find who has the needed expertise. The group may be interested in packaging expertise, for example. The knowledge platform enables group members to find people across General Mills who have packaging knowledge, and from this they can build a virtual team. Once the team is up and running, team members can store documents and use the Facebook-quality chat and collaboration tools to work virtually together. The platform also enables team members to capture knowledge from the projects on which they are working to ensure that any future team can build and refine from their earlier insights.

Reaching Out to Alliance Partners

However, the real scaling of the initial General Mills project came when the senior team began to create alliances with peers in other companies. Called Partners in Food Solutions (PFS), the alliance was launched with the goal of improving the capacity of African food companies to produce high-quality, nutritious, and safe food at affordable prices and to increase demand for the crops of smallholder farmers who supply those businesses. The hope was to create a "virtuous circle" of food processors, who could expand, hire, and source more product from smallholder farmers; of farmers and their families, who could use this extra income to pay school fees, get medical care, and start businesses; of store owners and others in the food supply chain, who would benefit from dynamic markets and greater demand; and of consumers, who could enjoy a more stable, affordable, and varied supply of nutritious foods.

First to join the alliance with General Mills was the U.S. food company Cargill and the nutrients company DSM. Whereas General Mills had limited presence in sub-Saharan Africa, members of the teams at DSM had already begun to build on-the-ground knowledge. The alliance members gained access to the platform, and by 2012, more than 500 people from across the PFS alliance companies were actively working on a number of projects. As Jeff Dykstra, who leads PFS, remarked:

> We are not trying to push our knowledge and expertise. It's a pull mechanism. This group is working on the ground in Africa defining the need, and then we ask who is interested in working on this. They simply raise their hand when something that interests them comes in.[11]

Over time, the alliance also began to attract a wider array of international NGOs that brought their expertise to the mosaic. One early technology NGO involved with the program was TechnoServe, which brought its capacity to screen and identify processing support in rural areas.

The alliance then began to broaden beyond food companies. For example, the investment firm Root Capital brought its knowledge and networks of investment funds. Root Capital's contribution proved crucial because a key issue that small African businesses face is that they often lack business acumen and a steady cash flow. Many also find it really tough to get a loan. What Root Capital was able to do was to develop investment funds specifically to support food processors, helping farmers to initially capitalize their business and derisk their investment.

The significant scale of PFS has enabled the alliance to work with over 40 food processors in Kenya, Zambia, Tanzania, Malawi, and

Ethiopia on over 120 projects sourcing from more than 100,000 smallholder farmers who support an estimated 600,000 family members. The PFS team helps the food processors on a range of projects, including improving packaging, helping to develop formulations for products so they retain flavor and optimize nutrients, and teaching about food safety and quality control and meeting food standards. "The technical and business expertise is so much more valuable than money," says Jeff Dykstra. "To help Africans feed themselves long term, you need to help build the capacities and the capabilities of a food industry that can compete with imports."[12]

The plan going forward is to broaden the alliances within PFS to include as many as 10 corporate partners and to work with 200 Africa-based food processors who purchase from more than 500,000 smallholder farmers in as many as 12 African nations.

Building Verification Processes in The Alliance on Human Trafficking

Every day, between 50,000 and 60,000 people in the world are trafficked. They can be forced to work against their will or consent to work but then find themselves in impossible situations.[13] A classic example is the experience of young men in rural areas of Bangladesh who are approached by labor agents to work on construction sites in the Middle East. They are charged an initial bond of $6,000 and then sent to Dubai, where they receive, on average, a monthly salary of $200. They are then forced to pay the agent $100, and once accommodation and living expenses are covered, they have less than $10 to send back to Bangladesh. Their return home is impossible because the agent holds their passports, and they cannot apply to the local consulate.

The plight of trafficked people has been on the radar screen of corporations for some time—and people who work in global recruitment and placement are particularly well served to understand the intricacies of this practice. For ManpowerGroup, this has been one of the social issues where the company believes its knowledge and know-how can make a difference. Headquartered in Milwaukee, the company is one of the biggest employers in the world, with more than 4.5 million people in work across many regions of the globe. With 4,000 offices in 82 countries, the company has extraordinary on-the-ground experience of what is happening in global labor markets. As David Arkless, a member of the executive board of the company and part of the team responsible for putting together the strategy and operational structure of the business, reflects:

> We operate ethically but are always coming up against illegal labor. I became more and more concerned about this—I cannot bear for these children to be forced into labor.[14]

This issue of labor conditions in supply chains can be complex. Take, for example, ManpowerGroup's own supply chain, which touches more than 15 million third-tier suppliers in vast webs of labor. It is clear that these massive supply chains are challenged by labor conditions around the world. They are also challenged by the uncoordinated nature of many of the players in a field, which includes NGOs and multilateral agencies such as the United Nations Development Program (UNDP).

Because of their global reach, what the team at ManpowerGroup was able to bring to the challenges of human trafficking was their coordinating and convening skills and on-the-ground knowledge. To do this, they began to convene an alliance of NGOs that work on human trafficking and corporations with vast supply chains. The first phase was creation of the Global Business Coalition against Trafficking (GBAT), in which CEOs from a large number of Fortune 500 companies including Ford, Coca-Cola, LexisNexis, Carlton Group, American Airlines, and ExxonMobil signed an agreement to end human trafficking. A group of NGOs endorsed by the United Nations also signed the agreement—including Verité and Polaris. The mission was to raise the game of U.S. corporations against human trafficking through ethical recruitment processes driven via their supply chain, as far back as their eighth-level suppliers, with a particular focus on bonded labor, abused migrants, and human-trafficked people.

As David Arkless says, "We need a serious bunch of organizations. The basic theory is this—unless you can mobilize a huge community of organizations, nothing is going to change."[15] The alliance then created a platform for communicating issues of trafficking, a process of verification and certification, and founded a lobby for public and private opinion to be placed in Washington.

The Power of Verification

Verification is crucial. When a CEO signs up to GBAT, he or she has to publicly state that his or her company is abiding by the mission and values of the alliance. The challenge then becomes one of checking. Arkless's view is this:

> The secret is to put in a verification process that does not cost hundreds of millions to run. Big companies hate to be audited and hate to be told they are doing a bad job.[16]

So the alliance developed a process of self-verification based on a set of principles and criteria drawn up by a number of NGOs, including Verité. Once the executives within a member corporation have performed the self-verification, they go back to the alliance and say that they are following the standards. The alliance then works with member NGOs to carry out random audits to verify self-certification, and if a corporation fails to meet the standards, it is asked to leave the alliance and is in danger of prosecution.

Creating Boundary Spanning at the Resilience Action Initiative

Every year, millions of rural dwellers are moving into the cities that are growing across the developing world and increasingly becoming the epicenters of resource stress in energy, water, and food. The extent of the crisis of cities is very clear to the community of scenario planners at Royal Dutch Shell, who since the 1970s have been monitoring the availability of natural resources such as oil and gas and water across the world. As a consequence of this, they became aware, perhaps before others, of the impact that the burning of fossil fuels would have on the climate and the environment.

The challenge is that building and operating resilient cities require an enormous amount of interconnected thinking and action taking. Often each part of the solution rests with a separate stakeholder, and "silo" thinking within these stakeholders can create different tribes, each with its unique mission and power relations. To solve these challenges, what is needed is what former Shell CEO Peter Voser has called "unusual partnerships." When these alliances begin to be formed and work, they have the potential to create innovation and to become a proof of concept.

Complementary Assets

An early example of this experimental approach to focusing on one location is the Resilience Action Initiative (RAI), an alliance launched at the World Economic Forum in February 2012. The focus of the alliance is to create and support resilient cities by bringing together corporations from sectors that play a role in the design and running of cities. Thus the alliance corporations include engineering companies (Siemens and Rio Tinto), chemical companies (Dow and DuPont), a strategic consultancy practice (McKinsey), a technology company (IBM), a consumer goods company (Unilever), an energy company (Shell), and a finance and insurance company (Swiss Re).

Early conversations suggested that a relatively unexplored area of opportunity in a city is to improve energy efficiency. Very often the challenge on the ground is not lack of technology solutions but rather one of integration among the different players and data sharing of proven business and financing models. To work on these opportunities, the corporations within the RAI alliance, like the Partners in Food Solutions Alliance, are using rapidly developing collaborative business models and open platforms that have the potential to create networks of knowledge flow among alliance partners.

The initial plan was to conduct a series of pilot studies designed to understand more clearly how a city can remain resilient in the face of acute threats such as floods and earthquakes, chronic threats such as constrained energy supplies, and unanticipated threats such as political transitions and economic transformations. The initial pilot study involves the city of Da Nang in Vietnam, where the alliance is working from the initial report of IBM's Executive Service Corps study of the city's transportation and water-supply systems that produced recommendations on integrated water management and food safety.

By June 2012, global and local energy-efficiency experts from seven RAI members (Shell, McKinsey, DuPont, IBM, Siemens,

Swiss Re, and Unilever) had met to share best practices and start the pilot. The teams from Shell and DuPont brought expertise from energy projects in large integrated sites; the McKinsey and IBM teams had experience in bringing new data, processes, and systems together; the Siemens team had experience in delivering technical expertise; the Swiss Re team understood risk assessment; and the Unilever team had experience in economics and implementation. By late 2012, a local technical and commercial team was being recruited, with a full-time project manager on board by early 2013. As Jeremy Bentham who heads up the scenario planning group at Shell explains:

> What is crucial is resilience both in institutions and in the resource systems. For this, collaboration will be crucial. We have to ask what business can do. They can take leadership and bring ideas and templates. Collaboration is crucial because these stresses go across the boundaries of private and public, of industry sectors, and of functional groups. This is difficult to do. For example, one challenge is the time frames for different institutions. So we need experimental activity, a bottom-up evolution. It's clear that the status quo is not an option. We need innovation and creativity.[17]

CONCLUSION

Most of the challenges the world faces come as issues that are complex, ambiguous, and involve many different stakeholders in their solution. Their solution requires people from across many organizations being both prepared and able to work together in a highly collaborative way.

These multistakeholder alliances can be tougher than paired NGO-corporation partnerships because they require many different corporations to work together. Thus, whereas traditionally corporations are seen as competing with each other, increasingly they are called on to collaborate if they are to build resilience in a fragile world. Often it is a senior executive or the CEO who takes the lead and begins to convene a group around a challenge the group is passionate about.

There is much to celebrate in corporations—some have honed world-class skills in innovation, scaling, and alliance building, and some are led by people who are passionate about leveraging these capabilities into the wider community. These are leaders who have created a compelling narrative, built a vision for the future, and honed clear measurement. It is to these leaders that we now turn.

PART V

REIMAGINING LEADERSHIP

Those who lead corporations have already experienced a decade of transitions and profound volatility, and as they look forward, there will be no obvious return to the status quo. These transitions, in energy, economics, and geopolitics, are already creating instability across the globe. As we shall see in Chapter 11, leaders are increasingly called on to overcome significant hurdles if they are to build resilient corporations for the long term. Some are faced with colossal performance pressure from their shareholders and the broader financial markets to think and operate in the short term, others are caught in a vortex where maximizing shareholder value has become the preeminent focus of the company, and most are faced with rising citizen activism and declining corporate trust.

It is not just across the wider world that these profound transitions are taking place. Within corporations, the dearly held hierarchical and traditional relationships between leaders and followers are under attack. As peer-to-peer communication strengthens and hierarchical decision making crumbles, followers are looking to their leaders to narrate a sense of purpose that is compelling and to model a way of being that is meaningful and authentic.

How will these changes affect what leaders do and how they are supported in their development? This question has been very much on my mind, and in answering it, I have been profoundly influenced by my own experience as a member of a number of communities where the future of leadership has been debated.

In 2011, I chaired the newly created Global Advisory Council on New Models of Leadership of the World Economic Forum (WEF). The council was created as the result of a growing belief within the WEF community that perhaps more than any other time in the history of the modern corporation, this is a crucial time for leaders to come forward and create a narrative of the future that is compelling and engaging. With membership from academics, corporate executives, and the heads of NGOs, what was clear was that our expectations of leaders are changing at a rapid pace.[1]

From 2008 onward, in my own research endeavor, the Future of Work (FoW) Consortium, my colleagues and I have debated the future of leadership with the many thousands of people who engaged with the research. We first debated the future of leadership in workshops in London, Mumbai, and New York and then opened up our online community platform FoWLab to hear what the wider community had to say. Many thousands of people from across the world engaged in a 48-hour online debate. What was overwhelming was the deep belief across the executives from more than 40 companies that joined us of the profound transitions that are happening right now in what we imagine leadership to be. There was broad agreement that the hierarchical command-and-control leadership style of the past could not hold up for the future. In its place would come a more transparent, authentic, and peer-based way of leading. What was less clear was how this could be developed.

The question of what this meant for leadership development was at the center of the debate I had at a leadership-development program led at London Business School by Doug Ready.[2] As leadership-development specialists, the participants debated the challenges that the old-style "tournament" career system was creating and the imperatives to building a way of supporting leaders' journeys through self-reflection and dialogue.

What about members of the young generation who will become the leaders in the coming decades—how do they see this transformation of leadership occurring? I was able to debate this question with members of an elective class I designed for London Business School MBA students that ran from 2011 onward. I came away from this experience with a visceral understanding of how these young people are facing up to the realities of a fragile world. I also came away with a perspective on how this generation could assume the mantle of leadership. I heard how many people in the class believe that corporations can and must play a more central role in the affairs of the world, I heard their disquiet with what they see corporate leadership becoming and their hopes for the emergence of a more authentic and purposeful leadership, and I could feel their concern about the pressures of being a leader and the hurdles they would have to overcome. Perhaps I should not have been surprised that when, at the end of the program, I asked how many wanted to become the leader of a large corporation, only a few put up their hands.

What I took away from these various debates was that we are truly in the midst of a transition from the old order to a new, emerging order. The old order was signaled by powerful leadership, supported by legions of PR-speak, and followed by employees prepared to engage in a "parent-child" relationship. What is coming is a new order where the hierarchies are becoming dismantled and followers are becoming more demanding. Yet this transition is by no means complete, and right now I sense that we are in a period of debate and exploration of where we will see new leadership role models emerging. In parallel with the transition of what a leader can be, the capital markets are putting leaders under extreme pressure for short-term performance, and ever more vocal citizens are forming themselves into worldwide communities of interest that are using the power of the crowd to influence corporate policy. Perhaps it is no surprise that so few of my MBA students want to become corporate leaders. I think this is a lost opportunity; if corporations are able to assume their full potential, then their leaders will play roles of great global significance. As we shall see in Chapter 12, this puts renewed focus on leadership authenticity and, in Chapter 13, on the extent to which leaders are able to create a worldview.

CHAPTER 11

TRANSFORMATION OF LEADERSHIP

The world in which corporations are taking action is subject to profound transformational forces. Leaders and the practice of developing leaders are not immune to these extraordinary transformational forces. Indeed, some of the leadership capabilities we hold dear are beginning to be swept away and in their place are emerging new ideas about what leadership can and should be.

These new ideas about leadership are transforming our understanding of the roles that leaders play, the tasks they will have to undertake to be adept, and the skills and competencies they need to develop. They are also transforming the daily behaviors of leaders as they interact with an ever widening array of people, from their external investors to their internal followers. It seems to me that of the many transformational forces that have the potential to reshape leadership, there are five that are particularly powerful:

1. The short-termism of the financial markets
2. Growing citizen activism
3. Declining corporate trust
4. The emboldened follower
5. Permeability and transparency

CHALLENGED BY THE SHORT-TERMISM OF THE FINANCIAL MARKETS

Corporations operate in the markets of the world—markets for finance, trade, and human capital. There is no doubt that markets can produce beneficial outcomes. As economists from Adam Smith to the present have noted, market systems create value for society in many ways—through more efficient use of resources, increased national prosperity, improved standards of living for citizens, and the propensity to encourage innovation, promote self-reliance, and give people an opportunity to find meaningful work. However, as we have seen, the consequences are not all beneficial—inequality and exploitation, environment damage, and financial instability.

There is a growing consensus that the market system in which corporations operate is in trouble. Some of those commentating on this failure are academics. Take, for example, Harvard Professors Joseph Bower, Herman Leonard, and Lynn Paine, who argue that the global market system is under threat from a variety of sources, including the velocity and opaque nature of capital flows, growing protectionism with regard to trade, inequality and extreme disparities of income caused in part by excessive executive compensation and weak or corrupt governments, and the inadequacy of existing institutions, including business governance and national institutions.[1] Others, such as Dominic Barton, global managing director of the consulting practice McKinsey & Co., see this from the perspective of the executive.[2] His views come from meetings with more than 400 business and government leaders across the globe. This is what he has to say:

> Those conversations have reinforced my strong sense that despite a certain amount of frustration on each side, the two groups share the belief that capitalism has been and can continue to be the greatest engine of prosperity ever devised—and that we will need it to be at the top of its job-creating, wealth-generating game in the years to come. At the same time, there is growing concern that if the fundamental issues revealed in the crisis remain unaddressed and the system fails again, the social contract between the capitalist system and the citizenry may truly rupture, with unpredictable but severely damaging results.

These concerns focus on the observations that corporations and the markets they operate are focused too much on the short term and can be overly zealous about maximizing shareholder value.

The Ticking Clock

This vision of the corporation with a single focus on quarterly earnings is not a pretty sight. A world where executives, in their constant search for efficiency, speed, and profit, demand that workers become hooked into an infernal cycle. A world that, though immensely materially rewarding for some, can be a crippling and inhuman experience for others. A world where ruthless, inhuman bosses can exploit and behave in an unprincipled way. A world of "Chainsaw" Al Dunlop, Tyco's Dennis Kozlowski, and Lehman Brother's Richard Fuld.

For sure, the dehumanizing of work through short-term market pressures is not a new complaint. What is more apparent, however, is the enormous pressures that can be created within corporations, propelled by an ever more powerful dynamic of global competition and indeed by the way investing institutions and corporate executives are rewarded. This pressure can erode the core of inner resilience and negate the issues of the external context. The argument is that this short-term pressure can place an unprecedented premium on leaders who are "unreasonable"—men and women who are ambitious and determined enough to go to extraordinary lengths to fulfill their mission to short-term investors and capital markets. They put it above all else. This is what some boards seek in their CEOs and, in turn, what CEOs seek in their subordinates. It often seems that for a time at least, such people are celebrated in the press. Collectively, their traits are bundled into the composite of the ideal leader: hard driving, ambitious, heroic, volitional, and male.[3]

The development of leaders in some corporations reflects this focus. The "tournament" leadership practices can create a context where ambitious fast-trackers collude with this process of dehumanization in return for the promise that they will get a turn at the helm and the possibility of extraordinary remuneration packages. Executives justify their actions by pleading powerlessness in the face of external forces. Some argue that the capital markets are relentless in their demands, they have no scope for choice, and the constraints of a market system leave no space for autonomous behavior.

It is not just leaders who suffer when the screws of short-term profits are tightened. Often the stress created by this constant focus on the short term puts enormous pressure on people across the corporation and leaves them with little of the emotional vitality that is so crucial to building a resilient inner core. A short-term focus places little emphasis on the growth potential of employees, focusing instead on simply exploiting their current capabilities.

Yet there is a growing debate that despite these short-term pressures, leaders are not as powerless as they might imagine. Indeed, some executives are taking action to overcome this short-termism. In doing so, they are facing up to significant hurdles. As Judith Samuelson, executive director of the Aspen Institute's Business and Society Program, remarked to me, "Short-termism is the 'engine of the beast.'" She sees it as a ticking clock that can define the purpose of a corporation, and the short-term time frame it creates becomes the time frame for the measurement of success. Short-term time frames—such as quarterly earnings guidance—set the clock ticking faster. This then has an impact on the incentivization of employees, the stock packages of CEOs, and the ways decisions between short-term gains and long-term legacy and resilience are made. It also creates frenzy on the part of investors.

As those in the Aspen Institute have argued, as long as most public companies provide quarterly earnings guidance, there is a "collective action" problem for the CEOs and boards that want to stop the practice. In a conversation I had with Judith Samuelson, she put it this way:

> I see confronting corporations on quarterly earnings guidance as a way to "open up the seam" of the short-termism problem that plagues most publicly traded companies. Providing earnings guidance (or forecasts) is not required, and ample evidence exists that managers who spend more time focused on meeting or exceeding the quarterly earnings estimates they have provided as part of their guidance are spending less time and money on research and development and hiring critical employees. In other words, they are abandoning their responsibility to ensure a publicly traded company's long-term survival or at least giving it short shrift. Coming up with that quarterly prediction siphons resources and energy away from building the capacity for the long haul. It is time

we stopped this practice of predicting the future and instead focus on communicating about and building value for the long haul.

Indeed, there are ways that executives and the corporations they lead are trying to overcome this short-termism. For some, particularly those in family ownership, such as U.S. commodities company Cargill and garment manufacturer Levi-Strauss, there has never been a requirement to post quarterly earnings forecasts. Yet even some of those corporations in public ownership have been able to step outside of the "ticking clock" by making the move to a longer-term view of their performance. At Unilever, Paul Polman made it clear from his first days on the job as CEO that he would not be predicting quarterly earnings. As he said at the Peter Drucker Conference in Vienna in October 2012:

> Our decisions are not made in 90 days. We have more important things to do; predicting quarterly earnings is a useless conversation. Fortunately, when I came into Unilever, I decided on the first day to abolish quarterly guidance—the only reason was I could not be fired on my first day. The share price went down 8 percent because the analysts thought this was a trick and mistrusted my motives. Short-termism is a drug, so we try to attract shareholders who want to join us in our endeavor. As a consequence of our action, our share price is less volatile, and our cost of capital has gone down. It's been important to work with the European government on this to create confidence for others and to ensure that the banking and financial industry is able to create a banking environment initiative that does not make short-term demands.

Polman certainly raised some eyebrows in the investment community by refusing to provide profit guidance for 2009 and 2010, pointing to the uncertainty created by the global economic downturn. However, Unilever still does not provide specific financial targets but rather publishes a short update on its sales performance without any specific guidance.

Polman is not alone, the CEOs at Coca-Cola and Ford have stopped issuing earnings guidance altogether, and Warren Buffett has had the practice stopped on all the boards of which he is a member. IBM's former CEO Sam Palmisano created a series of five-year road maps to encourage investors to focus more on whether IBM will reach its long-term earnings targets than on whether it exceeds or misses this quarter's target by a few pennies.[4]

What seems clear is that these hurdles of short-termism can be overcome, but to do so requires leaders to have a strong sense of themselves and their own values and the courage and determination to place the emphasis not simply on delivering short-term performance but also on building longer-term resilience. As we shall see, much of this is about the inner development of the leader and his or her capacity to think in a more longer-term and systemic way and his or her propensity to develop ha sense of authenticity and show courage when making tough judgment calls.

An Overzealous Focus on Shareholder Value

The pressures that markets put on leaders certainly can tip them to favor short-term performance over long-term resilience. These market pressures also can push them to maximize shareholder value beyond the needs of any other stakeholder, including employees and those working in the supply chain.

There is an argument that the only obligation of a corporation is to serve as the agents of the financial shareholders by maximizing the returns brought by the business. As economist Milton Friedman famously remarked, "The only business of business is business, and the only social responsibility of management is profit."[5] Thus, for example, the argument is that the decision to adopt environmental and social policies could destroy shareholder wealth because management might lose focus by diverting attention to issues that are not core to the company's strategy or revenue streams. Or taking a broader base of constituents into consideration may create a higher cost structure through, for example, paying employees a living wage rather than a market wage or not sacking people fast enough in an economic downturn. Or an executive team could bow to the pressure of NGOs and change the company's sourcing habits and by doing so increase the cost of the product and so lose customers to lower-cost competitors who have made no such decision.

This places leaders as bystanders; their role is to maximize share-holder value while some higher authority—preferably governments or NGOs—build resilience in a fragile world. In this argument, executives view themselves as fiduciaries for their shareholders and believe that spending money to benefit the public good is beyond what the law requires and would violate these duties.

How accurate is this argument? For Cornell Law Professor Lynn Stout, "Shareholder value ideology is just that—an ideology, not a legal requirement or a practical necessity of modern business."[6] Her view is backed by a growing body of research that disputes the wis-dom of simply maximizing shareholder value. Indeed, this research and commentary show how an overzealous focus on shareholders can have a negative impact on financial performance and can alien-ate potential investors, consumers, and employees.[7]

The fundamental question then becomes this: What is it that a corporation is there to achieve, and what role does the leader play in delivering this agenda? Is it indeed to maximize the return to shareholders at the cost of any other constituents? Here management philosopher Charles Handy has a rather interesting observation to make[8]:

> Two good ideas of the nineteenth century have unintended consequences. One is the joint stock company, and the other is limited liability. These two social inventions spurred unprec-edented economic innovation and growth, but they also put us on a dangerous course. By effectively separating the theo-retical ownership of a company from its management, the first turned shareholders into something more like punters at a racecourse. Using shares as betting slips on the nags of their choice, they behaved like neither trainers nor owners. As a result of the second, limited liability, managers gained their own license to gamble at no personal cost.

In reality, it is beginning to look like good companies can do both—they can both create an adequate return for their shareholders and also have a wider social agenda. This has become apparent in a series of recent research studies that examined firm performance and strategy. These studies have shown that over a period of time, the stock prices of corporations with sustainable and resilient agendas does not deteriorate. Instead, those with a sustainability agenda have been shown to conclusively outperform those without an agenda on sustainability. One study found that a U.S. dollar invested in a value-weighted portfolio of sustainable firms at the beginning of 1993 would have grown to US$22.6 by the end of 2010. In contrast, a U.S dollar invested in a value-weighted portfolio of unsustainable firms at the beginning of 1993 would have grown to US$15.4 over the same period.[9]

There is one more issue to be raised about the maximization of shareholder value, and that's the thorny question of who exactly financial shareholders are. What the careful analysis of shareholder groups has shown is that they are rarely a unitary, homogeneous group. Indeed, most economic interest in stocks is held by people, either directly or indirectly through pension funds and mutual funds. People are diverse in their needs, aspirations, and wishes. Whereas some will indeed want, as Handy says, to be "simply punters at a race course" with a quick turnaround, others will want the company they invest in to act in an ethical and socially responsible fashion. As Stout notes, the idea of profit maximization "reduces investors to their lowest possible common human (or perhaps subhuman) denominator: impatient, opportunistic, self-destructive, and psychopathically indifferent to the welfare of others."

The good news for those of us who would like to consider ourselves above subhuman is that there is a strong and important debate that reexamines shareholder value. There are a number of ways in which corporations' leaders are rebalancing shareholder values. Some, such as Unilever's Paul Polman, have actively sought to manage these investor groups. As Polman remarked at the presentation of the company sustainability results in London in 2012:

> It is hard to define a typical Unilever shareholder—some invest for long-term growth; others speculate—and it is my job to stick to a strategy rather than placate all investors. How could you run a company properly if you react to all these signals and try to please everybody? You try to have a strategy out there, and you try to attract shareholders who can relate to your strategy. CEOs need to do a better job attracting a shareholder base that fits their strategy. We have disinvited

some shareholders and invited some shareholders in. We have changed our shareholder base bit by bit. People who hold that share and see that model are very happy with that.

Others have addressed this issue through integrated reporting, where the company reports on the wider context of its operations.[10] In 2007, for example, Nestle CEO Paul Bulcke began issuing a global "Creating Shared Value" report every two years and, in 2012, migrated it to full reporting on an annual basis. This shows the progress of corporations on key resilience performance and indicators that include the impact on the environment (e.g., water usage), the impact on rural development (e.g., agriculture and commodities trading), the impact on customers (e.g., nutrition and health), and the impact on employees (e.g., well-being, engagement, training, and safety). Other corporations, such as Johnson & Johnson and IBM, are doing the same.

What does this debate mean for the development and practice of leadership? It seems to me that it both points to the need for courage and authenticity on the part of the leader and also refers to their capacity to understand the world in which they are operating and building alliances with the many stakeholders in their world.

FACED WITH GROWING CITIZEN ACTIVISM

It is not just shareholders who have a view of what a leader may or may not do. There are also increasingly connected and vocal communities of people who look closely at the rhetoric and actions of corporate leaders and don't always like what they see. Often these communities are addressing issues that corporations face that go more deeply into the psyche of how people across the world view the role and their expectations of corporations.

There have always been people and groups who have been interested in the actions of corporations. Yet, by the 1990s, and as some of the downsides of a head-long push for corporate growth became clearer, attitudes toward corporations and expectations of their actions began to be debated more widely. As a result, communities of people began to look to corporations to act in a way that builds resilience in their communities and addresses the challenges of an increasingly fragile world. Take, for example, environmental concerns. In 1971, the membership of the environmental campaign organization Greenpeace was 250 people; by 2000, it was over 1.7 million people, and the group was prepared to support causes and take radical action.

The group's target was the corporation. Those who led Greenpeace had become increasingly concerned about climate change in a fragile world and the oil companies, which they viewed as perpetrators of "oil addiction." They had U.S. giant ExxonMobil firmly in their sight. That year, members of Greenpeace released a pamphlet entitled, "A Decade of Dirty Tricks: ExxonMobil's Attempt to Stop the World Tackling Climate Change," in which they documented the corporation's funding for proxy groups that raised doubts about climate change. By 2003, they had sprung into action, raiding ExxonMobil headquarters in Irving, Texas, and unfolded a banner declaring the headquarters to be a global-warming crime scene.[11]

When it comes to how people feel about the actions of corporations and their leaders, Greenpeace supporters are not alone. Indeed, by 2004, more than 40,000 NGOs operated around the world, of which more than 90 percent had been formed since 1970.[12] Of these, around 6,000 were of the "attacking variety,"[13] prepared to take action against governments and corporations.

In part, these awakening citizen and consumer expectations are a consequence of the very same forces that have transformed corporations. Expectations have changed because people can communicate across communities of interest using newly developed global communications and monitoring and reporting technologies.

As a consequence, observations of corporate activities became more astute and, in many cases, more negative about corporate actions. Take, for example, corporate activities around climate change. Cynical observers argue that when executives talk about reducing their energy use, working positively with their supply chain, or solving global problems, they are simply going through a series of public relations stunts designed to allay legitimate fears on the part of employees or consumers about their business practices. In fact, the argument goes, corporations see as their only true role to increase shareholder value, and this "green washing" is simply there to cover up more seedy business practices. Or observers point to checkbook philanthropy as a means of simply trying to solve the very problems that businesses have created. Cynics see these initiatives as simply "bolted on." They are brought in superficially and, as a consequence, tend to be rather random in their focus and easily discarded when the going gets tough.[14]

With this cynicism comes a weakening of corporate legitimacy. The impact of this can be stark. If enough people disapprove of a company's actions, they can boycott the company's products, reduce the company's sales, and degrade the company's brand, as both Nike and IKEA discovered. It's not just customers who can act, governments and regulatory bodies can put pressure on corporations by restricting their freedom to operate. As personal investors or indeed through their savings and pensions, people can choose not to invest in the corporations they disapprove of, and this investor flight will serve to increase the corporation's cost of capital. Workers can show their disapproval by leaving the company or deciding not to join it. The potential business partners and suppliers of such corporations can show their disapproval through their unwillingness to trade with the company. Ultimately, a lack of confidence in leadership could lead to a decline in the valuation of a company and increase the risk of a hostile takeover.

DECLINING CORPORATE TRUST

Perhaps it is no surprise that in some countries citizens simply don't trust business. Studies of corporate trust in 2011 showed that in the United States, for example, trust in businesses was at an all-time low, with fewer than 50 percent of people saying that they trust corporations or CEOs.[15]

There are several explanations for this low corporate trust in the United States: the prolonged fighting between business and government, unemployment rates and a slower recovery than the country expected, and the nation's spot as the epicenter of many of the head-line crises of 2010, including the Gulf oil spill, product recalls, and the Security and Exchange Commission (SEC) investigation of Goldman Sachs. This reputational damage serves to weaken the legitimacy of corporations to operate in a wider sphere. The picture across industrial sectors is more complex. In general, people are more trusting of certain industrial sectors—notably technology, automobiles, and telecommunications—and have little trust in banks. There are also similar patterns across the world, for example, in China, where banks are credited with financing increased prosperity, 90 percent of people trust the banking system.

However, it is worth reminding ourselves that the understanding of attitudes toward corporations is rather intricate. At the very time people may say that they don't trust corporations, the paradox for most is that they willingly buy the goods they sell and often with great pleasure consume the services they offer. And this is not the only paradox. Although people outside corporations may not like and trust "big business," the vast majority of those working inside corporations feel proud to be members of them. We know this because every year in most corporations there are surveys of how employees feel about working with them. Typically, these surveys ask a whole raft of questions about how engaged employees feel about their work, what they think about their leaders and colleagues, and whether they would be proud to tell others that they work for that corporation. What's fascinating is that these surveys show that in many large corporations, a large proportion of people like to work there, they value their colleagues, and they are proud to tell others about the corporation.

These surveys also show the path to trust. By 2011, search engines ranked first as the place people go to for information about a company, followed by online news sources, and print and broadcast media. The data portray a savvy consumer who turns first to search engines to see what is available on the topic of interest and then seeks out traditional media to confirm or expand on what he or she has learned.

Reflecting on this, Richard Edelman, who leads one of the trust survey companies, believes that there are new expectations for governments, corporations, and leaders. The old expectations may have been of a "fortress framework" in which corporations protect their brands, control information, and give short shrift to partners, aiming simply to maximize returns solely for shareholders. In its place he sees new expectations emerging for companies to act collaboratively to benefit society, not just for their shareholders and to be transparent about their operations and profit engines.

The implication for leaders is clear. They have to work to ensure that they are empathic with the aspirations of communities of interest, even when those interests may not be the same as theirs. They also have to think about how best to engage and work with stakeholders. Both inevitably come back to the values and aspirations of the leader and to how the leader is able to show those values and aspirations in an authentic and trustworthy manner.

CONFRONTED BY EMBOLDENED FOLLOWERS

Leaders cannot lead without followers—and without followers, there can be no leader. This state of affairs has provoked my colleague at London Business School, Rob Goffee, to ask, "Why would anyone be led by you?"[16] If leadership is indeed about followers, what, then, do we know about the aspirations of followers over the coming decades? Those leading in the next decade will be leading Gen Yers; members of this generation are currently in their early adulthood and have emerging global traits that will shape them as followers, as indeed will they shape their expectations of leaders.

It seems that many of this Gen Y generation will want to take more control of their working lives than previous generations. In short, they want a different way of being and working, and many value a balance between their work and their life that will enable them to be personally resilient.[17] Increasingly, they look to their leaders to be role models living healthy, balanced lives. This generation values creativity and seems to naturally move toward meaningful work and a sense of purpose. Thus they will be excited and intrigued by leaders who have a personal narrative and strong values and purpose. Of course, this is also a generation that is deeply aware, perhaps more than any other generation before them, of the societal and resource challenges that will fall to them to confront.[18]

The daily context of Gen Y is increasingly influenced by the social media that envelops them. This has created a transparency of action that is fundamentally unlike the opaque hierarchies of the past. Thus, for Gen Yers, leadership is less about power and authority and more about following those whom they admire and from whom they feel they can actively learn. This became very clear during a worldwide conversation at the Future of Work Consortium about the future of leadership. This is what Tammy Johns, at that time senior vice president of innovation for global recruiter ManpowerGroup, had this to say about the sheer complexity of the leader's emerging role with Gen Y:

> The world is more transparent, so not surprisingly, young people are mobilizing (using technology and collaboration) to change the world. They care less about financial reward (though, contrary to popular belief, it is still important) and more about how things get done. They do not want a trophy for their work (boomers wanted them to be singled out to reward ourselves) but instead want to be able to make a difference, which is a much higher bar and a tougher leadership assignment.

This emboldened follower is not simply a Western phenomenon. In China, for example, there are rapidly rising expectations among Gen Yers, who are often more educated and ambitious than the generations that preceded them—and, as a consequence, more demanding. They are also fluent in the technologies that connect them to like-minded people around the world, so they have Western youth with whom to compare themselves.[19] In India, a recent corporate survey of Gen Yers placed work/life balance and meaningful work as the highest-ranking corporate benefits.

One of the consequences of this connectivity and transparency is that followers are demanding to be led in more equitable and democratic ways. They want their voices to be heard, and they want to be involved in making decisions. For them, the emphasis for leaders is less on command and control and more on cooperating and collaborating.

It seems that leaders increasingly will be operating in a world that is networked, interdependent, and transnational—a world where they as leaders are potentially weaker and their followers stronger. To succeed, the leaders of the future will need to find new ways of engaging with global problems and different models for collaboration and alliances.

SHAPED BY PERMEABILITY AND TRANSPARENCY

Glance at the daily papers in almost any country of the world, and it seems that progressively corporate leaders are resembling political leaders. Their names and faces are familiar, if not famous, and it's no longer possible for them to hide behind a gray corporate curtain and remain anonymous in their suits.

This "nakedness" is a consequence (perhaps unintended) of the extraordinary scientific and intellectual resources that are being developed. Ubiquitous connectivity is connecting billions of people across the world, the tools of conviviality are creating opportunities for swarms of citizens to share ideas and information, and the tools of monitoring are enabling data to be collected and analyzed. Together these resources are bringing to the surface a degree of sensitivity and transparency unheard of years ago. These scientific and intellectual resources are transforming workers and corporations. They are also profoundly transforming leadership and creating challenges and opportunities along the way.

First, the challenges. Even now, a corporate leader can be known more for the Twitter storm he or she creates than for the work of his or her highly professional public relations agencies. In the past, expert advertising and a great public relations team would have created an aura that could serve to envelope a leader in a cloak of purposeful respectability. The public relations team could write the leadership scripts, and the advertising agency controlled the media persona. This is no longer the case. Social technology such as Twitter is creating total transparency that is able to show to anyone who wants to look the extent of alignment between a leader's rhetoric and his or her everyday actions.[20]

At the same time that corporate leaders are becoming transparent to the point of being naked, the voices from within and outside the corporation are becoming harsher and louder and are carrying further.[21] The disrobing of leadership has happened at an extraordinary pace. As Harvard's Kennedy School of Government Professor Barbara Kellerman[22] reminds us,

> When John Kennedy was in the White House, the American people had no idea that he was a reckless and tireless bounder. When Franklin Roosevelt was in the White House, the American people had no idea that he was essentially paralyzed and confined to a wheelchair. And when Woodrow Wilson was in the White House, the American people had no idea

that he was so severely disabled by a stroke that during the last 18 months of his presidency, his wife, Edith Bolling Galt Wilson, in effect governed the country.

It seems that followers' familiarity with and disrespect for their leaders, coupled with their own feeling of entitlement, are sapping the authority of leadership and draining leaders of much of their historical power and influence.

Yet with this transparency and connectivity come opportunities for leaders, and in order to seize these opportunities, leaders will need to be both authentic and able to craft a purposeful narrative. For those able to do this, transparency creates extraordinary occasions for their real selves to be demonstrated and revealed and for the narrative of their passion, goals, and values to be heard across a vast arena. This social media transformation is shifting the focus from old-style leadership as commander and controller toward the leader as influencer, shaper of virtual communities, boundary spanner, and builder of alliances.

In debating the future role of leaders at the WEF, the Council on New Models of Leadership was much influenced in our thinking about social media and leadership by Max Levchin, one of the council members. Levchin was the cofounder of PayPal and erstwhile vice president of engineering at Google. As might be expected, he has a clear view of how the transparency of social media will transform leadership—and for the better. In the initial council report we wrote, this is how Max Levchin describes that transformation[23]:

> Social media offers leaders the chance to communicate from a platform where their constituents are effectively their peers. It is an opportunity to pull back the curtain, to connect with their audiences directly, to be human, emotional, and vulnerable. It is a chance for leaders to earn the trust of their charges by being and communicating among them.
>
> Feedback loops are being shortened from days to minutes. The conversation is changing from a one-way, one-shot interpretation by a professional, but ultimately disenfranchised news reporter, to a dialog with deeply motivated, passionate participants. Social media offers a chance to create and curate the image of a leader in a deeply authentic way. It creates an

opportunity for a leader to speak with a single, honest voice, connecting with their critics, debating with their doubters, and personalizing their message in a meaningful way.

Indeed, there is growing evidence that leaders who are connected have an advantage.[24] Yet, as late as 2010, 64 percent of American CEOs were not using social media of any kind for the purpose of connecting with their boards, employees, and customers.[25]

As Levchin describes, there are real opportunities for leaders to have their voices heard and to demonstrate to the world what they believe to be purposeful and important. In doing so, the notion of the "naked leader" brings to the fore the centrality of authenticity. With no place to hide, leaders are increasingly judged by their every-day actions, by the judgement calls they make under pressure, and by the alignment between what they say and what they do. This is why, as we shall see in Chapter 12, a leader's authenticity and capac-ity to create a narrative that describes himself or herself to others become so central.

CONCLUSION

Leading a resilient corporation is fundamentally about courage—the courage to overcome the hurdles of short-termism and an overzeal-ous focus on shareholder values, the courage to address ever more active citizens, and the courage to create a narrative that connects the present with the future in a compelling way. Those who follow leaders know it when they see it—it is evident in the way that leaders describe themselves, in the judgment calls they make under pressure, and in the stories they weave about the future. It is this authentic leader who will become so crucial for the future.

CHAPTER 12

THE LEADER'S JOURNEY TO AUTHENTICITY

Followers want to hear about and understand their leader's personal journey and the values he or she espouses, they want to hear the leader's story and passion, and they want to understand the story that connects the leader's own life and history with the actions and choices he or she makes. This authenticity is not easy. Often, particularly in the "tournament" process of selecting leaders, it is advantageous for leaders to construct a near-perfect description of themselves and their lives, leaving aside the failures and moments of self-doubt. Moreover, leaders who have introvert personalities are more likely to prefer to keep their own stories and personal lives out of the public domain, and there is evidence that more introverts are moving into the leadership roles that historically had been the domain of extroverts.[1]

Yet, despite this, there are leaders who have been able to narrate their own lives and values in a way that others find authentic and believable. We heard this earlier in Paul Polman's explanation of his own motivation[2]:

> We have become a "we generation"; we wanted it all, and in doing this, we have stolen resources and taken away job opportunities from the next generation. We now have to fix it. We can make a difference. We can try to correct and put the world on a better path. We have to try this.

What is interesting here is what Polman has to say and what he has chosen not to say. When asked what motivates him, Polman did not frame the answer in economic or strategic terms—although he has set clear goals for both. Instead, he chose to tell a story of his own childhood and how his personal values shaped the way he thinks about corporations. His is not a Pollyanna account of his life and his values. He is prepared to acknowledge some of the negative aspects of the legacy his baby-boomer generation has left for those who take over. By doing so, he is signaling to those who are following him that there is a thread that connects his experiences, beliefs, and values right through to his actions and goals as a leader. This thread is important both to himself and to his followers. For his followers, it creates a story they can relate to. For himself, it builds a description of him that he can access under stress.

For some leaders, their narratives are so compelling that they can reach forward for decades. As we saw earlier from Antoine Riboud the founder of Danone:

> A company's responsibility does not end at the door to the factory or the office. The jobs it provides shape whole lives. It consumes energy and raw materials, and in so doing, it alters the face of our planet. The public will remind us of our responsibilities in this industrial society.[3]

It is this belief about the resilience of communities and the world that has guided the current CEO and that drives the actions of many workers at Danone. Leaders who are taking the reins from others often have a story to tell that in some way connects the legacy of the past with the present and then into the promise of the future. Here is how Standard Chartered Bank's current CEO Peter Sands describes this continuity with the past:

> The heritage and values of Standard Chartered Bank are clearly expressed in its brand promise: "Here for good." Fundamentally, what drives me is to shape the organization simultaneously to be very effective in terms of performance, a great place to work, and something that is actually a force for good.[4]

For some leaders, these ideas and narratives come from profound personal experiences or "crucibles" that have transformed their own way of looking at the world.[5] Recall how Google's Jared Cohen built the idea of working with violent gang members from his own experience of interviewing rebels in the Middle East, which brought him insight and empathy. As he poignantly reflects, "They were broken souls who would rather have had a pen in their hand."[6]

In the age of the "naked" leader, empathy, reflection, and narrative will become ever more central. When leaders describe a storyline that connects the past with the future in a personal and resonant way, they are signaling their authenticity to their followers. However, although these words are indeed important, what followers are particularly sensitive to are the deeds that follow and the judgment calls that leaders make when they are confronted with tough situations that test their espoused values.

AUTHENTICITY AND JUDGMENT CALLS

A follower judges a leader's authenticity in part on the extent of the gap between knowing and doing. As Professors Jeffrey Pfeffer and Robert Sutton discovered, knowing and saying that something is important do not necessarily mean that a leader will act on that knowledge.[7] This knowing and doing gap can become particularly apparent when a leader is confronted with a judgment call for which the outcome is unclear. It is at this point that the capacity of a leader to call on her strong, authentic values can be the defining point of her career.

When leadership scholars Warren Bennis and Noel Tichy examined how leaders make tough judgment calls, they found that leaders most likely to make good judgment calls are those who know most about themselves and are most authentic to this self-knowledge.[8] It is this self-knowledge that helps them to understand how they learn, how they face reality, and how they watch and listen. It also seems to depend on how willing they are to improve. Those who tend to make good judgment calls are able to use this self-knowledge and capacity to improve and to build strong teams around them and indeed to then mentor and coach others on how to make better judgments.

What is particularly interesting about these leadership insights is what occurs when these leaders act under the pressure of time. It comes as no surprise to learn that often a leader's decisions have to be made quickly and under much stress. This means that, inevitably, rather than engaging in a deep analytical process to determine the latitude of the decision, most leaders fall back on their internal mental frameworks or heuristics and their inner storylines and narratives. Thus the stronger and more values-based their internal narrative and heuristics, the more likely they are to use those values as a basis for decision making. And, of course, the more publicly they describe those values as commitments to others, the more likely they are to stand by them when the going gets tough.

BARRIERS TO A LEADER'S JOURNEY TO AUTHENTICITY

Narratives and self-knowledge are the bedrock of a leader's authentic development. This development takes place through a process that we might call their *inner journey*, which is the internalization of what the person has experienced. Indeed, as a large number of psychologists and psychoanalysts have found, the authentic life is the examined life.[9]

There is a journey to authenticity. Leaders become authentic when they experience *crucible experiences* that test them and help them understand more profoundly the world around them. They become more authentic when they have time to reflect and in this process of self-reflection learn more about themselves and what they care about. They become authentic when they have the opportunity to fail and to learn from those failures. And they become authentic when those around them are frank and open in their observations.

Yet there are many barriers within corporations that can severely reduce a leader's capacity to become authentic—extreme pressure destroys the time for reflection, and the sycophancy of those around can reduce the chances of truthful feedback.

It's hard to develop the habits of self-reflection when faced with the everyday realities of corporate life and the sheer and unrelenting pressure many potential leaders face—constantly barraged by endless e-mails, spending weekends traveling, and answering the phone throughout the night. These are certainly the symptoms of a globally connected world, but the pressures it creates have an impact on potential leaders—affecting their personal lives and making it really difficult for them to create deep, authentic relationships with others, be they friends, partners, or children. The cycle between work pressure and family life can easily turn caustic under extreme work pressure, eliminating the vital opportunities for reflection and conversation that are so important to a leader's sense of authenticity.

What's more, the corporate power structures and hierarchies can make self-reflection complicated. It can be hard to develop an authentic self when faced with the sycophantic followership that can accompany the staircase to the top. In many corporations, the currency of leadership is power, and it is positional power that creates the legitimacy for behaviors and provides the cover for action. Yet, at the same time, power can be a real impediment to the open and deep feedback that can be so crucial to personal learning.

HOW CORPORATIONS SUPPORT THE LEADER'S JOURNEY TO AUTHENTICITY

It has never been more important for those who will become leaders to be able to develop values they can express in an authentic way and then be able to act on those values, even when under tough judgment calls. Yet the capacity to take this journey is often hampered by extreme work pressure and sycophancy. Corporations that are able to overcome these barriers and create space for the inner journey do so in a number of ways:

1. They experience the "edge of the system."
2. They open up to "crucible experiences."
3. They engage in reflection and dialogue.

Experiencing the "Edge of the System" at Novo Nordisk

My World Economic Forum (WEF) colleague Massachusetts Institute of Technology Professor Otto Scharmer describes the importance of potential leaders being exposed to what he calls the *edge of the system*. It is in this reality that insight is created as we walk in the shoes of others.[10]

To understand how executives deal with these edge-of-the-system experiences, Boston College psychologist Philip Mirvis followed a group of vice presidents from the Danish pharmaceutical company Novo Nordisk when they visited health centers in São Paulo. These centers ranged from a world-class children's cancer facility, to an overcrowded hospital serving thousands of patients a day, and to a makeshift clinic in one of Rio's *favelas*.[11]

Mirvis, in his research on authenticity, has argued that while these edge-of-the-system experiences are vital, it also takes inner questioning to make a difference and create an opportunity to transform how people see the world and how they shape their personal narratives. With the Novo Nordisk group, he saw this inner questioning take place as the teams participated in what they called "community diagnosis." After each visit, the executives took time out to reflect on what they had seen and to analyze their understanding of these insights. They thought about what it meant to them and what it meant for leading a resilient corporation into the future. Often they found that these experiences confronted their own value systems and made them think more deeply about their own leadership roles and how others create a narrative for themselves. Mirvis reports one participant recounting:

> Dr. Parelli of the cancer clinic said something that touched me deeply. "We open our doors to all children, no matter their insurance or what their families can pay. We use state-of-the-art technology and cure many of them. Still, some die. I want these children to know they are dying because of their disease, not because they are Brazilians.
>
> He built a diabetes clinic from nothing. How? Real passion and belief in what he's doing. There was no complaining about resources or roadblocks. Nothing got in the way of his vision and drive.[12]

In reflecting on a leader in a cancer clinic, the executive was confronted with his own experiences of resources and roadblocks and rather uncomfortably realizing that someone with significantly fewer resources was still able to create a way of thinking about being a leader where "nothing got in the way of his vision and drive."

These individual reflections seem to be crucial to act as a contrast between the narratives of others and the narratives of self. However, Mirvis also observed that this is not just an internal process. When the executives talk to each other about their experiences, they also lift the debate from their own individual insights and lessons to a wider collective consideration and learning. Mirvis saw that by sharing with others, these executives had an opportunity to test out their own values and attitudes.

The Novo Nordisk group made these experiences even more powerful by following them up with meetings with government officials and local executives. This proved to be crucial because it enabled the experiences to be seen in the context of a worldview and of multiple stakeholders. In thinking about their own leadership journeys, often these executives came away deeply touched by the leadership journeys of others and the courage they had shown.

These experiences of the edges of the system can be profound because they encourage people to come to grips with the social, moral, and environmental impacts of their corporations. And it is no surprise, as Mirvis's research has shown, that a leader's personal outlook on society itself shapes the pace and trajectory of the leader's company's resilience agenda.[13] As we saw in the quote from Paul Polman earlier, it is often through reflection on a leader's own experiences and history that insights and courage about the role of the corporation are constructed.

Opening Up to Crucible Experiences at Hindustan Unilever

Potential leaders also need to experience what have been called *crucible experiences*. Looking back on my own life, in my second year at university, I hitchhiked across the Middle East—through Turkey, Syria, and Jordan—with only a hundred pounds in my pocket. This was to prove to be a crucible experience, teaching me empathy—how life could be for others—and also testing my own sense of self. This empathy is crucial. As Wharton Business School's Stewart Friedman has observed, "It is well established that human relations develop and deepen as people see themselves in another person and see another in themselves."[14]

I was reminded of my own experiences when listening to Dan Goleman, a member of the WEF Global Advisory Council on New Models of Leadership, who had this to say:

One is stepping outside one's comfortable life—living abroad on a shoestring, for example, or otherwise getting to know reality on the fringes. Living in a culture different from our own surfaces hidden norms and lets us see our own culture through the lens of other eyes. That's good practice for analyzing any system. And living on the cheap strengthens our own adaptability and makes us more comfortable with the unknown and with risk. Another competence-builder might be a period of social service—that is, diving into a role where others' needs come first rather than just looking out for number one, such as working for a NGO in the poor world. Still a third would be an experience that requires taking a contrarian, skeptical position—standing up for a minority view.[15]

I am sure that you have had your own crucible experiences, a time when you have been pushed out of your comfort zone and perhaps even had to confront aspects of yourself with which you are uncomfortable. Often these crucible experiences contain dilemmas that have to be faced or unpalatable truths that have to be confronted.

In some companies, these crucible experiences are part of the early development of future leaders. Take, for example, the practice at Hindustan Unilever (HUL) of the "rural stint." I first heard about this from Sunny Verghese, CEO of Olam, which is a large Asia-based commodity company. I was interviewing Verghese as a member of a CEO panel at Singapore's Human Capital Summit back in 2010. I asked him what experiences had been most crucial to his development as a leader. In 1982, he had received an MBA from the prestigious Indian Institute of Management Ahmedabad, and so I had rather expected him to start with that. Rather unexpectedly for a leader who is known for his general management expertise, he talked instead about the time he had spent as a young graduate in an Indian village. During a six-month period, he had lived in a village in rural India really learning to understand and empathize with the lives and hopes and expectations of the villagers. He went from village to village demonstrating the firm's products, learning firsthand how customers used them, and immersing himself in the Indian ethos and customs. It was a leadership perspective that would run deep and stay with him through his career, and it was this insight, he said, that made him the CEO he is now and created the depth and clarity of values that has been a mark of his leadership at Olam.

The rural stint that Sunny Verghese experienced more than 20 years ago has been a cornerstone of development at HUL and continues to this day. As one of India's largest consumer products companies, the company has more than 1 million retail outlets across India, and this makes it a natural place for crucible experiences. Leena Nair, executive director at HUL, sees it this way:

> Sensitizing young managers to the ground realities that many of them never get a feel for while growing up in large cities. The experiences they have in these villages stay with them through their careers, and this has gone a long way in making them more human managers. The rural stint has been a part of the management training program for over 30 years now and certainly has a role to play in the quality of leadership HUL has consistently produced over the years.[16]

Even with its long and prestigious history, the decision to keep the rural stint was not an easy one. It's a lengthy experience, and young recruits who had been educated overseas do not expect to be walking the streets selling packets of soap, tea, and shampoo to the wholesale trade in Indian villages. Indeed, it remains as tough an assignment as it was for Sunny Verghese 20 years ago. Trainees still travel extensively through the hottest months and the Indian monsoon, sharing the life of a traveling salesman, staying in the same lodges, eating the same food, and drinking the same suspiciously colored liquids that traders offer them in the market.

Yet the rural stint remains, somewhat reduced to six to eight weeks—but it is still an important part of the 12-month training program that encourages graduates to live in a village in rural India and contribute to the local community. These days, during their time in the villages, the trainees engage in village life—building supply chains to eliminate middlemen for local produce, raising awareness of the benefits of hand washing, educating the community about family planning, and teaching in the village school.

These rural stints have proved to be crucial to the development of future leaders. As the leadership-development team told Stephen Remedios, "Throw three or four young managers into a remote village and charge them with a challenging task and you will be surprised with what they come up with." As Remedios reflects, "Benefits accrue over many years in situations where least expected. One of the most commonly heard phrases at HUL is 'When I was in my rural stint.'" Indeed, I saw this firsthand,[17] Sunny Verghese may be one of Asia's most celebrated leaders, but when asked about his leadership philosophy, it was about his time as a young man in rural India that he spoke. As many others have found, it is an experience that stays with leaders through their entire careers and provides insights they can reflect on in the years to come.

Engaging in Reflection and Dialogue at Standard Chartered Bank

These catalyst experiences have very little value on their own; it is the process of understanding and internalization that creates opportunities for them to be understood and subsumed within the scope of the person's whole authentic character. Inevitably, this process of internalization is husbanded through deep and high-quality conversations with others. It would seem that perhaps more than any other community of people, those who are or who will become leaders desperately need conversations and reflections with talking partners. They need people who are prepared to be open and honest with them and who understand the pressures they face.

Take, for example, Standard Chartered Bank (SCB), where for the last 20 years Geraldine Haley has been involved in stewarding the development of the leadership cadre. This starts from the top, and the orderly succession of long-serving CEOs has played a strong role. Successive CEOs (Rana Talwar from 1998 to 2001, Mervyn Davies from 2001 to 2006 and then chairman from 2006 to 2009, and Peter Sands from 2006 to the present) have worked to create continuity in explaining what the role of the bank can be. At the center is the phrase, first coined in 2010, "Here for Good," that reflects both the core of resilience that is crucial to the bank and the values it would want to have in its communities.

These explicit statements of the values and principles of the bank have served as a touchstone for the leadership-development practices.[18] As Geraldine Haley comments:

At the bank, people have the opportunity for extraordinary experiences. They can work with many different nationalities and generations. So the compelling dimension that holds this disparate group of people together is their sense of purpose. We ask all our leaders, "What is your core purpose? How does this align with Here for Good?" We want them to bring their whole self to work. We expect them to make a difference in the world they live in.[19]

Although there are many ways the bank supports authentic and purposeful leadership, in Haley's experience, there are four leadership practices that have made the most significant impact. These are the ways that new senior hires are supported in their first 100 days, the way that authentic leadership teams are built, the impact of narratives, and the ways leaders are supported in reflecting on the many dilemmas and judgment calls they face.

Reflecting on the First 100 Days

One of the challenges in supporting a leader cadre is that whereas those in charge of leadership succession typically expect to develop around 70 to 80 percent of their leaders from within the corporation, the remaining 20 percent come in from outside as senior hires. This percentage typically increases when, like SCB, the firm is growing rapidly or moving into a new sector or geographic area. The influx of new ideas and skills is crucial to refreshing leadership, but it also can create confusion if new joiners struggle to align their behaviors with the values and principles of the corporation.

Clearly, values-based external selection processes can play a key role in identifying people with values most likely to be aligned with those of the firm. Yet, even with careful selection, the initial socialization period can be a make-or-break period for many executives. In order to combat this, for newly appointed senior executives at SCB, coming from both inside and outside the firm, the emphasis is on it being a "make" rather than a "break" experience. The way these odds of success are increased is by working closely with all new senior executives who are joining the senior global level for their first 100 days. As with many onboarding programs, a central part of the experience of new executives is a five-day global program taught by the bank's leaders. This is a crucial opportunity to hear from the executive team how its members behave and live the corporate purpose on a day-to-day basis.

What is perhaps more unusual is that during the first 100 days, every new senior executive at SCB is assigned a personal internal facilitator. The purpose of the facilitators is to work very closely with the executives. They do this by supporting the executives in significant events, for example, accompanying the executives to their first team meetings and then reflecting with them on how the meeting went. The role of facilitators is to encourage the executives to consider their own sense of authenticity, to reflect on how they come across to others, and to think about how this is aligned with the corporation's values.

Authentic Leadership Teams

Building inner strength and authenticity is crucial for a leader, yet, in reality, most of the success and failure leaders experience comes as part of the way they lead their own teams and work as members of the executive teams. At the early stages of their coming together, some of the more commercially crucial teams have full-time facilitators working with them. One established practice is that within these business meetings there is always space for people to get to know each other. To do this, they are encouraged to create a storyboard time when they talk about their lives and what has shaped and influenced them. As Haley remarks:

> If we want teams to behave in a different space, then we have to create an opportunity for them to understand each other more through open and inclusive listening. They must have challenging conversations, and we accelerate the process of storming by knowingly creating bonds that hold firm during these tough conversations.[20]

What has become clear is that these threads of conversations that are created at the beginning of team formation often have a profound impact on the behavior of the team. These first meetings can be tricky, so almost always there is a facilitator with the team who typically then joins the team a couple of times a year. The facilitators have one constant message: the leader must be "red hot on context," which means that the leader needs to deeply understand the context in which the team is working and understand the cultural nuances and values of the team. It is this empathy and understanding that bring credibility to the leader and the team and put them in a better space to become high performing.

Narratives and Leadership Authenticity

One-to-one coaching and team support play a key role in developing resilient and purposeful leaders at SCB. So too does the responsibility of the leaders of the bank to be open and honest about their own professional and personal journeys, the challenges they have encountered, and the difficulties they have faced. To do this, executives have to be prepared and able to create their own personal narratives that describe what they stand for, how they have learned, and what they have gotten wrong. As Haley remarks:

> This personal narrative builds deep self-awareness, and it can also be powerful and cathartic. It is a powerful process for building authenticity because there are lots of myths about senior leaders, and this debunks these myths by really showing their vulnerabilities and mistakes. It also creates less distance between leader and follower. This is important because increasingly in the transparent and connected companies in which leaders are operating, their role is less about power or status and more about being open and prepared to share challenges. This reduces the distance and creates a sense of closeness.[21]

For Mike Rees, CEO of Wholesale Banking, this personal narrative means teaching on the bank's onboarding program and cofacilitating the bank's top 200 training program. As part of this class, Rees talks openly and candidly about his own personal journey and the mistakes he has made. This means sharing how his childhood has influenced him, his own marriage, and the impact the pressure of the job has had on his family. He believes that in opening himself up in this way, he is acting as a role model for others to do the same. By doing so, he has developed what Noel Tichy has called a "teachable point of view" that conveys his ideas and values and energizes others to help them make clear and decisive judgments.[22]

Confronting Dilemmas and Judgment Calls

Engaging in crucible experiences and being coached and mentored both can play a role in supporting an executive on his or her inner journey. Reflecting on the SCB experience, there is one other practice that Haley believes has made a significant contribution—and that is the practice of supporting groups of executives to work through dilemmas and judgment calls.

The idea is to challenge and to really put to the test the principle of the bank's core value statement—"Here for Good." Questions take the form of "How can we be a 'force for good' by working with the client to ensure that our environmental and social standards are met?" and "What will be the impact on the community if we choose not to be involved?" As with all dilemmas, the outcome is not always clear. In some instances, the right thing to do may be to refuse credit to an existing client. In other cases, executives must weigh the balance of any environmental or social impacts and the ability to mitigate them against the benefits that a project would bring to the economy and surrounding communities. As Warren Bennis and Noel Tichy have found in their study of leadership decision making, understanding how these judgment calls are played through can be crucial in supporting the values and principles of executives.[23]

CONCLUSION

In a world of ever-growing transparency and Gen Yer's expectations of a compelling leadership narrative, a leader's capacity to be authentic and purposeful becomes crucial. Yet, on the leader's journey, there are many barriers to this—extreme work pressure deprives them of the opportunity to really reflect, and surrounded by the power structures, it's hard not to be sycophantic. Yet, as we have seen, it is possible within the corporate structure to create opportunities for potential leaders to explore who they are and how they relate to others.

CHAPTER 13

◆

THE LEADER'S JOURNEY
TO A WORLDVIEW

When we reimagine leadership, we can imagine leaders who are capable of taking a worldview, who can see beyond the boundaries of the corporation into the world outside, who are able to take a perspective that has a longer time viewpoint, and who see the complexities in the world and by doing so acknowledge the interdependencies. Leaders are increasingly engaged in multiple layers of the external context: from the global (e.g., carbon emissions and climate change), to the regional (e.g., demography and population growth), and down to the national and local (e.g., recession, unemployment, and dysfunctional political systems). Thus they are becoming increasingly detached from their specific locations, contexts, and society and instead are embracing and internalizing the needs of many contexts and many societies. It is this that takes them on the journey to a worldview. As my fellow member of the World Economic Forum (WEF) Global Advisory Council on New Models of Leadership and psychologist Dan Goleman describes, "We will need leaders with a dual capability of attention: both alert to subtle, telling signals as well as a larger systems awareness." For him, the leaders most able to get beyond shared blind spots will do so through a willingness to search out and understand the interrelatedness in the systems in which they operate:[1]

> When one sees these issues in a systemic way, then it's easier to make decisions that consider the many, not the few, and for the long term, not just the present. Tomorrow's leaders

will need to go beyond the limits of the systems within which they operate today to see what those systems might become.

The challenge for leaders is to get a handle on the sheer complexity of what is ahead. The problems they will face do not present themselves with black-and-white solutions, nor are they easily amenable to rational and overly logical thinking. Instead, they come as messy, complex, interrelated sets of factors in which action in one sphere is likely to lead to unintended consequences in another. In other words, they are often embedded in larger systems of interrelated factors. Here is how my WEF colleague Otto Scharmer describes this[2]:

> The collective dimension of leadership requires leaders to think, sense, and act beyond the boundaries of their own institutions. Leaders must be able to co-sense and co-create at the level of the whole ecosystem. Corporate leaders need to think and act on the scale of their extended enterprise. NGO and government leaders need to think beyond the silos of their own traditional focus and geography. The biggest leadership challenges today deal with this contradiction between eco-system reality and ego-system awareness. The leader's new work is about helping people and communities to move from ego-system awareness (generating well-being of a narrow interest group) to eco-system awareness (generating well-being of the whole). The process of moving from ego-system to eco-system awareness requires a profound intellectual, emotional, and social journey, a journey to our real sources of presence and self.

HOW CORPORATIONS ENCOURAGE A WORLDVIEW

There are three ways that those trying to stretch the worldviews of executives are approaching their development:

1. They stretch the time span of discretion.
2. They encourage diverse networks.
3. They create alliance-building skills.

Stretching the Time Span of Discretion at Royal Dutch Shell

It is important for executives to think into the future, but it's tough to take a longer-term, complex view when constantly faced with short-term pressures. What becomes important is to strengthen what might be called a *temporal perspective*—the capacity to imagine over an extended period of time.

Elliot Jaques, a founding member of the Tavistock Institute of Human Relations in London, described this temporal perspective as the "time span of discretion" and argued that it operates at three levels of temporal maturity.[3] The first level is the capacity to work at an operational level where the themes of work are to add value for the present and where the results of work become apparent within a time horizon of less than two years. The second level is the capacity to operate beyond the operation level to embrace the organizational level. Here the themes of work are the development of strategy and of strategic intent, and the focus is on the longer-term objectives of the organization. In this second level, the individual is operating at time horizons that can stretch up to 10 years. The third and highest level is the potential to operate at a strategic level where the focus is on long-term strategic functioning and the sustained viability of organizations for future generations. In this level of cognitive functioning, the time frames can exceed 25 years.

What will be increasingly important in leadership is to find and develop people capable of operating at the longest time span of discretion. Jaques believed that these levels develop and unfold over the career of a leader as he or she makes the transition from seeing one perspective to seeing more complexities, more opportunities, and more challenges.

For some companies, operating at the longest time span of discretion is particularly crucial. Here is how the Chairman Jorma Ollila of Royal Dutch Shell described this in a speech he gave in New York in October 2012 on the occasion of the Financial Times Business Book of the Year awards ceremony:[4]

> If we are going to meet our future global challenges, leaders in both business and government will need to develop certain critical traits. The old ways of doing business and governing

are unlikely to get us where we need to go. In this new era, leaders need to be humble enough to want to see through the eyes of others and understand what drives them. They need to be wise enough to recognize that their success depends on accommodating the interests of others. They need to be far-sighted enough to distinguish trends and real disruptions from everyday volatility. And they need to be resilient enough to tackle the inevitable challenges of a turbulent world.

Supporting this approach of far-sighted thinking has been crucial to the success of Shell. From the early 1970s, the executives began to realize that traditional forecasting of oil reserves and their impact was creating a too narrow and restricted view of the future. Theirs is an industry that tends to move slowly—witness the slow transition from coal to liquid fuel—but it also can move fast, as the U.S. shale gas revolution has shown.

At the same time, the Shell executives had become aware of the way the U.S. military had created and discussed a number of "unthinkable" futures during the cold war, including the possibility of nuclear war. What the military had begun to realize was that these unfolding scenarios were able to move military thinking from simple, one-dimensional models of the future to something much more dynamic and complex. As Jaques had found, it is possible to extend the time span of discretion by extending cognitive thinking. Realizing the potential of this way of thinking, the Shell executive team brought the concept of unthinkable futures from the arena of war to the arena of business.

In the first scenarios, the Shell team explored a number of possibilities, including an Arab oil embargo and the impact this would have on escalating oil prices. By thinking through these possible scenarios and rehearsing their attitudes and plans with executives across the world, the Shell executives were able to move quickly when in 1973 this scenario played out. As a result, Shell was the first oil company to act on the impact of the oil shock. Since that time, a succession of scenario planners—including Pierre Wack, Kees van der Heijden, and Arie de Geus—has developed and refined this way of thinking.[5] Peter Schwartz, one of the pioneers of scenario development at Shell, puts it this way[6]:

To be an effective planning tool, scenarios should be written in the form of absorbing, convincing stories that describe a broad range of alternative futures relevant to an organization's success. Thoughtfully constructed, believable plots help leaders to become deeply involved in the scenarios and perhaps gain new understanding of how their organization can manage change as a result of this experience. The more involved leaders get with scenarios, the more likely it becomes that they will recognize their important but less obvious implications. Moreover, scenarios with engrossing plots can be swiftly communicated throughout the organization and will be more easily remembered by decision makers at all levels of management.

By 2010, the scenario had two distinct visions of the future—Blueprint and Scramble.[7] The Scramble scenario showed a world in 2030 in which nation is pitted against nation in a scramble for the remaining energy resources of the world. As a consequence of this unfettered scramble, there are rapid rises in carbon dioxide levels and more extreme climate change. In the alternative Blueprint scenario, nations and corporations work more collaboratively together, and the emerging global alliances result in resources being husbanded and major investments being made in the alternative-energy sector.

Over the years, I have worked with Dr. Cho Khong, current chief political analyst in the global business environment team. He describes the situation this way:

> The process of scenario building is really about casting a wide net and then narrowing it down; ideally, we want the issue at hand to be as challenging and significant as possible. Good scenarios are ones that explore the possible, not just the probable—providing a relevant challenge to the conventional wisdom of their users and helping them prepare for the major changes ahead. They will provide a useful context for debate, leading to better policy and strategy and a shared understanding of and commitment to actions.[8]

The decades of successive scenario planners at Shell have probably gone farther than any other community in constantly putting time and resources into taking a longer-term worldview. What seems to be crucial is the balancing of the facts and conversation.

Enhancing Foresight Through Facts and Conversation

Each scenario process begins with a worldwide search of experts who are studying and analyzing trends—be that population growth, social trends, the melting of the icecaps, or the frequency of unusual weather events. What is powerful is the sheer variety of the facts, trends, and narratives that are brought together. These facts are then assembled into possible trends and refined in conversations between the scenario team and internal and external experts. The facts are debated in a succession of preliminary workshops that provide an opportunity for key decision makers at Shell to think through the implications of the key trends. During this process, the trends are refined into scenario narratives. Often these dialogues include both diverse internal groups—with people of different ages, functions, seniority, nationality, and experience—and provocative external perspectives. This can be crucial, as Cho Khong remarks:

> The audience not only consists of senior executives and experts but all people who are curious by nature and who are highly motivated to acquire a deeper understanding of themselves and the world around them.[9]

Over time in this collective dialogue process, the knowledge and narratives about the future are exchanged, and the group begins to build a deeper mutual understanding of the central issues.

Yet, as decades of scenario planners will attest, the value is not simply in the facts and trends. Although they provoke and frame, the lasting value comes from the conversations and group dialogue they enable and encourage. The scenarios establish a wonderful frame to think about the future, and it is the conversations and the exchanges of ideas and insights that really create the opportunity for internalization of these ideas. For a corporation such as Shell, where coordinated action often takes place under pressure, these group dialogues enable leadership teams to collectively arrive at a worldview and a confirmatory perspective. Watching these conversations, Cho Khong remarks, "Often they leave the workshops saying, 'We need to get moving on this,' with a more cogent and courageous sense of the actions they need to take."

It seems to me that the scenario planning process at Shell and the succession of dialogues that support the scenarios are a profound example of how a worldview can be supported across vast populations of executives and future leaders. What is clear from those who have managed this process is that it is the combination of diverse facts and group dialogue that is key.

Group Dialogue

Picture for a moment what takes place in one of the Shell scenario workshops. Over the years, I have participated in a number of these scenario workshops, and although there are some differences, there are also commonalities. The commonalities are that about 30 people are invited to spend a day or a half-day together sitting so that they can see each other clearly—sometimes, but not always, in a circle. It is interesting to reflect on what is going on in these groups. To help me understand this more, I turned to physicist David Bohm, who in 1996 wrote, *On Dialogue*, a treatise on how thought is generated and sustained on a collective level.[10] His contention is this:

> Communication can only lead to the creation of something new if people are able to freely listen to each other, without prejudice, and without trying to influence each other. Each has to be interested primarily in truth and coherence.

Bohm's ideas on dialogue and group processes have been very influential to the generations of organizational development specialists who have supported the scenario planning process at Shell. Bohm believes that sustained thinking on a collective level can only happen with groups of between 15 and 40 people who are prepared to engage in a process of dialogue. The quality and nature of this dialogue are crucial. As a scientist, Bohm had seen that often group conversations are "almost like a Ping Pong game, where people are batting the ideas back and forth and the object of the game is to win or to take points for yourself." Like those who support the scenario process at Shell, he believes that what is crucial is to create a dialogue where there is "something more of a common participation, in which we are not playing a game against each other, but with each other. In a dialogue, everybody wins."[11]

Much of what Bohm describes as dialogue I have experienced in the Shell scenario workshops. I have experienced how the conversation within the group is unfolding and recursive rather than linear and directed, giving me time to reflect on the subtle implications of my own assumptions and creating a context that is relaxed, nonjudgmental, and curious. I have experienced that what this creates is an increasing sensitivity within the group of similarities and differences as we listen more carefully to each other.

These group dialogues are rather extraordinary experiences, and as a psychologist, I am fascinated by what is happening within them. Since the 1970s, the successive scenario teams at Shell have been deeply influential in helping people across the world to extend their time spans of discretion and develop a more complex worldview.

Encouraging Diverse Networks

Watching the scenario process unfold at Royal Dutch Shell, Cho Khong is very clear that what can also boost an executive's worldview is the breadth, depth, and diversity of their own networks. He reflects:[12]

> Those who bring the most to the conversations are those who are able to draw from many sources of insight. Those with restricted and narrow networks have as a result a paucity of ideas.

Therefore, it is perhaps no surprise that over the years, the leadership team at Shell has attempted to broaden executive networks in a number of ways. The executives have ensured, for example, that talented young people have an opportunity to attend the scenario workshops, and indeed they rotate people through the scenario teams. There is also an understanding that developing external links, for example, into academia and with experts, members of NGOs, and community leaders, is crucial to building a worldview.

There is a similar focus on executive networks at Standard Chartered Bank (SCB). As Geraldine Haley remarks, "It is these networks that can provide leaders with crucial insight and analysis of what is going on around the world."[13] Some executives are using peer-based networks such as the WEF, others are taking time to sit on the boards of NGOs, and still others are becoming actively involved in government-public partnerships. These peer networks create an opportunity to accelerate real-time business insight and horizon scanning. They also create an opportunity to learn how others are experimenting—and to learn both their successes and failures.

It is clear how important these relationships and networks are to many of the people I have described in this book. Think about how Franck Riboud at Danone reached out to Muhammad Yunus or how the networks that Google's Jared Cohen created early in his working life proved to be such a spur to action later on.

Much of my own research over the last decade has been about the nature and evolution of networks and what it takes for people to build those networks. In an early book on cooperation, *Hot Spots*, I described how I saw that the teams that were alight with energy and innovation inevitably contained within them diverse networks of relationships that enabled team members to access new sources of knowledge and from this to make innovative combinations.[14] In the follow-up, *Glow*, my attention turned from the corporation and the teams within in it to the individual as I showed how highly accomplished people tend to create opportunities in their lives to reach out to others who are different from themselves.[15] I explored the ideas of relationships and networks in the coming decades in *The Shift*, where I described how important it is to build both tight, intimate networks (which I called the *posse*) and big, diverse networks (which I called the *big-ideas crowd*).[16]

When leaders only have small, dense "clique" networks, their view of the world tends to be bounded. In contrast, those who are able to develop a worldview do so by connecting to broader networks. There are many benefits that accrue to leaders who are able to create well-structured networks—they are more able to access people with specific resources, they experience information benefits because they are connected to people who know about opportunities,[17] they are able to have early access to these opportunities faster than those who are less connected, and the nature of the reciprocal relationships in these networks can build trust and norms of cooperation.[18]

Building Broad and Diverse Networks at Arla Foods

In some companies, encouraging people to build broad and diverse networks and to take a worldview starts as soon as they join. I saw this at Arla Foods, which is a cooperative owned by 7,200 Swedish and Danish milk producers with production facilities in 13 countries, sales offices in a further 20 countries, and brands that include Arla, Castello, and Lurpak. Like many strong country-based companies, as the Arla business has expanded, the executive team had to reimagine leadership for the future. Team members did this by first identifying the four leadership competencies they believed would be crucial in the future—continuous learning, global mind-set and capacity to be open-minded, continuous personal development, and network building. Next, they went about finding people with the potential to develop these leadership competencies.

They began by recruiting young people who had already shown their curiosity and potential to take a worldview. They scrutinized carefully their résumés to find experience of those already working or spending significant time in an international context. Once they had made this initial selection, they put the candidates through a barrage of psychometric tests to identify their values and attitudes and a one-day assessment to focus on their curiosity and open-mindedness.

Once these young people had been brought into the corporation, the challenge was to help them develop their networks and take a worldview. To do this, the leadership-development team prepared a two-year program that included three eight-month stints working outside their functional backgrounds and outside their home country. The young people spent time in countries such as Argentina, Canada, Russia, and Sweden, building networks and establishing a couple of relationships that they could take with them to their next project. During this two-year program, the skills and capabilities of the group were strengthened through five one-week sessions in project management, personal training, and leadership training. Group members then had an opportunity to bridge this knowing-doing gap by working in small teams on two major projects. Each of these projects lasted for six to eight weeks and encouraged group members to focus on an important business issue and challenges that Arla is facing.

What this highlights for me is the sheer scale of investment some companies are prepared to make to ensure that they have leaders for the future who have a worldview, are curious, and are building diverse and rich networks. I talked to the group head of human resources, Ola Arvidsson, about why the leadership team at Arla continued to make this investment. He described a range of benefits. As they had hoped in the initial planning, people do indeed develop a global and holistic mind-set and certainly become more open-minded. Interestingly, the habits of continuous personal development that are so much a part of the experience seem to stick, and it seems that the skills supported through the program become basic ways of working. Perhaps most important, the richness of the networks is a huge benefit. Each member of this diverse cohort builds strong relationships with each other, but through the assignments and the projects, they also have an opportunity to build diverse networks across the world.[19]

Allowing Serendipity at LG

I recall vividly sitting in an executive session in Hong Kong with my colleague, Sumantra Ghoshal. It was the early 1990s, and we were there to lead London Business School's Global Business Consortium program. Ghoshal and I were both converts to the idea of the importance of leadership networks, so we had gathered in that room six potential leaders from six corporations around the world. Our plan was to take this group of 36 leaders to Europe, South America, and Asia to really understand how the world was changing and to see what this would mean for their own and for other corporations. We began by asking each executive to recount a personal experience that illustrated their character.

All the stories from the executives that afternoon in Hong Kong had something interesting about them. Yet what really struck me most was the story from one of executives from the Korean company, Lucky Goldstar. He described how he had been encouraged, as a potential future leader, to take a paid year off from work. I think at that point many of the executives in the room imaged that he would have spent the year engaged in an executive program at Harvard Business School or the Sloan program at Massachusetts Institute of Technology. This is where the surprise came. Instead of this conventional path, he described how he had decided to use the year to understand more about his passion, which was for opera. I recall at this point in his explanation glancing around the room to see a look of bewilderment and some amusement on the faces of the other executives. I could image them thinking about asking their own bosses if they could take a year to visit the opera houses of the world.

I've reflected often on that conversation and told the story a number of times to my students. I've also brought the story up to date from the 1990s. By 2012, Lucky Goldstar had changed its name to LG, and the opera-loving executive had run a large chunk of the European electronics business, a business, by the way, with global revenues of US$50 billion and an operating profit of US$1 billion. What was interesting was that building a worldview was crucial to the expansion of LG into Europe, and for the opera-loving executive, the experience of a year out played a crucial role in developing this worldview. But it was not in the planned way of the Arla executives; instead, it relied on *serendipity*—the casual, in-the-moment experiences and unstructured, unplanned meeting of people.

Let's for a moment imagine what happens to a young high-potential Korean executive in his year experiencing operas. In his global wanderings, he gets to know a diverse crowd of people, and over time, they introduce him to other people. He meets and gets to know opera singers and opera lovers, conductors and producers, fund raisers, and directors—in fact, that huge global community that creates opera seasons around the world. He also moves around the world—as opera becomes an ever more global phenomena with productions in New York, London, Sydney, Beijing, and Vienna. And, of course, he deeply experiences a process of production in a field that is very different from his own, with its own sensibilities, style, and creativity. During that year, he has the opportunity to build his own *big-ideas crowd*—that diverse community of people from across the world engaged in work that is very different from his own. How, you might be thinking, does this diverse network support him after his year of opera? What is clear is that during that year, he has strengthened his worldview. He has learned about creative sensibilities—something that proves crucial to LG as it designs and launches electronic products for the Western market. He meets with conductors and watches orchestras—broadening his ideas about how complex coordination takes place. He learns to speak English and lives in places across the world, and as he does so, he makes friends with other music lovers. And, perhaps most important, he learns the importance of being able to create relationships across boundaries and from this to develop his own personal worldview. His may not be the planned experiences of the Arla executives, but in its own way it is likely to be as rewarding.

Alliance Building at Save the Children

For some people, their experience of the edges of the system has changed their lives. Here is WEF council member Jasmine Whitbread, CEO of Save the Children, describing her experience: [20]

> When I first switched sectors and moved to Senegal (from Boston, where I was working for Thomson Financial), I found myself sitting in the Dakar Education for All conference in 2000, in a ballroom full of representatives from NGOs of all shapes and sizes indulging, as I then thought, in a chaotic airing of views of what had to change to reach a mind-boggling 120 million children then out of school. This was far from the analytical, process-driven, project-managed, tightly budgeted approach to leadership I was used to in the private sector, and I frankly doubted its efficacy—for a start, who was in charge? But less than a decade on, the number of children out of school had dropped by nearly half—which could never have happened without that coalition for change.

As Jasmine Whitbread found, experiencing the edge of the system took the theory and logic of building self-awareness to the deep reality of what it means to face an experience that was testing and profoundly disturbing to her status quo. It is this experience of working at the edge of the system that can be so crucial to developing and acting on a worldview. These diverse networks and the multistakeholder collaborations they involve have continued to be crucial to Jasmine Whitbread as she and her executive team attempt to recreate Save the Children as a twenty-first-century organization. An NGO such as Save the Children may have a clear purpose, but it needs to partner with corporations to create scale and build capability. In reinventing Save the Children as a twenty-first-century organization, she and her team have reached out to a range of venture partners who can leverage their own unique capabilities. Thus, for example, a team at the consultancy group BCG has worked on strategy, members of the head-hunting firm Egon Zhender have worked on top talent and board development, and lawyers at Freshfields have advised them on their merger with other voluntary organizations.

Reflecting on her own experience of alliance building, she makes a couple of observations. First, one of the arts of alliance building is knowing which to choose: "There are now dozens of these multi-stakeholder initiatives, and part of the leadership nous is backing the one where you have the greatest potential to achieve the biggest impact." Next, she believes that there is a set of leadership capabilities that seem to be crucial to alliance building:

> These cross-sector collaborations can be daunting and messy challenges, with everyone coming from a slightly different perspective and no one in change. The leadership posture needed to make a decent fist of this is not an easy animal to describe, but you know it when you see it—a curious mix of audacity and humility, patience (with process) and impatience (with outcomes), tight on principles and loose on control.[21]

For Jasmine, this alliance building will be crucial for the future of organizations such as hers:

> We need this experience to kick in fast to supercharge the last few years of campaigning focused on the current set of Millennium Development Goals. And we need to tap into this experience in agreeing on the next set of "big issues" that need to be agreed on post-2015. Unlike the last set of goals, which were largely created in the UN with some NGO collaboration, the next set will be created by a multistakeholder collaboration. If only we can stop this watering down of goals or accountability, a wider and joint leadership effort to improve the world has got to be a good thing.

This is why places like the Clinton Global Initiative and the WEF are so important. By focusing on big global issues, they move the debate forward and create forums for discussion. I can see this in the Davos forum of the WEF. Every year, many thousands of leaders descend on a tiny Swiss resort to meet and debate, argue, and agree.

They represent governments, international and multinational agencies, NGOs, social entrepreneurs, and universities. It would be naive to think that none of this is about business, growth, and profitability—it's the easiest way for leaders to meet their clients and suppliers. But it's more than this. Collected in that snow-bound ski resort are the very stakeholders in many of the emerging challenges the world faces. The debates, which range from small roundtable conversations to large panel discussions, focus not simply on profit maximization but also on making the world a safer and more equitable place. These forums create real opportunities for diverse alliances to be forged.

CONCLUSION

Increasingly, the practice of leadership will take place in a context that is potentially both global and almost certainly one that has to consider the longer term. In corporations where this is seen as crucial, a host of leadership initiatives is taking place to stretch both the temporal perspective of a future leader and to increase the aperture of their perspective.

CHAPTER 14

THE END OF THE LOVE LETTER

I began with a love letter to corporations. The letter arose from my own curiosity about corporations and those who work in them, a curiosity that dates back more than 40 years from my own corporate initiation at British Airways to latterly as a business professor at London Business School. During this period, I have been both inspired and astounded by corporations and those who lead them. More recently, my own research into the way that the landscape of corporations has and will change has begun to highlight the extraordinary forces that are shaping corporations, bringing with them both challenges and opportunities.

It is becoming increasingly clear that corporations are dominating our world. They deliver goods and services to the outer-most reaches of the globe, and their supply chains touch the lives of billions, shaping consumer aspirations as they do. For me, the corporate experience that began back in my early corporate days had a tacit promise that these ever-growing corporations would bring plenty to consumers and investors. In some aspects, this promise has been delivered.

These vast corporations have indeed brought plenty of goods and services and in doing so have forged the capacity to create extraordinary mechanisms of coordination and delivery. They have built the capability to bring together some of the most talented people in the world and have created places for them to research and develop ideas and to innovate. Moreover, the sheer variety we have seen across corporations—their unique structures, values, practices, and processes—has created a gigantic Petri dish for constant experimentation and has bolstered their capacity to innovate and change.

It now seems that these corporate capabilities are becoming ever more crucial. Faced with a fragile and volatile world, intelligence and wisdom are the most valuable assets that any individual, group, or society can have. The very best corporations are finely tuned to make the most of the intelligence and wisdom of millions of brains; indeed, some have created crucial collaborative tools for orchestrating this intelligence. Well-being and happiness are the most important goals that intelligence can be directed toward, and corporations can be one of the tools for delivering this. For most people, relationships are the source of much of what we value, and corporate life can create extraordinary opportunities for the formation of deep and profound, wide and diverse networks of relationships.

The argument I have made in this book is that corporations also can form the context for communities of people to make a positive difference in the world. They do this by seeing their role as steward-ship and renewal rather than exploitation and of interconnectivity and cooperation rather than independence and competition.

We stand at the fork in the path. Now is the time to build a vision of what a corporation can be. To do this, we need profound imagination and radical ideas to ensure that the yet-unrealized posi-tive potential of corporations can be brought to the fore.

I hope that I have delivered on at least some of my side of the bargain I promised in the love letter—to build an argument for what the role of corporations could and should be and to provide some ideas and examples that could be the basis for inspiration and action. Now to the role that you can play.

TO THOSE WHO LEAD

If you are a current or aspiring leader, you may want to reflect on the words of Harvard University's Barbara Kellerman when she says, "Leadership is in danger of becoming obsolete. Not leaders—there will always be leaders—but leadership as being more consequential than followership."[1] It would seem that the very forces that are transforming corporations are also transforming what leadership is becoming—ever more transparent and ever more accountable. Indeed, there is a pos-sible future where large corporations and those who lead them will become less trusted, less powerful, and more highly regulated.

Faced with becoming obsolete, now is the time to seize the opportunities these transformational forces are creating and to be willing to think bigger and more expansively. This thinking is not just about what happens inside a company. As I have shown, it will also be necessary to consider new forms of engagement outside the corporation to preclude corporations from ignoring issues as insidious as unemployment and gross income inequality.

As leaders of some of the most complex and sophisticated institutions currently in the world, it falls to you to make a difference. If you are to make a difference, then you have obligations to meet and commitments to fulfill.

The initial leadership commitment I have described here is to commit to employees and shareholders that you are building a corporation that is fit for the future. This means that it can withstand the external shocks that are an inevitable consequence of this volatile world and also reap the extraordinary benefits that a joined-up, innovative, and creative world is bringing. Leaders who meet their commitments to building a corporation fit for the future do so by continuously strengthening inner resilience. They do this by relentlessly amplifying the intelligence and wisdom of everyone in the community, by enhancing their emotional vitality and well-being, and by creating opportunities to harness the excitement and innovation of diverse networks and deep relationships.

Is this commitment enough? Will it be enough for you as a leader to feel that you have built for future generations and have devoted your time to a legacy that is worthwhile?

The answer to this question is less about organizational capability and more about the moral compass that guides you and the principles and values you strive to live by. Every leader knows (or at least should know) what it takes to build a resilient corporation. Moreover, as we have seen, the sophistication of the rapidly advancing technology of connectivity and knowledge transfer means that increasingly, hierarchical leadership is obsolete. Highly connected and talented employees are ever more capable of doing much of the strategic heavy lifting that was previously the domain of those in the executive suite.

Faced with decentralized decision making and resource allocation and with ever more active followers, the "obsolete leader" label may on the face of it seem concerning. In fact, for those who are able to, it creates a wonderful space for leaders who aspire to more. This expansion of aspiration is crucial. What will differentiate leadership in the coming decades is not just what the leaders choose to do within their corporations but also what they choose to do in the world. And it is here that the question of a moral compass comes in. Placing the corporation in the context of the whole world raises questions as to what the role of a corporation is, what the obligations are to those in the supply chain, and whether those who lead a corporation should engage themselves and their resources in wider issues such as youth unemployment and climate change. There is a rational answer to these moral questions. As I reported earlier, large-scale studies of corporate return on investment show that those who take an active role in their communities tend to deliver higher capital returns. However, although these studies are important to know, I don't think that this is the whole point. I believe that it is the combination of an economic imperative and the moral compass of leadership that should act as a steer to ensuring that the corporation is anchored in its neighborhoods and supply chain and has the will and the capacity to address global challenges.

How best to achieve this wider aspiration is essentially a question that can only be answered in the context of the specific conditions of a corporation. It is a question that leadership teams are called on to ask of themselves. Throughout this book I have provided ideas and stories that I hope will inform and inspire these conversations. However, I realize that many of these stories are about initiatives that are in their infancy and about projects that are not yet fully scaled. As a consequence, many will not yet be capable of making the real difference they have the potential to make. To reach this potential, we have to think on a much bigger scale. Here corporations and those who lead them are at a distinct advantage. As I have shown, perhaps more than any other institutional form in the world today, large corporations have extraordinary research and innovation capabilities, a deep capacity to scale and mobilize, and a growing understanding of what it takes to build alliances across multiple stakeholders. It is these capabilities that will enable the nascent ideas and projects described in this book and the many others that are happening in parallel to be scaled in such a way that the potential of corporations to be a force for good can be fully realized.

Looking more closely at almost every example I have given of how corporations are building inner resilience, anchoring in the community, or addressing global challenges, there has been a significant role for leaders. These leaders are setting aspirational goals for others to follow, they are making resource-allocation decisions that encompass a wider community of people, they are supporting and role-modeling compassion and involvement, and they are reaching out to a vast array of stakeholders to join them on this grand adventure. These are leaders who are determined to create positive strength both within and outside the boundaries of their corporations. They are part of a rapidly growing vanguard of people who want to make a positive difference.

I can sense this momentum growing, I can hear it in the conversations leaders are having with their peers, and I can read it in the plethora of books about these topics that have been published in the last couple of years. It seems that the zeitgeist of corporate narrative is changing to embrace a wider role for corporations.

In thinking about this broader role, it seems to me that leaders are confronted with some important questions. The first is how to become part of this vanguard and how to join the narrative. As we know, when courage is required, joining with like-minded peers and developing a wide and diverse network of relationships are crucial. Of course, the question is also how best to avoid the sycophancy of power and the homogeneity of corporate success that can so easily blind one to the dangers ahead.

The second question is rather more profound. Leadership is a creative act—for which leaders are educated and for which they are prepared over a lifetime of learning. The way you choose to lead says much about your relationship with yourself. Do you have access to the courage to stand against short-term market pressure or to be courageous in the face of some of the worst aspects of capital markets? Are you able to listen to those within the corporation and the supply chain who want to create something they are proud of?

How can you make your leadership a lifetime of learning? What might this lifetime of learning mean for you? What are the crucible experiences that would have the potential to transform the way you see the world? What are the courageous conversations and group dialogues that would help you to think about yourself? What are the judgment calls that would strengthen your moral compass?

TO THOSE WHO FOLLOW

The world of those who work in corporations has changed and will continue to change profoundly. Over the course of your working life, you can expect the point at which you retire to move steadily later, and as a consequence, for many people, the extent of a working life will be a marathon rather than a sprint. This brings your capacity to develop and to access your inner resilience and emotional vitality to the fore. At the same time, across the global labor market, the hollowing out of work will put an increasing premium on highly skilled work while making the early stepping stones to a career ever more difficult to find. Thus, for anyone with aspirations for a good working life, the capacity to amplify their intelligence and wisdom and to harness the knowledge embedded in diverse connections will be key. But this is not all. As workers, parents, and caregivers, we are also guardians of a world that is becoming ever more fragile. It will be increasingly difficult to deny or indeed to avoid some of the more unpleasant aspects of this fragility.

In tandem with these broader changes has come a steady transformation of the relationship between employee and employer. More than a decade ago, I predicted the end of what I called the *parent-child* working relationship. What I meant by this was the end of a relationship where the tacit agreement was that the corporation is the "parent" and the worker is the "child." In its place, I believed, would emerge an *adult-to-adult* working relationship, where both employer and employee would assume greater responsibility. Since that time, this transition in the nature of the relationship between employee and employer has been gathering momentum. I believe that, taking many factors into consideration, this constitutes the best way to manage this relationship. However, it does have profound implications for working lives. It does mean that workers have to be prepared and able to take more responsibility for their own working life (with no parent to direct them) and at the same time be more accepting of the consequences of these choices (with no parent to shield them from these consequences). In the context of the ideas and cases in this book, there are a number of aspects of being a follower that now can be strengthened to ensure that you are up for a purposeful and rewarding working life.

Although the transition to the adult-to-adult relationship may be less cozy, it does have the effect of bringing to the fore the power of followership. In fact, there has never been a time when followership has been more powerful. Thus how best can you and your colleagues use this newfound power? I want to think about this in three ways— in how you think about your own working life, in how you think about those who lead, and in how you think about the relationship of the corporation to the wider world.

On this working marathon, it makes sense to engage in work that builds your inner resilience. As I have shown, you achieve this by amplifying your intellect, enhancing your emotional vitality, and creating opportunities to develop deep and broad networks. More specifically, you may want to ask of yourself these questions: Does the work I do stretch my thinking and encourage me to engage in experimentation and innovation? Is the relationship I have between my work and my personal life creating and enhancing a positive source of energy? Am I working in a collaborative way with others and in a way that is creating rich and deep relationships? If the answer to any of these questions is no, then you will want to think deeply about the work you are doing and the corporation with which you are working.

You also may want to consider your relationship with those who lead your team, your business, and your corporation. This is a relationship that has changed profoundly and that I believe will continue to change. It is symbolized in the shift from parent-to-child to adult-to-adult. I believe that this is a positive and important transition—but it does have implications for followers. As adults rather than children, you can expect that more decisions will rest with you. It is you who will have to actively decide how best to develop your skills, what roles will enable you to do this, and which corporations will be best able to provide a context for resilient development. This entails a purposeful and active way of making decisions and acting. As adults, you also may want to be articulate about what it is you want from your leaders, what you can expect leaders to do, how you expect them to behave, and the leadership narratives that you will find most compelling.

Earlier I quoted Barbara Kellerman: "Leadership is in danger of becoming obsolete. Not leaders—there will always be leaders—but leadership as being more consequential than followership."[2] Her view is that joined-up, intelligent, insightful, purposeful followers will become more consequential than leaders. Looking back to the practices that support *wise crowds*, it is possible to understand her thinking on this topic. Collaborative technology has created a platform that has fundamentally tipped the balance from hierarchical command and control to peer-to-peer decision making and resource allocation. In reality, what this means is that the top-down and hierarchical relationship between leaders and followers has evolved into wise crowds of followers interacting more openly and purposefully with each other. My advice is to make full use of these collaborative technologies—join communities of practice, engage in crowd sharing, and find interesting people. By doing so, you will discover that your collective voice on matters that you believe to be important will carry much farther and be listened to more carefully.

This leaves the question of what you personally believe to be important. In a sense, this brings us back to the third question I posed: how you think about the relationship of the corporation to the wider world.

For this, you will need to think into the future. Of course, as the Shell scenarios described, the future is unknowable, but enough of the default path is known for us to have some understanding of this:

> This is a world of 9 billion people and of extraordinary demographic swings—in Japan, more than 22 million people will be over 75 years of age, whereas the predicted growth rates in Nigeria will lead to a 50 percent population growth, resulting in a country of over 390 million people, the majority of whom will be under the age of 30.
>
> It is a world of cities—by 2025, in Asia alone there will be 10 hypercities with more than 25 million citizens, including Jakarta, Dhaka, Karachi, Shanghai, Mumbai, and Lagos. In China by 2050, there will be 500 more cities and 100 more airports.

It is a world of unprecedented consumption that will suck in vast amounts of natural resources—right now, the middle class in the United States buys 67 items of clothing a year; by 2050, that consuming class will be joined by billions of others; by 2030, the consuming middle class of China will rise from the current 300 million to 800 million, and in India it will be 583 million.

A world of rapidly diminishing natural resources—by 2050, many scientists predict that the major oil and gas reserves will have run out, followed by coal in 2112.

A world of water shortages—by 2030, global water requirements will be 40 percent above the current supply; much of the current supply comes from "fossil water" that cannot be replenished and from mountain snows that are rapidly melting, so by 2025, more than 1.8 billion people will be living in water-scarce regions.

A world of climate extremes—the 0.6 degree shift in temperature that occurred in the last century as a result of rising carbon dioxide levels will be dwarfed by global warming that the most optimists modeling put at 1.8 degrees and the more pessimistic at 4.0 to 5.0 degrees. This would lead to the melting of the arctic ice caps and extreme drought conditions.

Of course, none of this default path could happen: we could live healthly into our 90s, learn to curb our consumption, invent new ways of feeding ourselves and new energy sources, innovate our way out of climate change, and learn how to provide meaningful work for our young people. Yet, as I have argued, if any of this is to happen, it will be in part because corporations—either acting on their own or in alliances with other corporations or in complex multistakeholder strategies with governments and NGOs —are able to make this work. It is in all our interests to have good companies doing good work.

What role could you play? In a sense, the key to this is in the move to the adult-to-adult relationship and the capacity to take more personal responsibility. This means, for example, when you are interviewed by a new company, asking explicitly what the leaders of the company are actually doing in the three areas I have described—how they build resilience in their employees, what they are doing in their neighborhood and supply chains, and how they are addressing the challenges of a fragile world. And don't take the public relations "greenwash"—try to find out exactly what they are doing. These are important questions to ask because executives are very influenced by what people are interested in when they join their companies. There is a shortage of talented people with job-ready skills, so make your aspirations clear.

Next, when you are working for a company, find out what the company is doing in the three spheres of resilience. Most companies are doing something—although perhaps on a limited basis or at a piloting stage. Consider which of the areas I have described in this book are of interest to you and where your passion lies. Think back to the researchers at General Mills and how they realized that they had skills they could use in the service of others. Get involved, and join other communities that interest you.

Finally, as consumers, become more conscious of the values and purpose of the company from which you are buying. My guess is that in the coming years there will be an increased call for corporations to bring value to the world and a more sophisticated monitoring system to ascertain whether the rhetoric is followed by action.

I began to work on this book when my earlier research into the future had shown with such clarity what the default path could look like. There is no doubt that it is possible to destroy resilience within corporations—just as it is possible to destroy resilience in the communities and environments of the world. However, as I have shown, it is also possible to create places of work where people thrive, to build communities that are strong and positive, and to create a world that we could be pleased to leave to the coming generations.

My greatest fear is that we are embarking on the default path with our eyes closed. My greatest hope is that the global corporations and those who lead and work in them have the innovation, courage, and determination to provide the key that unlocks at least some of the problems of the world.

ACKNOWLEDGMENTS

I'd like to begin by acknowledging my colleagues at London Business School, a place that has been my academic home for more than two decades—and in particular Andrew Likerman and Apurv Bagri for their support and goodwill and my colleagues Dan Cable, Rob Goffee, Gareth Jones, Andrew Scott, and Mike Blowfield, who were all sources of great conversation. A big thank you to Patti Luong, who has kept my schedule under control in the two years I was writing this book. The elective MBA on the future of work that I direct at the school has been a huge source of inspiration, and I'd like to thank successive years of engaged and enthusiastic students who helped me to see the future of corporations through their eyes.

For over five years, my team at the Hot Spots Movement has worked with me to develop the Future of Work (FoW) Consortium and to prepare the corporate cases that I describe in this book. I would particularly like to thank Julia Goga-Cooke, who worked with me on the FoW Consortium; Tina Schneidermann, who leads the Hot Spots Movement group; Marzia Arico, for her creative inspiration; Max Mockett, for his work on the changing context of work; in particular, Haniah Shaukat, who did a great job working on the case studies; and Jayna Patel, for keeping the whole structure working.

More than any other book I have written, this one has been tough and complex. My corporate research and writing have always been about the "inside" of the corporation—the practices, processes, culture, leadership, and structural architecture that create high-performing, cooperative corporations. With my last book, *The Shift*,

I had looked at the "outside" and what it meant for people, and in this book, I wanted to understand what these shifts mean for corporations. Thus I had to look more closely at what happens outside a corporation in terms of its supply chain and neighborhoods, and I had to think more profoundly about leadership than I had ever done before. As a result, I needed to reach out to a much larger "big-ideas crowd." This turned out to be incredibly exciting—but also very daunting.

This is a book about corporations, so it is no surprise that it is corporate and nongovernment organization (NGO) executives who are at the center. Many people gave their time, ideas, and insights. I would like to thank at Arla Foods, Ola Arvidsson, group head of human resources; at Unilever, CEO Paul Polman and Gail Klintworth, who is the chief sustainability officer; at Safaricom/Vodafone, Joel Roxburgh, who was the head of sustainability at the Vodafone Group; Christele Delbe, head of corporate responsibility at the Vodafone Group; and Claire Alexandre, head of commercial and strategy, mobile payments at Vodafone; at Infosys, Sanjay Purohit, who is senior vice president and global head of products, platforms, and solutions; and Nandita Gurjar, who is the global head of education and research; at BT, Caroline Waters, who was director of people and policy; Nigel Perks, who was chief human resources (HR) officer at BT Global Services; and Vivian Leinster, head of people and organization development at BT Global Services; at Deloitte, Cathy Benko, vice chairman; at TCS, N. Chandrasekaran, CEO; Nupur Singh, director of HR for the United Kingdom and Ireland; and Anshoo Kapoor, talent management; at Royal Dutch Shell, Cho Khong, chief political analyst at Shell International; at Save the Children, CEO Jasmine Whitbread and Joan Coyle, HR director; at John Lewis Partnership, Laura Whyte, personnel director; at Danone, Muriel Penicaud, vice president for human resources; and Nicolas Rolland, learning and digital transformation director; at Standard Chartered Bank, Jeanette McKenna, community investment manager at Seeing Is Believing; Mark Devadason, group head of sustainability and regions corporate affairs; and Geraldine Haley, group head for future organization and leadership effectiveness; at DSM, Fokko Wientjes, sustainable development and program director of the DSM-WFP partnership; and Alba Tiley, sustainability engagement officer; at Partners in Food Solutions, Jeff Dykstra, founding executive director; at Boston Consultancy Group, Craig Baker, partner and managing director; at Manpower, David Arkless, president of global corporate and government affairs; and Tammy Johns, former head of strategy; and at the RAI Initiative, Norbert Both, vice president for corporate communications at Shell.

Many of the cases I describe have purposeful, authentic, and courageous leaders somewhere in the story. So I wanted to really look more deeply at how these ideas about the future and about resilience would play out in the leadership arena. I was fortunate to be asked to chair the newly launched World Economic Forum's Global Agenda Council on New Models of Leadership. I'd like to thank Gilbert Probst, Selima Benchenaa, and Carsten Sudhoff from the World Economic Forum. I also would like to thank the council members who engaged in the long conversations about leadership: Mario Alonso Puig, a fellow at Harvard Medical School, based in Madrid; Dan Goleman of Rutgers University; Hori Yoshito of Globis Institute Japan; Nancy Koehn of Harvard Business School; Ralph Krueger, who coaches the Canadian ice hockey team; Max Levchin, who was vice president of engineering at Google Inc.; John Maeda, who was the president of Rhode Island School of Design; Charlene Li, author on social media and technologies; Nick Udall, CEO of Nowhere Group, London; Jasmine Whitbread, CEO of Save the Children International; Ndidi Nwuneli, founder of Leadership Effectiveness Accountability and Professionalism (LEAP) Nigeria; Bob Sutton, Stanford University; and Otto Scharmer, based at MIT.

This book has taken me out of my comfort zone—and as a result, more than any other time in my writing career, I have reached out to people to look at an early draft. I want to particularly thank those people who read early drafts of the book and provided incredibly useful feedback and insight about how I could make the argument clearer: the social philosopher Charles Handy; Nigel Boardman, partner at Slaughter and May; Caroline Michel, CEO of PFD; Clare Chapman, group people director at BT; Hugh Mitchell, chief human resources and corporate officer at Royal Dutch Shell; Eric Brunelle, chief solution architect at SAP; Diana Robertson, professor of legal studies and business ethics at the Wharton School; Sabine Vinck, associate dean of executive education at London Business School;

journalist Simon Caulkin; Andrew Scott, professor of economics at London Business School; Richard Straub, chair of the Drucker Foundation; Stefan Stern, formerly director of strategy at Edelman; London Business School MBA student Luen Lien Choong; Tammy Johns, formerly senior vice president of Global Workforce Strategy at Manpower; executive board member Julie Hill; Ben Emmens, former director of HR services at People in Aid; Ioannis Ioannou, assistant professor of strategy and entrepreneurship at London Business School; and Jody Heymann, dean of UCLA's Fielding School of Public Health. Their initial feedback was very helpful, and as I result, I hope I have been able to follow their advice and made this book less complex and clearer than the initial draft I sent them.

As always, my "posse" helped and supported me—Tammy Erickson, Gita Piramal, Peter Moran, Gary Hamel, Dominic Houlder, Tobsha Learner, and Dave Ulrich. Thanks for giving me so much support and ideas over the years and to Nigel Boardman for his combination of love and wisdom.

My children, Christian and Dominic Seiersen, continued to remind me of how much I say, "I'm never going to write another book!" (and for those who heard about their career aspirations in *The Shift*, Christian did study history and is still determined to build a career around writing and research, and Dominic is studying medicine at University College London). My literary agent, Caroline Michel from PFD, kept me moving along whilst being a wonderful friend, aided and abetted by Tim Binding's endless cups of coffee and wonderful sentences that helped me through some of the darkest hours of rewrites, and my editor at McGraw-Hill, Knox Huston, who determinedly brought simplicity by ruthless cutting. I want to particularly thank my Japanese editor, Ai Nakajima, at President in Tokyo not just for this but also for her determination to get the message about the future into Japan.

I have had to venture far outside my comfort zone in writing this book. This has been by far the most intricate of my writing endeavors, and I owe a huge debt of gratitude to everyone who over the last four years has provided the wisdom and energy to keep me on track.

RESOURCES

The issues I've raised in this book are complex and far-reaching. As such, reading this book is only the first step on your journey, and I hope that you will want to explore the issues I have raised here further by using the resources listed below.

You can start by downloading the workbook that accompanies this book. The workbook is designed to help you think more deeply about the issues raised in *The Key* by providing probing questions that can lead to decisions and actions. You can download at www.lyndagratton.com/books/the-key.

If reading this book has increased your interest in planning the way your organization should operate in future, consider joining the Future of Work Research Consortium. Run by my team at the Hot Spots Movement, the consortium brings together professionals from leading global organizations to forecast what the future of work will look like and how corporations need to adapt their work practices to build the kind of resilience I have talked about in this book. To find out how you can join, visit http://www.hotspotsmovement.com/get-involved.

Perhaps the questions raised by *The Key* are topics that you feel your organization as a whole should be thinking about and discussing. My FoWlab Jams are a powerful and effective way of doing this. FoWlab Jams enable you to engage your employees in an informed, focused, real-time debate and promote creative conversations. My team provides a facilitated virtual space where your employees can feel free to collaborate and experiment on any topic you choose. Go to http://www.hotspotsmovement.com/future-of-work/benefits.html.

ENTER THE DEBATE

If you have any ideas or questions prompted by reading this book, I would love to hear from you via any of the channels listed below:

> *Twitter.* Follow @LyndaGratton on Twitter for the latest articles and updates. You can also follow @HSpotM for new research and ideas.
>
> *Facebook.* Discover a range of fresh multimedia content and interact with like-minded professionals on the Lynda Gratton and Hot Spots Movement Facebook pages.
> http://www.hotspotsmovement.com/the-key.html
> http://www.lyndagratton.com/books/97/116/The-Key.html

ENDNOTES

Preface

1. R. Reich, *Supercapitalism: The Transformation of Business, Democracy and Everyday Life* (New York: Vintage Books, 2008).
2. G. Lodge and C. Wilson, *A Corporate Solution to Global Poverty: How Multinationals Can Help the Poor and Invigorate Their Own Legitimacy* (Princeton, NJ: Princeton University Press, 2006).
3. Ibid.
4. S. Moss, *Chocolate: A Global History* (London: Reaktion Books, 2009).

Chapter 1

1. United Nations Population Division, "World Population Prospects: The 2010 Revision," international seminar entitled, "Population Estimates and Projections: Methodologies, Innovations, and Estimation of Target Population Applied to Public Policies," United Nations, New York, 2010.
2. C. Marson, "10 fool-proof predictions for the Internet in 2020," National Science Foundation, Washington, 2010; available from: http://www.networkworld.com/news/2010/010410-outlook-vision -predictions.html (accessed July 17, 2013).
3. Some, like Columbia University economist Jeffrey Sachs, see it creating a real opportunity for global conversations and problem solving around the world. Available from: http://www.project-syndicate.org /commentary/connectivity-for-all (accessed July 17, 2013).
4. R. Florida, "The World Is Spiky." *Atlantic Monthly* 296(3):48–51, 2005.
5. D. Autor, "The Polarization of Job Opportunities in the U.S. Labor Market: Implications for Employment and Earnings," Brookings Institute, Washington, DC, 2010; available from: http://www.brookings .edu/research/papers/2010/04/jobs-autor (accessed July 19, 2013).

6. R. Rajan, *Fault Lines: How Hidden Fractures Still Threaten the World Economy* (Princeton, NJ: Princeton University Press, 2011).

7. From G. Lodge and C. Wilson, *The Corporate Solution to Global Poverty: How Multinationals Can Help the Poor and Invigorate Their Own Legitimacy* (Princeton, NJ: Princeton University Press, 2006).

8. The World Bank, "Poverty Overview," http://www.worldbank.org/en/topic/poverty/overview (accessed July 19, 2013).

9. Kofi Annan, Address to the United Nations, "We the Peoples, The Role of the UN in the 21st Century," January 1, 2010.

10. Ibid.

11. R. Wilkinson and K. Pickett, *The Spirit Level: Why Equality Is Better for Everyone* (London: Penguin, 2010).

12. R. Rajan, *Fault Lines: How Hidden Fractures Still Threaten the World Economy* (Princeton, NJ: Princeton University Press, 2011).

13. Intergovernmental Panel on Climate Change, "Fourth Assessment Report: Climate Change 2007," Geneva; available from: http://www.ipcc.ch/publications_and_data/publications_and_data_reports.shtml (accessed July 19, 2013).

14. Her Majesty's Government, "The Impact of a Global Rise of 4°C (7°F)," Met Office, London; available from: http://www.metoffice.gov.uk/climate-change/guide/impacts/high-end/map (accessed July 19, 2013).

15. The "Stern Review on the Economics of Climate Change" is a 700-page report released for the British government on October 30, 2006 by economist Nicholas Stern, chair of the Grantham Research Institute on Climate Change and the Environment at the London School of Economics (LSE) and also chair of the Centre for Climate Change Economics and Policy (CCCEP) at Leeds University and LSE. Available from: http://webarchive.nationalarchives.gov.uk/20130129110402/http://www.hm-treasury.gov.uk/stern_review_report.htm (accessed July 19, 2013).

Chapter 2

1. B. Swanson, "Economic Abundance, Real and Imagined," *Forbes*, October 8, 2012; available from: http://www.forbes.com/sites/bretswanson/2012/10/08/economic-abundance-real-and-imagined (accessed July 19, 2013).

Part II

1. M. W. McCall and M. M. Lombardo, *Off the Track: Why and How Successful Executives Get Derailed* (Greensboro, NC: Center for Creative Leadership, 1983).

2. B. Groysberg, *Chasing Stars: The Myth of Talent and the Portability of Performance* (Princeton, NJ: Princeton University Press, 2010).

3. R. S. Burt, *Brokerage and Closure: An Introduction to Social Capital* (Oxford, UK: Oxford University Press, 2005).

4. J. Nahapiet and S. Ghoshal, "Social Capital, Intellectual Capital, and the Organizational Advantage," *Academy of Management Review* 23(2):242–266, 1998.

5. L. Gratton, *Hot Spots: Why Some Teams, Workplaces, and Organizations Buzz with Energy—and Others Don't* (San Francisco: Berrett-Koehler Publishers, 2007).

Chapter 3

1. Dev Patnaik, CEO of Jump Associates, gave me this example.

2. S. Bisson, "Information Overload," *The Guardian*, May 28, 2003; available at: http://www.guardian.co.uk/technology/2003/may/29/onlinesupplement.insideit (accessed July 17, 2013).

3. I. Illich, *Tools for Conviviality* (London: Marion Boyars, 2001).

4. C. Shirky, *Cognitive Surplus: Creativity and Generosity in a Connected Age* (London: Penguin Books, 2010).

5. J. Rifkin, *The Empathic Civilization: Global Consciousness in a World in Crisis* (New York: J.P. Tarcher/Penguin Putnam, 2010).

6. We interviewed Nandita Gurjar on November 7, 2012 via a telephone call.

7. M. Granovetter, "The Strength of Weak Ties," *American Journal of Sociology* 78(6):1360–1380, 1973.

8. A. Huff et al., *Leading Open Innovation* (Boston: MIT Press, 2013).

9. L. Huston and N. Sakkab, "Connect and Develop: Inside Procter & Gamble's New Model for Innovation," *Harvard Business Review* 84(3):58–66, 2006.

10. R. Wageman, "Interdependence and Group Effectiveness," *Administrative Science Quarterly* 40:145–180, 1995.

11. S. Caulkin, "Bust Bureaucracy by Liberating People to Manage Themselves," Leader, Columbus, OH; available at: http://www.leader.co.za/printarticle.aspx?s=6&f=1&a=2305 (accessed April 5, 2013).

Chapter 4

1. Chartered Institute of Personnel and Development (CIPD), "Absence Management Survey 2011," CIPD and Simplyhealth, London, 2012; available at: http://www.cipd.co.uk/hr-resources/survey-reports/absence-management-2012.aspx (accessed July 17, 2013).

2. S. Turkle, *Alone Together: Why We Expect More from Technology and Less from Each Other* (New York: Basic Books, 2011); and S. Gain, *Quiet: The Power of Introverts in a World That Can't Stop Talking* (New York: Crown Publishers, 2012).

3. S. Mennino, B. Rubin, and A. Brayfield, "Home-to-Job and Job-to-Home Spillover: The Impact of Company Policies and Workplace Culture," *Sociological Quarterly* 46:107–113, 2005.

4. Organisation for Economic Co-operation and Development (OECD), "Families Are Changing," OECD Family Base, Paris, 2011.

5. According to Catalyst Research, in 2012, whereas 50 percent of graduates joining corporations were women, the number of women in management positions was around 30 percent and in board positions around 10 percent. Moreover, the proportions seem to be remaining the same. Available at: http://www.catalyst.org/media/catalyst-2012-census-fortune-500-no-change-women-top-leadership (accessed July 17, 2013).

6. G. Desvaux, S. Devillard-Hoellinger, and P. Baumgarten, *Women Matter* (New York: McKinsey & Company, 2007).

7. T. Erickson, *Plugged in: The Generation Y Guide to Thriving at Work* (Boston: Harvard Business School Press, 2008).

8. H. J. Wolfram and L. Gratton, "Spillover Between Work and Home, Role Importance, and Life Satisfaction," *British Journal of Management* 25:77–90, 2012.

9. World Health Organization (WHO), "Closing the Gap in a Generation: Health Equity Through Action on the Social Determinants of Health," WHO, Geneva.

10. M. Kivimäk, S. T. Nyberg, G. D. Batty et al., "Job Strain as a Risk Factor for Coronary Heart Disease: A Collaborative Meta-analysis of Individual Participant Data," *Lancet* 380(9852):1491–1497, 2012.

11. Regus, "A Study of Trends in Workplace Stress across the Globe," Regus.com; available at: http://www.regus.co.uk/images/stress520full-520report_final_designed_tcm7-21560.pdf (accessed April 5, 2013).

12. G. Becker, "A Theory of the Allocation of Time," *Economic Journal* 75(299):493–517, 1965.

13. J. Schor, *Plenitude: The New Economics of True Wealth* (New York: Penguin Press, 2010).

14. C. Murphy, "Secrets of Greatness: How I Work," *Fortune*; available at: http://money.cnn.com/popups/2006/fortune/how_i_work/frameset.8.exclude.html (accessed April 5, 2013).

15. S. Turkle, *Alone Together: Why We Expect More from Technology and Less from Each Other* (New York: Basic Books, 2011).

16. J. Dutton, *Energize Your Workplace: How to Create and Sustain High-Quality Connections at Work* (San Francisco: Jossey-Bass, 2003).

17. D. Cable and K. Elsbach, "Why Showing Your Face at Work Matters," *MIT Sloan Management Review* 53(4):10–12, 2012.

18. Interview conducted with Caroline Waters in London on May 23, 2011.

19. C. Mainemelis, "When the muse takes it all: a model for the experience of timelessness in organizations." *Academy of Management Review* 26(4):548–565, 2001.

20. J. Batelle, *The Search: How Google and Its Rivals Rewrote the Rules of Business and Transformed Our Culture* (New York: Penguin Books, 2005).

21. A. Deutschman, "The Fabric of Creativity," *Fast Company*, December 1, 2004.

22. D. T. Campbell, "Blind Variation and Selective Retention in Creative Thought as in Other Knowledge Processes," *Psychological Review* 67:380–400, 1960.

23. D. K. Simonton, "The Continued Evolution of Creative Darwinism," *Psychological Inquiry* 10:362–367, 1999.

24. J. Gershuny, O. Sullivan, and Y. M. Kan, "Gender Convergence in Domestic Work: Discerning the Effects of Interactional and Institutional Barriers from Large-Scale Data," *Journal of Sociology* 45(2):234–251, 2011.

25. Cathy Benko (Vice Chairman and Managing Principal, Deloitte LLP), in discussion with author, December 2012.

26. C. Benko and A. Weisberg, *Mass Career Customization: Aligning the Workplace with Today's Nontraditional Workforce* (Boston: Harvard Business School Press, 2007).

Chapter 5

1. M. Nowak and R. Highfield, *Super Cooperators: Altruism, Evolution, and Why We Need Each Other to Succeed* (New York: Free Press, 2011).

2. Y. Benkler, "The Unselfish Gene." *Harvard Business Review* 89 (7–8):76–85, 2011.

3. M. Nowak, "Fives Rules for the Evolution of Cooperation." *Science* 314(5805):1560–1563, 2006.

4. L. Gratton and T. J. Erickson, "Eight Ways to Build Collaborative Teams." *Harvard Business Review* 85(11):100–109, 2007.

5. L. Gratton and S. Goshal, "Integrating the Enterprise." *MIT Sloan Management Review* 44(1):31–38, 2002.

6. M. Biosot, M. Nordberg, S. Yami, and B. Nicquevert, *Collisions and Collaboration: The Organization of Learning in the ATLAS Experiment at the LHC* (Oxford, UK: Oxford University Press, 2011).

7. European Organization for Nuclear Research (CERN), "Computing," 2013; available at: http://public.web.cern.ch/public/en/lhc/Computing-en.html (accessed April 5, 2013).

8. Ibid.

9. G. Paul, "The Colleague Letter of Understanding: Replacing Jobs with Commitments," Management Innovation eXchange, 2010.

10. Interview with Nupur Singh in London, May 2012.

11. Interview with Robert Kovack in London, October 2011.

12. S. Ghoshal and P. Moran, "Bad for Practice: A Critique of Transaction Cost Theory," *Academy of Management Review* 21(1):13–47, 1996.

13. D. Eden, "Self-fulfilling Prophecy as a Management Tool: Harnessing Pygmalion." *Academy of Management Review* 9(1):64–73, 1984.

14. M. Nowak, *Evolutionary Dynamics: Exploring the Equations of Life* (Boston: Harvard University Press, 2006).

Chapter 6

1. M. Chandler, "Hsieh of Zappos Takes Happiness Seriously," Graduate School of Stanford Business School, Stanford, CA.

2. T. Hsieh, *Delivering Happiness: A Path to Profits, Passion, and Purpose* (New York: Business Plus, 2010).

3. E. Glaeser, *Triumph of the City* (New York: Penguin Press, 2012).

4. Independent research from NEF Consulting reinforces the role that the John Lewis Partnership has played in the revitalization of town centers.

5. M. J. Sandel, *What Money Can't Buy: The Moral Limits to Markets* (New York: Farrar, Straus and Giroux, 2012).

6. D. Ariely, *The Upside of Irrationality* (New York: Harper Collins, 2010).

7. D. Ariely, *Predictably Irrational* (New York: Harper, 2009).

Chapter 7

1. J. Hansegard, "IKEA's New Catalogs: Less Pine, More Pixels." *Wall Street Journal*, August 8, 2012.

2. S. Bissell, "Incentives to Education and Child Labor Elimination: A Case in Bangladesh." In G. K. Lieten, R. Srivastava, and S. K. Thorat (eds.), *Small Hands in South Asia: Child Labour in Perspective* (New Delhi: Manohar, 2004), pp. 269–290.

3. UNICEF (2012) *IKEA, UNICEF programmes reach 74 million children in India*, UNICEF Press Release. Available from: http://www.unicef.org/media/media_65718.html (accessed May 10, 2012).

4. Available at: https://www.danone.com/en/our-vision/danone-a-unique-model.html (accessed April 9, 2013).

5. C. K. Prahalad, *The Fortune at the Bottom of the Pyramid* (New York: Pearson Prentice Hall, 2006).

6. M. E. Porter and M. R. Kramer, "Creating Shared Value." *Harvard Business Review* 89(1–2):62–77, 2011.

7. L. Hashiba, "Innovation in Well-Being: The Creation of Sustainable Value at Natura." Management Innovation eXchange, 2012; available at: http://www.managementexchange.com/story/innovation-in-well-being (accessed April 9, 2013).

8. Ibid.

9. Natura was ranked as the eighth most innovative company by *Forbes* in a survey published in July 2011. It also has been ranked second in the sustainable assessment carried out by Corporate Knights in 2012.

10. B. Seale, "Blending Being Well with Well-Being." *DirectSellingNews*, January 1, 2012; available at: http://directsellingnews.com/index.php/view/blending_beingwell_with_well_being (accessed April 9, 2013).

11. Ibid.

12. D. Mello and L. Hougland, "Companies Work to Save the Amazon Forest." Infosurhoy.com; available at: http://infosurhoy.com/cocoon/saii/xhtml/en_GB/features/saii/features/economy/2012/07/10/feature-03 (accessed April 9, 2013).

13. B. Seale, "Blending Being Well with Well-Being." *DirectSellingNews*, January 1, 2012; available at: http://directsellingnews.com/index.php/view/blending_beingwell_with_well_being (accessed April 9, 2013).

14. K. Rawe, "A Life Free from Hunger: Tackling Child Malnutrition." Save the Children UK, London.

Part IV

1. L. Gratton and S. Ghoshal, "Beyond Best Practice." *Sloan Management Review* 46(3):49–57, 2005.

2. J. Schumpeter, *Capitalism, Socialism, and Democracy* (New York: Harper, 1975; orig. pub. 1942).

Chapter 8

1. R. Goffee and G. Jones, *Clever: Leading Your Smartest, Most Creative People* (Boston: Harvard Business School Press, 2009).

2. K. Rawe, D. Jayasinghe, F. Mason et al., *A Life Free from Hunger: Tackling Child Malnutrition* (London: Save the Children, 2012).

3. DSM Press information; available at: http://www.dsm.com/content /dam/dsm/cworld/en_US/documents/hidden-hunger.pdf (accessed April 14, 2013).

4. Interview with Fokko Wientjes, November, 2012

5. L. Gratton, *Hot Spots: Why Some Teams, Workplaces, and Organizations Buzz with Energy—and Others Don't* (San Franscisco: Berrett-Koehler, 2007).

6. Interview with Fokko Wientjes, November, 2012

7. Ibid.

8. B. Einhorn, B. (2012). *Why Is Google's Eric Schmidt Going to North Korea?* Business Week.

9. Pew Research Center report; available at: http://www.pewforum.org /future-of-the-global-muslim-population-main-factors-age-structure .aspx (accessed April 13, 2013).

10. E. Knickmeyer, "The Arab World's Youth Army." Foreign Policy; available at: http://www.foreignpolicy.com/articles/2011/01/27/the _arab_world_s_youth_army?page=0,0 (accessed April 13, 2013).

11. D. Kerr, "Google Ideas Tackle Violent Extremism." Cnet; available at: http://news.cnet.com/8301-1023_3-57421608-93/google-ideas-tackles -violent-extremism/ (accessed April 13, 2013).

12. E. Spivack, (2011). *Jared Cohen on shattering misperceptions of violent extremists.* Poptech. Available from: https://poptech.org/blog/jared_ cohen_on_shattering_misperceptions_of_violent_extremists (accessed October 11, 2012).

13. J. Guynn, "Google Ideas Exploring How Technology Can Address Global Troubles." *Los Angeles Times*, July 17, 2012; available at: http:// articles.latimes.com/2012/jul/17/business/la-fi-google-ideas-20120717 (accessed April 13, 2013).

14. J. Peterson, "Google Maps Global Arms Trade." *The Daily Callers*, August 7, 2012; available at: http://dailycaller.com/2012/08/07/google -maps-global-arms-trade/ (accessed April 13, 2013).

15. M. Useem, "Jared Cohen: Google Ideas Director Fuses Technology and Statecraft." *Washington Post*, November 28, 2011; available at: http://www.washingtonpost.com/national/on-leadership/jared-cohen -google-ideas-director-fuses-technology-and-statecraft/2011/11/28/ gIQAk9Ld8N_story.html (accessed April 13, 2013).

16. R. Carroll, "Google to Tackle Internet Crime with Illicit Networks Summit." *The Guardian*, July 17, 2012; available at: http://www

.guardian.co.uk/technology/2012/jul/17/google-tech-knowhow
-internet-crime (accessed April 13, 2013).

17. Jasmine Whitbread was interviewed in February 2012 in Switzerland.
18. Craig Baker was interviewed in June 2012 in London.
19. Jasmine Whitbread was interviewed in February 2012 in Switzerland.
20. Jasmine Whitbread was interviewed in February 2012 in Switzerland.

Chapter 9

1. Paul Polman, CEO of Unilever, was interviewed by Adrian
   Wooldridge, management editor and "Schumpeter" columnist for
   The Economist, at Fourth Global Drucker Forum in Vienna in 2012.
   Available at: http://www.youtube.com/watch?v=vgpaHKCohio&
   feature=youtu.be (accessed July 17, 2013).
2. A. Ignatius, "Captain Planet." *Harvard Business Review* 90(6):112–
   118, 2012.
3. Gail Klintworth (Chief Sustainability Officer at Unilever) in discussion with author, London, November 2012.
4. Ibid.
5. Ibid.
6. T. Johns and L. Gratton, "The Third Wave of Virtual Work." *Harvard
   Business Review* 91(1):66–73, 2013.
7. A. Ignatius, "Captain Planet." *Harvard Business Review* 90(6):112–
   118, 2012.
8. Gail Klintworth (Chief Sustainability Officer at Unilever) in discussion with author, London, November 2012.
9. Quoted in M. Beer, *Higher Ambition: How Great Leaders Create
   Economic and Social Value.* (Boston: Harvard Business School Press,
   2011)
10. T. Suri and W. Jack, "The Performance and Impact of M-PESA: Pre-
    liminary Evidence from a Household Survey." Unpublished paper,
    2009.
11. W. Jack and T. Suri, "The Economics of M-PESA: An Update." Con-
    sortium on Financial Systems and Poverty, University of Chicago, 2010.
12. W. Jack and T. Suri, "Mobile Money: The Economics of M-PESA."
    NBER Working Paper No. 16721, National Bureau of Economic
    Research, Cambridge, MA, 2011.
13. N. Hughes and S. Lonie, "M-PESA: Mobile Money for the 'Un-
    banked.'" *Innovations* 2(1–2):63–81, 2007.
14. Christele Delbe (Head of Corporate Responsibility at Vodafone
    Group) in discussion with author, September 2012.

Chapter 10

1. L. Gratton, *Hotspots: Why Some Teams, Workplaces, and Organizations Buzz with Energy—and Others Don't* (San Francisco: Berrett-Koehler, 2007); and L. Gratton, *Glow: How You Can Radiate Energy, Innovation, and Success* (San Francisco: Berrett-Koehler, 2009).

2. D. Acemoglu and J. Robinson, *Why Nations Fail: The Origins of Power, Prosperity, and Poverty* (New York: Random House, 2012).

3. J. Bower, H. Leonard, and L. Paine, *Capitalism at Risk: Rethinking the Role of Business* (Boston: Harvard Business School Press, 2011).

4. G. Lodge and C. Wilson, *A Corporate Solution to Global Poverty: How Multinationals Can Help the Poor and Invigorate Their Own Legitimacy* (Princeton, NJ: Princeton University Press, 2006).

5. Ibid.

6. This was clear in the 2011 Edeleman report on trust. Available at: http://www.cipr.co.uk/sites/default/files/Trust percent20Executive percent20Summary_FINAL.pdf (accessed July 18, 2013).

7. C. Shirky, *Cognitive Surplus: Creativity and Generosity in a Connected Age* (New York: Penguin Press, 2011).

8. J. Ruggie, "Taking Embedded Liberalism Global." In David Held and Mathias Koenig-Archibugi (eds.), *Taming Globalization: Frontiers of Governance* (Cambridge, UK: Polity Press, 2003).

9. P. Diamandis and S. Kotler, *Abundance: The Future Is Better than You Think* (New York: Free Press, 2012).

10. A. Wolk, *Advancing Social Entrepreneurship: Recommendations for Policy Makers and Government Agencies* (Aspen, CO: Aspen Institute, 2008).

11. Jeff Dykstra (Executive Director, *Partners in Food Solutions*) in discussion with author, November 2012.

12. Ibid.

13. U.S. Department of State, "Trafficking in Persons," report, Washington, DC, 2012; available at: http://www.state.gov/documents/organization/192587.pdf (accessed July 18, 2013).

14. David Arkless (President, Global Corporate and Government Affairs of ManpowerGroup) in discussion with author, December 2012.

15. Ibid.

16. Ibid.

17. Jeremy Bentham (Head of Scenario Planning at Shell) in discussion with the author, October 2012.

Part V

1. World Economic Forum, Council on New Models of Leadership, http://reports.weforum.org/global-agenda-council-on-new-models-of-leadership/.
2. D. Ready, L. Hill, and J. Conger, "Winning the Race for Talent in Emerging Markets." *Harvard Business Review* 86(11):62–70, 2008.

Chapter 11

1. J. Bower, H. Leonard, and L. Paine, *Capitalism at Risk: Rethinking the Role of Business* (Boston: Harvard Business School Press, 2011).
2. D. Barton, "Capitalism for the Long Term." *Harvard Business Review* 89(3):84–91, 2011.
3. S. Ghoshal and P. Moran, "Bad for Practice: A Critique of the Transaction Cost Theory." *Academy of Management Review* 21:13–47, 1996.
4. D. Barton, "Capitalism for the Long Term." *Harvard Business Review* 89(3):84–91, 2011.
5. M. Friedman, "The Social Responsibility of Business Is to Increase Its Profit." *New York Times Magazine*, 1970; available at: http://www.colorado.edu/studentgroups/libertarians/issues/friedman-soc-resp-business.html (accessed July 17, 2013).
6. L. Stout, *The Shareholder Value Myth: How Putting Shareholders First Harms Investors, Corporations, and the Public* (San Fransisco: Berrett-Koehler, 2012).
7. R. G. Eccles, I. Ioannou, and G. Serafeim, "The Impact of a Corporate Culture of Sustainability on Corporate Behavior and Performance." Harvard Business School working paper, Cambridge, MA, 2011.
8. C. Handy, "The Unintended Consequences of Good Ideas." *Harvard Business Review* 90(10):36, 2012.
9. R. G. Eccles, I. Ioannou, and G. Serafeim, "The Impact of a Corporate Culture of Sustainability on Corporate Behavior and Performance." Harvard Business School working paper, Cambridge, MA, 2011.
10. There is early work by Robert Eccles at the Harvard Business School, the International Integrated Reporting Committee, and Aviva Investors. For reference, see R. Eccles and M. Krzus, *One Report: Integrated Reporting for a Sustainable Strategy* (New York: Wiley, 2010).
11. S. Coll, *Private Empire: ExxonMobil and American Power* (New York: Penguin Press, 2012).

12. M. Edwards, *Civil Society* (Cambridge, UK: Polity Press, 2004).

13. G. Lodge and C. Wilson, *A Corporate Solution to Global Poverty* (Princeton, NJ: Princeton University Press, 2006).

14. P. Moran, "Is Your Social Reputation True, False or Schizophrenic?" *Academy of Management Review* 40(1):1–12, 2012.

15. For example, in 2011, the Edelman Global Trust indicator that compares data from the last decade across the world showed that trust in businesses in the United States is at an all-time low.

16. R. Goffee and G. Jones, *Why Should Anyone Be Led By You? What It Takes to Be an Authentic Leader* (Boston: Harvard Business School Press, 2006).

17. I have written about Gen Yers and their expectations in my blog at www.lyndagrattonfutureofwork and no doubt will continue to do so. The way in which this generation will make choices as it moves into parenthood will be very fascinating to observe.

18. T. Erickson, "Gen Y in the Workforce." *Harvard Business Review* 87(2):43–49, 2009.

19. B. Kellerman, *The End of Leadership* (New York: HarperBusiness, 2012).

20. B. George, "How Social Networking Has Changed Business." HBR Blog Network, 2010.

21. D. Tapscott and D. Ticoll, *The Naked Corporation* (New York: Free Press, 2003).

22. B. Kellerman, *The End of Leadership* (New York: HarperBusiness, 2012).

23. Max Levchin, World Economic Forum, Council on New Models of Leadership, http://reports.weforum.org/global-agenda-council-on-new-models-of-leadership/.

24. Q. Huy and A. Shipov, "Social Media's Leadership Challenges." HBR Blog Network, 2010.

25. Weber Shandwick's 2010 study, "Socializing Your CEO: From (Un) Social to Social," was one of the earliest quantitative explorations of CEO engagement through social media. The analysis revealed that most of the CEOs from the world's largest companies—64 percent— were not using social media. That is, they were not engaging online with external stakeholders and thus were missing out on opportunities to deepen their company reputations and customer relations.

Chapter 12

1. S. Cain, *Quiet: The Power of Introverts in a World that Can't Stop Talking* (New York: Viking Press, 2012).

2. Paul Polman, CEO of Unilever, was interviewed by Adrian Wooldridge, management editor and "Schumpeter" columnist for *The Economist*, at the Fourth Global Peter Drucker Forum in Vienna in 2012; available at: http://www.youtube.com/watch?v=vgpaHKCohio &feature=youtu.be (accessed July 17, 2013).

3. Riboud quote can be found at: http://ecosysteme.danone.com/ danone-ecosystem-fund/genesis-and-mission/a-vision-of-danone-s -role/ (accessed April 2012).

4. Quoted in M. Beer, *Higher Ambition: How Great Leaders Create Economic and Social Value.* (Boston: Harvard Business School Press, 2011)

5. W. Bennis and R. Thomas, "Crucibles of Leadership." *Harvard Business Review* 80(9):39–46, 2002.

6. This is from Jared Cohen's speech at the 99 Percent Conference in May 2011.

7. J. Pfeffer and R. Sutton, *The Knowing-Doing Gap: How Smart Companies Turn Knowledge into Action* (Boston: Harvard Business School Press, 1999).

8. W. Bennis and N. Tichy, *Judgment: How Winning Leaders Make Great Calls* (New York: Penguin Group, 2007).

9. For an overview of this line of thinking, see, for example, J. Hollins, *Creating a Life: Finding Your Individual Path* (Toronto: Inner City Books, 2000).

10. O. Scharmer, *Theory U: Leading from the Future as It Emerges* (San Francisco: Berrett-Koehler, 2009).

11. P. Mirvis, "Executive Development through Consciousness-Raising Experiences." *Academy of Management Learning & Education* 7(2):173–188, 2008.

12. Quotes from P. Mirvis, "Executive Development through Consciousness-Raising Experiences." *Academy of Management Learning & Education* 7(2):173–188, 2008.

13. P. Mirvis and B. Googins, "Stages of Corporate Citizenship." *California Management Review* 48(2):104–126, 2006.

14. S. Friedman, *Total Leadership: Be a Better Leader, Have a Richer Life* (Boston: Harvard Business School Press, 2008).

15. The Goleman chapter can be read at: World Economic Forum—Council on New Models of Leadership: http://reports.weforum.org/ global-agenda-council-on-new-models-of-leadership/.

16. This quote is from S. Remedios, *Eight weeks in a village goes a long way in making compassionate leaders—Hindustan Unilever's Rural Immersion Program,* Management Innovation eXchange. (2011).

17. Ibid.
18. R. Eisenstat and F. Norrgren, *Higher Ambition: How Great Leaders Create Economic and Social Value* (Boston: Harvard Business School Press, 2011).
19. Geraldine Haley (Group Head, Future Organization & Leadership Effectiveness at Standard Chartered Bank) in discussion with author, May 2012.
20. Ibid.
21. Ibid.
22. N. Tichy and E. Cohen, "How Leaders Develop Leaders." *Training and Development* 51(5):58–63, 1997.
23. W. Bennis and N. Tichy, *Judgment: How Winning Leaders Make Great Calls* (New York: Penguin Group, 2007).

Chapter 13

1. World Economic Forum, Council on New Models of Leadership, http://reports.weforum.org/global-agenda-council-on-new-models-of -leadership/.
2. O. Scharmer, *Theory U: Leading from the Future as It Emerges* (San Fransisco: Berrett-Koehler, 2009).
3. E. Jaques, R. O. Gibson, and D. Isaac, *Levels of Abstraction in Logic and Human Action: A Theory of Discontinuity in the Structure of Mathematical Logic, Psychological Behaviour, and Social Organisation* (London: Heinemann Educational, 1978); and E. Jaques, S. Clement, and R. Lessem, *Executive Leadership: A Practical Guide to Managing Complexity* (Oxford, UK: Blackwell, 1994).
4. Speech given by Jorma Ollila at the Financial Times Business Book of the Year Awards Ceremony, New York, October 2012.
5. P. Wack, "Scenario's Unchartered Waters Ahead." *Harvard Business Review* 63(5):73–89, 1985; K. Heijden, *Scenarios: The Art of Strategic Conversation* (London: Wiley, 1996); and A. P. de Geus, *The Living Company: Growth, Learning and Longevity in Business* (London: Nicholas Brealey, 1997).
6. Peter Schwartz at the Global Futures Forum General Meeting on Building Resilience in the Face of Future Shocks, September 12–15, 2010, in Singapore.
7. Shell energy scenarios to 2050; available at: http://www.leader.co.za/printarticle.aspx?s=6&f=1&a=2305 (accessed July 15, 2013).
8. Dr Cho Khong (Chief Political Analyst in the Global Business Environment team, Shell International) in discussion with author, November 2012.

9. Ibid.
10. D. Bohm, *On Dialogue* (London: Routledge, 1996).
11. Ibid.
12. Dr. Cho Khong (Chief Political Analyst in the Global Business Environment team, Shell International) in discussion with author, November 2012.
13. Geraldine Haley (Group Head, Future Organization & Leadership Effectiveness at Standard Chartered Bank) in discussion with author, May 2012.
14. L. Gratton, *Hot Spots: Why some Companies Buzz with Energy and Innovation—and Others Don't* (London: FT Prentice Hall, 2007).
15. L. Gratton, *Glow: How You Can Radiate Energy, Innovation, and Success* (San Fransisco: Berrett-Koehler, 2009).
16. L. Gratton, *The Shift: The Future of Work Is Already Here* (London: HarperCollins, 2011).
17. M. Granovetter, *Getting a Job: A Study of Contacts and Careers* (Cambridge, MA: Harvard University Press, 1974).
18. J. S. Coleman, *Foundations of Social Theory* (Cambridge, MA: Harvard University Press, 1990).
19. Ola Arvidsson (Group Head of Human Resources Arla Foods) in discussion with the author, October 2011.
20. World Economic Forum, Council on New Models of Leadership, http://reports.weforum.org/global-agenda-council-on-new-models-of-leadership/.
21. From the piece by Jasmine Whitbread in: World Economic Forum, Council on New Models of Leadership, http://reports.weforum.org/global-agenda-council-on-new-models-of-leadership/.

Chapter 14

1. B. Kellerman, *The End of Leadership* (New York: HarperBusiness, 2012).
2. Ibid.

INDEX

ABOUT THE AUTHOR

© Lukas Kroulik

Lynda Gratton is a professor of management practice at London Business School and considered the leading global voice in human resources. She is the founder of The Hot Spots Movement and directs the Future of Work Research Consortium with more than 60 corporate members from across the world. Gratton is ranked by the Thinkers50 as one of the top 15 business thinkers in the world. She is a Fellow of the World Economic Forum and has chaired the WEF Council on the Future of Leadership.